Thinking Outside the Box

Thinking Outside the Box

BRAD FRIEDEL

with Malcolm McClean

First published in hardback in Great Britain in 2009 by
Orion Books
an imprint of the Orion Publishing Group Ltd
Orion House, 5 Upper St Martin's Lane,
London WC2H 9EA
An Hachette Livre UK Company

1 3 5 7 9 10 8 6 4 2

A CIP catalogue record for this book is available
from the British Library.

ISBN: 978-1-4091-0061-4

Printed in Great Britain by Clays Ltd, St Ives plc

The Orion Publishing Group's policy is to use papers that are natural, renewable
and recyclable and made from wood grown in sustainable forests. The logging and
manufacturing processes are expected to conform to the environmental regulations
of the country of origin.

Every effort has been made to fulfil requirements with regard to reproducing
copyright material. The author and publisher will be glad to rectify any omissions
at the earliest opportunity.

www.orionbooks.co.uk

To my mom and dad; Tracy, Izabella and
Allegra; and to my friend and mentor
Tim Harris

Contents

1

The Box

Ordinary riches can be stolen, real riches cannot. In your soul there are infinitely precious things that cannot be taken from you

Oscar Wilde (1854–1900)

My job has changed hardly at all since its roots in late Victorian England. It's an unusual kind of job with an unusual kind of workspace, one which measures just 16.5 metres by 40.3 metres. It's a place they call 'The Box'.

Just in case I should forget where my workspace begins and ends, white lines are drawn onto the green surface. It's a place which allows no room for executive frippery, punctuated as it is only by a white spot situated in the central area. A spot which will be used should I or any of my colleagues have been adjudged to have committed a misdemeanour.

I am very protective of this space, even though at times it can be a solitary existence. In fact, my colleagues spend most of their time with their backs turned towards me. I don't believe it's because I am unpopular – honestly. It's just that I am a specialist in my field. They rely on me to make crucial decisions and interventions.

In a world where many people have become accustomed to flexible and virtual working, I cannot hot-desk or log in from

1

home. To do my job I have to be there, and in a quaint throwback to the nineteenth-century roots of my profession, a long whistle blows to denote the start of my shift. I continue working until I hear two short toots of the whistle followed by a final prolonged one. Then I may go home.

I'm at my happiest when I go home with a clean sheet. It's funny how in a business which talks telephone numbers, if I can achieve a zero I can be considered a hero.

Of course, I am a goalkeeper by trade. Currently, the last line of defence at one time European champions Aston Villa. It's a position which brings with it a fantastic privilege: it offers me the opportunity to be both participant and observer. It has conditioned me to notice and given me time to think. It has helped me to understand the value of reflection and analysis, on the field and off the field; in my chosen sport, in business and in life.

Being a goalkeeper gives you quite a unique perspective on things. You are part of a team yet somehow separate; there are no grey areas, with success or failure being measured in real time; and you have a physical job which you can only do well by paying attention to your mental well-being. A great goalkeeper has to have the keys to a great mindset. To be able to work well in the box, I believe you have to be able to think 'outside of the box'.

It can be an unforgiving job. I am held immediately and publicly accountable for misdemeanours, mistakes and misjudgements. What I do for a living may appear to be simple. Yet think about it, I have to apply an intuitive understanding of geometry and the laws of physics. I'll make continuous and instantaneous risk assessments about the action I should take in relation to the flight of a spheroid object. That's what my job is really all about. Then, in an instant, I get to find out if my assessment of my own physical capability was correct. If I get all of the calculations right I will have fulfilled my function. I will have made a save; cleared the ball; caught it; or done just enough to allow one of my colleagues to clear our lines.

For a goalkeeper, there is no hiding place. Yet I would not trade the goalkeeper's view of the world for anything. It is a view which I have had to fight for; a view which is informed by being an

American in a so-called minority sport; a view which has been made richer by periods of being enmeshed in foreign cultures; a view which I've developed in periods of adversity as well as success.

It's a view that I want to share with you, by taking you on the journey I have made. It's a journey which continues both as a professional and as a person. From my days playing international soccer against the likes of Brazil and Argentina for $35 a day, through my five-year work permit battle, to my establishment as a Premier League regular, and much, much more. It's a journey which I hope will give you some unique insights into football that you wouldn't normally get; I will show how football is really a metaphor for life and in doing so put the game into perspective. It's a fantastic game which has given me an incredible life. Yet one day it will stop. Maintaining perspective is important for everyone. It is especially important for a professional footballer and in particular for those at the top of the football pyramid. For a short time you live in a cotton wool kind of world where you are at the height of your powers. Is it any wonder that players feel that they are invulnerable? Of course, none of us is and sooner or later it will end. It could end for any one of us at any time.

From my goalkeeper's view of the world I'm beginning to glimpse a new kind of future. One which, perhaps, has more in common with the Victorian entrepreneur–philanthropists, many of whom laid down the foundations of this game. This game of football, which, almost by default, has rewarded me with a lifestyle and a family environment beyond my wildest dreams.

It is true that the extraordinary amounts of money in the game today make doing my job incredibly lucrative, and I have no complaints about that. The *real* value though, is that it has opened up doors and brought forward ideas and opportunities which are enriching my life and the lives of my family members. I have long ago ceased to be excited by the material wealth that my profession brings. I have taken a view where I take little pleasure and have little interest in being ostentatious. I take more pleasure in providing material comforts for those who enjoy them more than I do. Don't get me wrong, I have my indulgences of sorts, yet I prefer to keep them in perspective and focus on the things that are really important to me.

I'm no saint either. I've made my share of mistakes and though I like to help people if I can, I will make difficult or unpopular decisions when I need to. Yet I've just reached a stage in my life where the nonsense and frippery that surround professional footballers, and the unrealistic lifestyles that are associated with them, are just not something that I buy into any more. I know that my days of playing football will end and that there is definitely still an exciting life beyond.

If you like, I am thinking *outside of the box*. I think it is a state of mind brought about by the remarkable and unusual things that have happened to me in the pursuit of a dream to play football in the best league in the world. A state of mind brought about by being part of something and yet independent. Separate yet connected. Participant and observer.

A goalkeeper's view of the world.

The Darwen Controversy

In November 1875 two wealthy entrepreneurs, John Lewis and Arthur Constantine, brought together a group of like-minded, well connected friends in a room above the Leger Hotel in Blackburn, Lancashire.

These 17 men formed a football club, Blackburn Rovers, which would compete alongside well-established rivals in the town, Blackburn Olympic and Blackburn Road FC. In the early years the club struggled to become established, with games being played in several locations before the team rented a piece of farmland at nearby Oozehead, long before their eventual move to their current home at Ewood Park.

By 1879 the club had progressed sufficiently to enter the FA Cup for the first time, only to be knocked out in the third round taking a 6–0 thrashing from Nottingham Forest. Yet the club had consolidated and began to have ambition. In 1880 the committee took a controversial decision. They agreed that they would select players from outside of Blackburn to fill in for members of the team who were unavailable to play. This was considered a major violation of an important principle of the Lancashire Football Association, to which The Rovers were affiliated.

The Rovers committee remained undeterred, and at the start of the 1881 season they did the unthinkable. They persuaded a player by the name of Fergie Suter to transfer to them by offering him improved terms. This move was controversial enough, involving the movement of a player using financial inducement. What made it even worse was that the player concerned was brought in from neighbouring club Darwen. Almost a full five miles away.

What transpired was years of bitterness, not just between the two clubs, but between the townspeople of Blackburn and Darwen as well. When the teams were drawn together in the fourth round of the Lancashire Cup, the bitterness meant that they were unable even to agree on a date for the match. Consequently, both teams were ejected from the competition.

The Darwen controversy drew attention to the issues emerging in a game that was developing rapidly in the late Victorian era. The issues of professionalisation and the free movement of players. Things which still cause controversy even today. Things which have had a massive impact upon my own life and led me to circumnavigate the globe many times, before I was able to settle in the place where all the controversy really started – Blackburn Rovers.

It is ironic that in the eight years I spent at Blackburn there were no players from nearby Darwen and only one was from Blackburn itself, that was the young Matt Derbyshire. Precious few were even from England – in fact in 2007–08 there were just four out of 35 players. Like most Premier League squads today, ours was like the United Nations. As well as our English players we had a Scot, a couple from Northern Ireland and a Welshman, representing the Celtic nations. In addition we had players from the Republic of Ireland, Holland, the Congo, Turkey, New Zealand, Australia, Paraguay, South Africa, Norway, Georgia, Switzerland, Germany, Sweden, Grenada and of course the good old U S of A. The Blackburn Rovers committee really started something when they dared to take a player from outside of the town.

At about the time of the Darwen controversy, a small settle-ment on the edge of the Great Lakes was becoming established. Bay Village, Ohio, USA, had only 50 years earlier been reclaimed from the woods by the founding Cahoon family. Some one hun-dred years later it was my great good fortune to be born there. Great good fortune in every way except, that is, if you wanted to become a top-class professional footballer. In football terms, my birthplace caused as much controversy as the Darwen episode. The issues of professionalism and the free movement of players began to dominate my life, almost my every waking moment.

Yet here I am, a veteran of two Olympic Games, three World Cups, with 82 international appearances, and more than 300 Premiership games and, on 29th November 2008 at Villa Park, I played my 167th consecutive Premiership game, breaking David James' all-time record of 166.

That represents an achievement of course. Yet for me it is a win against the odds, a battle I would not lose as obstacle after obstacle was placed in the way of my dream to play in the Premiership. Out of adversity comes strength and now that I can reflect on how it all happened I can see how I have grown as a player and as a person.

Getting to where I wanted to be has indeed been a battle. There have been moments of triumph and days of despair. They say that in life it is not how far you fall, it is how high you bounce. In my life I have always tried to bounce after that fall.

This is my story. In fact this is more than just my story. It's a series of insights and observations that will take you inside the world of professional football and which I hope will demonstrate that whatever it is that you do for a living, by taking notice of what is happening there is always something to learn.

For that reason, I'm going to recount the story not necessarily in the order that it happened. This story will take you around the world; it will take you back in time and look forwards towards the future; it will take you behind the scenes in the biggest league in the world. It's a story which draws on my own past to envision a new kind of future. It's the story of how I began to think – outside of the box.

2

The Wonder Years

See the children run as the sun goes down, among fields of
gold

'Fields of Gold', Sting

Nostalgia. It's the sugar coating we sometimes put on the past,
which makes it seem better than it was. It's the eradication of
unfavourable events, the sanitisation of our awkward moments
which enables us to reflect on an era of near perfection: our
childhood.

For me, my childhood was a period of wonderment. I was lost
in a world of sport and adventure. A world in which I felt safe and
secure.

Only now, as I reflect on my past, can I fully appreciate the role
that loving parents play in smoothing out the troubles and overcoming the obstacles that could get in the way of an idyllic childhood. As a family, we had our triumphs and tribulations, our ups
and our downs, yet Mom and Dad did all that they could to make
sure that when I look back on those early years, I don't need the
benefit of nostalgia. These truly were the wonder years …

Genetic Legacy

Bay Village, Ohio, the 1970s

Leonard Friedel, my dad, fixed a basketball hoop to the outside wall and went inside for a drink. Moments later he heard the excited cries from my mom Susan who was outside: 'Hey, Len, get out here, you just gotta see this.' Dad ran outside and observed what was happening. I was two and a half years old and curious about this hoop thing that Dad was building. Mom had picked up a ball and thrown it in my direction. I instinctively caught it and threw it back. So now she threw one to the side, then to the other side, then up and then wider. Each time I caught the ball without moving my head or my eyes. Mom shouted some big words over to Dad which I later found out were 'coordination' and 'peripheral vision'. Of course, I was just happy to have pleased my parents. I had no idea that these big words, which were their genetic legacy to me, would help me to get a job.

When my mom wasn't teaching, she was working in the dry-cleaners. When she wasn't working in the dry-cleaners she was drilling the high school girls' dance team, the Rockettes. She took them to perform at football grounds with marching bands and touring them around the country, going to places to perform from Disneyworld to Chicago to Philadelphia. Somehow in the spaces in between, Susan Friedel found the time to create a loving home for me and my sister Kim and of course my dad.

My dad Leonard was a provider. He is a principled man who at one stage almost lost everything, and in his efforts to keep things together came close to losing his life. Mom and Dad just got on with things, and maybe their approach to their most difficult times seeped into me through some form of osmosis. Both had a tremendous work ethic and whatever their problems they refused to quit. When the going got tough – and it did get very tough at one stage – they made sure that we became stronger by binding us together as a family unit.

I was born and raised in Bay Village, Ohio, a small community of about 17,000 people sitting on the banks of the Great Lake Erie, which separates the United States from Canada. It was the place that the legendary crime fighter Eliot Ness came to settle after Prohibition was lifted in the US in the 1930s. It brought to an end a life spent fighting crime against some of America's most wanted gangsters, including Al Capone. Ness could not have gotten further away from crime than Bay Village. Consistently, it is ranked as one of the safest places in the whole of the United States. For example, in 2005 only two violent crimes were recorded and as for property crimes such as burglary and car theft these hit the heady heights of six recorded incidents.

It's not surprising then that Mom and Dad had no problems letting us kids roam about the streets. It was, and still is, a community of picket fences and beautifully painted clapperboard houses. A genuine community where people really do look out for each other. With the school system ranked in the top 3% in the United States it is a fantastic place to raise a family.

As if this were not enough, for me the weather has to be the best weather in the world because it has four very distinctive seasons. We would get cold winters with beautiful snowfalls; a marvellous springtime which brought the lakeside back to life; wonderful hot summers; and to top it all a golden fall.

There was no other place to be than in the outdoors, and I remember that day in, day out, we kids were outside all of the time, constantly trying all sorts of activities. My dad tells me that he had me on snow skis at the age of two. On a trip to Colorado, I had these things strapped to my feet. My mom says that I skied perfectly down the slope, stopped and said, 'OK. I've skied, now I want to go back to the playhouse.' I didn't even think about it as I was growing up, but balance was another of the natural blessings given to me by my parents.

From the first possible moment, it was just common practice that kids signed up for everything that was on offer. So from the age of three or four, my buddies and I were into every conceivable sport and activity. We did Cubs, Weebeloes and Boy Scouts; kayaking, rafting and canoeing; basketball, baseball, ice hockey, football, gymnastics and of course soccer. Somehow, we found time just to be kids and to do the kind of things that kids do. My great friends were the Way triplets Beth, Steve and Brad. One time on the way home from school there had been a fall of apples. One of the triplets picked up an apple and threw it at me. I returned the compliment and soon there were apples flying everywhere. I unleashed an apple curveball, which bypassed everybody and smashed through the church window. When it was reported that four kids were seen running from the scene – three triplets and a tall redhead kid – there was no need to send for Eliot Ness to solve this one. It was blatantly obvious who the perpetrators were. Our parents made sure that we spent the next few weeks repaying our debt by cleaning the church windows. Perhaps it is this kind of honour system that keeps the crime statistics so low in Bay Village. Growing up in Midwestern Ohio was as natural, innocent and ordinary as you can get. Though there were many episodes of us just being normal kids, it was sport that took up most of my time.

I spent a lot of my time in Bradley Park, close to my home. I was one of the taller boys so I guess I had a natural advantage in sports. All I know is that I just loved playing sport. I didn't mind too much which sport, and I didn't mind too much who I was playing with – often I would play with boys who were older than me. As long as I was playing I was happy.

By the age of eight, I had joined an ice hockey team, Bay Hockey, and began travelling to play games away from home. We even went to play in the Silver Sticks, which is the US national championships. I was very confident in myself, and had no problems being alone; meeting new people; being in a room with complete strangers. That's how I've always been and I guess it stems from this early period.

Both my parents had been athletic. Mom was a swimmer representing Miami University of Ohio. Dad won a scholarship as an American football running back at Colorado State University. When you think about it, Mom's sport was all about coordination and graceful movement, while Dad's was about athleticism and courage. Luckily, I got a bit of both of them in my genes. They were useful in all sorts of sports and all sorts of positions, yet this combination, coupled with the peripheral vision that Mom had noticed the day she tossed a ball at me, and the balance that kept me up on skis, was suitable for one position more than any other.

Sparklers & Firecrackers

When I joined my first soccer team, the Sparklers, it was the start of something that was to take hold of my life in a way that I could not have imagined. In time, I graduated from being a Sparkler to being a member of the Firecrackers. Sometimes, I would play as a forward, but by the time I was 13, I had made my home in goal.

Early on, Dad's business was going well, and when things were good we enjoyed a good lifestyle. Dad always had a wanderlust and liked to take us as a family on quite adventurous trips. We would ski a lot in places like Aspen, Buttermilk, Keystone, Vail and above the timberline in Arapahoe on our many trips to Colorado. He liked Europe, and London in particular, and when we went there on vacation when I was nine, he promised that he would take me to my first soccer match. We boarded a rickety London Underground train. It was packed and noisy. People were shouting and chanting and we got sprayed with beer as an over-exuberant fan laid into his six-pack.

I was really excited as I took in the sights and sounds walking towards the stadium along the old Wembley Way. There were these odd accents all around. The guttural Scouse of the Liverpool fans and the sing-song Cockney of the West Ham United fans. Policemen in pointed helmets were chasing skirmishing fans in through the entrance of the toilets and then out of the exit on the other side. I was excited and entranced by all of this as it was like watching an episode of *The Keystone Cops*.

The noise and the colours in the stadium were unforgettable. Some 90,000 people had turned out to watch Liverpool face West Ham United in the curtain-raiser to the 1980–81 season, the Charity Shield. Terry McDermott scored the only goal of the game, and Liverpool took the Shield home. That was an experience that I would never forget. Afterwards, I told my dad that it was my dream to play for Liverpool and to play at Wembley Stadium, and from then on I became a full-time Liverpool supporter.

Back home as I moved towards my teens, the Firecrackers had developed into a really good team under Spanish coach Juan Gonzalez, and won the State Championship before giving a good account of ourselves in the regional competition. Juan had a son, Jay, who at that age was a tremendous player and in amateur circles was a wanted man. We were good friends, and together we went to trials for East West, the best team in the area. This team was the be-all and end-all for me at the time. They had all the best players in the whole of northeastern Ohio.

There may have been some politics involved in the selection process, who knows? A big part of it was, I think, who could afford to pay for the travel and who couldn't. All I know is that I couldn't. Dad had been involved in a business deal which went bad and the person responsible fell foul of the law. Justice may have been done, but Dad had to sell our house and file for bankruptcy and we had moved to a smaller rented home. On top of this Dad developed health problems as a result of all the stress. Mom was working hard to keep our heads above water. They talked to me and my sister and said, 'We will be in this together. We will do different things, and life will go on.' So we swapped our life of travel and foreign vacations for something altogether more simple. Instead of buying fancy decorations for our Christmas tree, we made our own. We made cookies and popcorn the old-fashioned way. We scrimped and saved, but we were together and that's all that mattered. In an odd way, this is the time when we were closest as a family.

Meanwhile, Jay, being the tremendous player that he was, got selected right away. I was an unknown with the wrong sort of financial profile. What's more, I was still only 13, and trying out for an Under 14s team. I went away from the trial feeling really down and dejected. I didn't think that I had performed the way I could have done, nor did I feel that I had been given a proper look. It was as if they had a preconceived notion of who they were going to select. I was upset. I so much wanted to join East West. As my other friends had already received calls to let them know they had been selected and I had received none, the writing was on the wall for me to read. I had not made the team.

A few days later, out of the blue, I got a call. Tom Firth, the director of East West, said it was up to me to prove him wrong and that I could come along and play for their 'B' team. In truth, I think that Jay had a word in his ear. One thing was for sure, they didn't want to lose Jay Gonzalez, and as a result I got a glimmer of a chance.

I didn't like a lot of things about the way Tom Firth operated. I played in the 'B' team for about a year, and then when I started improving as a player, he suddenly wanted to be my best pal. He wanted to bask in the reflected glory. I have to be honest and fair though; being with East West took me to another level. It gave me my first taste of international travel as a footballer as we played in tournaments in places like France, Cuba and Canada. In fact the trip to France could have seen me quit soccer altogether. We were at the Toulon Soccer Festival, and there was a basketball team in town. They came over and asked, 'Do any of you Americans want to play basketball?' A few of us joined in a game, and I scored over 40 points against a very good team. They asked me if I wanted to come over and play for them, and I called home to tell Mom and Dad. I did return home though, and it was while I was playing in a small tournament in Virginia that a freak gust of wind was to influence my whole future.

An assistant coach from University of California, Los Angeles (UCLA), Dean Wurzberger, was at the tournament to check on a particular player. There must have been a lull in the play, and he turned to look over to our game. As his eyes hit on a tall goalkeeper, having had virtually nothing to do in the game, I punted the ball. There was a tremendous wind behind me and the ball just flew. It got me noticed, and Dean began asking questions about me.

I was in high school at the time when I began to become aware that UCLA were scouting me. In two years' time they would be in need of a goalkeeper and Sigi Schmid, the head coach, took a 6,000-mile round trip to take a look at me. There are very strict rules about what they can and cannot do in terms of making an approach. Everything has to be documented to make sure that no money changes hands and that a player does not compromise his amateur status.

In those days in the States to have interest from UCLA was like having a Premier League club such as Manchester United scouting you. They must have seen something that others didn't. Sure I was being scouted by other colleges, but they were not as prestigious as UCLA. Indiana was somewhat interested, but it didn't look like they would offer a scholarship. Anyhow, Jurgen Sommer was their keeper and we were of a similar age and he was very good. Cleveland State was looking. They had a decent soccer programme, but it was not what you would call amazing. Then there was University of San Francisco (USF) and Maryland but, remarkably, nothing was as concrete as UCLA.

The Earth Moves for Mrs Friedel

When I was 17, UCLA followed the proper procedures and was allowed to offer me an all expenses paid three-day visit. California was a long way away, and Mom, having lived all of her life in small town Ohio, decided that it was no place for a young man to go alone. She had real concerns about a boy from a 'button-down collar' type of community heading for the bright lights. So, together we boarded the plane to Los Angeles.

Our plane was delayed and we were late arriving in LA. We were met at the airport by people from UCLA, who seemed almost in a frenzy. They said, 'Come on, come on, hurry up, we are going to a volleyball game.' Mom and I looked at each other quizzically: 'A volleyball game?' We couldn't understand the fuss that was being made about a volleyball, game. All we had ever known was high school volleyball, which was OK, but nothing to write home about.

Very quickly, they rushed us to dinner, and then took us out to Pauley Pavilion. It was a huge set-up, wall-to-wall with people, for this girls' game. There were stands full of excited students, bands and cheerleaders. It was like the ticket of the century for this game. It was UCLA, the no. 1 team, playing the no. 2 team, Stanford. It was just an unbelievable experience; we had never seen anything like it for a volleyball game.

While I was staying with the team, Mom stayed at a hotel. The coaches showed her around and tried to impress her. Mom, being a schoolteacher, wanted to know all about the ins and outs of the academic programme, and eventually said, 'Look. Would you let me walk around the campus on my own and sit in on some classes?' So that's what she did. That's when she fell in love with UCLA herself. She saw normal, well-adjusted kids in an incredible environment, with amazing opportunities opening up for them. She thought that I should get a degree in architecture and play a little soccer along the way.

As for me, I just felt that the whole thing was fantastic. I looked through the names of the current players. Many were in the full US national team; the weather was amazing; the campus was flanked by Beverly Hills, Bel Air and Westwood; and then there were the girls. It was just the most amazing place.

I had offers of basketball and tennis scholarships from colleges in Ohio. These were closer to home and offered a paid education. I was a good basketball player, but I don't think I would ever have been good enough to become a professional. In any case, the truth is that after my visit to UCLA, my mind was made up. My mom, despite sitting through an earthquake on her last night in LA, gave me her blessing. I was thankful that she liked it because it saved a fight. I was going anyway. Once I had made up my mind that UCLA was the place for me, nothing was going to stand in my way.

Of course this was all immensely exciting, but it was played out against a backdrop of family dramas. I already touched on the fact that we had gone from a comfortable middle-class way of life to one in which we had constant financial struggles, while my father tried to recover from a financial collapse.

My sister Kim and I had a tremendous relationship when we were growing up. She is three years older than me and always looked after me. One of the highlights for her, though very embarrassing for me, was when I was a high school freshman and she was a senior and we performed together in the school production of *Anything Goes*. What was I thinking? I can't sing and I can't dance. She must have had something good on me to get me to do that. She was a good athlete, but she will be the first to admit that she was a total klutz. Nobody has fallen down stairs more than Kim. She has broken arms and ankles and damaged her knees. Despite this, her tolerance to pain and the sight of blood is next to zero. She would scream and shout and cry.

When you break a bone, you can scream and shout and eventually everything will be mended. Kim knew about this more than most. However, when somebody's dignity is violated; when they are robbed of their self respect; and when nobody screams and shouts about it, you have to wonder if the scars can ever be mended.

Unfortunately Kim suffered an ordeal, which I believe is the root of the problems she has had in her life. She suffered a traumatic experience involving a distant family member related by marriage. Our extended family closed ranks and the whole episode was swept under the carpet. Wouldn't we all do things differently if we had the chance to turn the clock back?

I know my mom and dad would. At the time they were going through the mill just to survive and to keep our extended family together. Their emotional and mental energy was drained. We had a strong extended family and that's how things were done. I think that the way Kim saw it was that nobody cried out for her pain, and I would have to agree with her on that.

After that she developed a lot of insecurities. When I was 15, I got a call from one her college friends. She said that my sister was really struggling with some health issues, and that I had to get her out of college. I was in high school. I'd only just learned what the words these girls were using to describe the illness meant. I felt I had to spill the beans to Mom and Dad. Mom, being a teacher, was well versed in these things and knew just what to do. They collected her from college, and slowly tried to help her to get well.

Today my sister and I hardly speak. This is the one part of my life that leaves me feeling empty and hollow. Kim chose a path in life which I have a hard time being a part of. In time I sincerely hope that together we can remedy this situation.

In November 1989, a letter landed on the doormat of the little rented house that was now the home of the Friedel family. It was postmarked Los Angeles, California. Now, there are all sorts of combinations in terms of the support that a college can offer. Scholarships have three elements to them: they can offer room and board, tuition and books. In those days, UCLA tuition alone was $16,000 a year to out-of-state residents, and then you had to find somewhere to stay, feed yourself and buy books. As a family, it was a time when we were struggling financially, so everything hinged on what was in the offer letter. They offered me room and board for the first year. That was great. They offered a two-thirds scholarship. This meant that I still had to find something like $5,000, but once you register as a state resident in California, this goes down to about half. I'd stopped reading by the time it got to the part where it mentioned that I was also going to get the books paid for. Somehow, some way I was going to find the money to make up the tuition fees. I was going to California.

On scholarship, having your books bought for you is a great thing. With books costing maybe $400 depending upon which courses you were taking, an enterprising student might open up a second-hand market for textbooks.

My high school girlfriend was a lovely girl called Kerri Kitchen who was two years younger than me. From the November she had seen it coming: once the summer came I was leaving for California. I remember we had a great going away party with all my friends who were going off to college. There was a tinge of sadness in leaving the relationship behind, but overall, I felt happy and excited. At this stage I had no inkling that soccer could become a career. I just saw the move to UCLA as a natural progression in my sport and my life.

There was an emotional farewell, with everybody coming to see me off at the airport. Most kids get driven to college and dropped off, so it's a big thing when a boy from Ohio boards a plane bound for California. I said my goodbyes – Mom, Dad, sister Kim, Kerri my girlfriend and Grandma. I held on tight to the money I'd saved up from working over the summer. It was $1,600. In Beverly Hills terms, this was the equivalent of next to nothing. Mom and Dad gave me one piece of advice, which they still give me today: 'Be safe, and stay happy.'

As I boarded the plane and looked back towards the people

who were closest to me, it signalled the end of a fantastic period in my life. It signalled the beginning of a period that was to take me way beyond anything that I could have imagined.

Mom and Dad had raised me, educated me and sheltered me during a topsy-turvy period in their lives. For them there had been some difficult years.

For me, thanks to Mom and Dad, those will always be the wonder years.

3

The Call

> It was the best of times, it was the worst of times, it was the age of wisdom, it was the age of foolishness, it was the epoch of belief, it was the epoch of incredulity
>
> *Charles Dickens*, A Tale of Two Cities

A tale of two cities. If only it had been that easy. So much had happened to me since, as a young kid, I had boarded that plane bound for Los Angeles in 1989. By the time Anfield beckoned it was 1997 and I had made my home in cities across the world. In an attempt to get my international appearances up to the required level to qualify for a work permit, I had travelled hundreds of thousands of miles. I would have needed to plant a forest the size of Wales to offset my carbon footprint.

When the call came it did indeed become a tale of two cities. New York and Liverpool. Two cities whose destinies had become entwined over time now held the key to my destiny. Only a trip to New York and some contractual wrangles stood in the way of my dream to make the journey to Liverpool to play for the club that I had followed from afar as a boy. It was a call which changed my life. It was a call which signalled the beginning of a period that could have been written by Charles Dickens himself. A period in which I would experience incredulity, develop belief, witness wisdom as well as foolishness. It was to be the best of times and the worst of times …

At Last Anfield Beckons

It was 20 December 1997. Just five days to go to Christmas and the streets of Columbus, Ohio, were decked with boughs of holly. It was cold and overcast and the best place to be was in bed, which is exactly where I was. The night before I'd just returned from an international training camp in San Diego, California. Columbus was cold and I was tired. I needed a lie-in.

At 6.30 a.m. the phone purred with that long kind of comforting American ringtone. *Prrrrrrrrrrrrr ... Prrrrrrrrrrrrr*. Comforting it may be, but at 6.30 a.m. all the possibilities flash through your mind. You imagine that something bad has happened. One possibility didn't enter my mind as I reached for the phone. That's strange because it was a possibility that I had thought about every single day for five years.

Slowly, I pulled the phone onto my pillow and up to my ear. My mumbled half 'Hello' was interrupted. Somebody was shouting and screaming down the phone. In an instant I leapt out of bed. It was almost as if the shouting and screaming was some form of contagious disease which had transmitted itself down the phone line. I began hollering, punching the air and repeating the words of my agent Paul Stretford who was on the other end of the line: 'The work permit came through. I'm going to L-i-v-e-r-poooool.'

To say that I was elated just does not do justice to the way I was feeling. I felt I had reached the highest heavens. As I continued my jig around the room, phone still in my hand, Paul jigging away on the other end, I looked over to my live-in girlfriend Jenny Benzle. She had propped herself up in bed. Half-dazed with sleep, there was no mistaking the expression on her face. It was more than the look of tiredness. It was a look of devastation.

I put down the phone and made the grand announcement. 'We are off. I've got my work permit,' I shouted, trying to wrap her up in my elation. Her response was a hesitant 'Oh?' I said, 'I'm going. I *have* to go.' Though she was later to come over to Liverpool for a short time, our relationship effectively died the moment I took that phone call.

While I was in one room calling my parents saying, 'We are going to Liverpool,' she was in another room telling her parents, 'We are going to Liverpool.' The difference was in the delivery. I said it like a kid whose Christmases had all come at once. Jenny announced it in the manner of a doctor delivering an unfavourable prognosis.

Lovely as she was, her nature was that of a homebody. We had dogs and a home close to her family. That was all that she wanted really. Ohio was her world, and you can't blame her for that. One phone call, two responses, but come hell or high water, I was going.

I was going, provided I could resolve one small snag. To do it I had to get to New York and the offices of Major League Soccer (MLS). The next morning I boarded a plane to New York determined to do whatever it was that I had to do.

Reflections in the Clouds

Leaving Jenny behind, half-heartedly packing boxes for the move, gave me a chance to reflect on all that had happened over the past five years. I sat on the plane and looked back on a roller-coaster, helter-skelter period of one frustration after another, which could be brought to a head if I could just do the business in New York. There was a tension in the pit of my stomach as I settled into my seat, so I reminded myself what it was all about – this work permit hell I had been through.

I wondered if things might have turned out differently had a Bristol City player named Tinnion not knocked Liverpool out of the FA Cup in a replay at Anfield in 1994. It was that result which piled on the pressure for Graeme Souness when he was the Liverpool manager and saw him resign. With it went my hopes of signing for Liverpool at that time after a lot of effort from Graham Smith, who was then my agent, and Bob McNab, the former Arsenal player who had moved to California.

It's funny how relatively small incidents thousands of miles away can trigger off a sequence of events which have seismic effects. According to chaos theory, a butterfly flapping its wings on one continent can create a movement of air which gradually increases so as to cause a hurricane on another continent. In a way, Tinnion's goal created just that kind of 'butterfly effect'.

With Liverpool out of the equation, Nottingham Forest, Newcastle and Sunderland all failed at the work permit stage. I was not too upset about the Forest situation. After all, at the time I had only one international cap to my name. But these latter two failures were beginning to get to me big time.

At that time the requirement was that you played 75% of your country's international fixtures. This made it hard for me. The policy of the US coach was to alternate goalkeeping duties between me and Tony Meola. As a goalkeeper you don't get the luxury of being subbed into games all the time. So this was my argument. Surely a situation like this should be taken into account when considering the work permit application. No such luck. No goalkeeper in America could possibly get near the 75% figure. There was some dispensation for young players and, at 23 years old, I felt I was young for a goalkeeper, a position where it is not uncommon to play into the late thirties. Yet this was not considered a factor for me either.

I got so frustrated and angry at the whole situation. As I sat on the plane thinking back, I wondered why this situation had persisted, where I was turned down time after time, appeal after appeal. So many football people were adamant that I was good enough to play in the Premier League: Brian Clough, Graeme Souness, Peter Reid and Paul Bracewell, Kevin Keegan, and these were hardly novices at the game. Sunderland went to incredible lengths to get me to sign for them. I remember I was on international duty in a backwater somewhere in the middle of Uruguay, South America. Paul Bracewell said he was coming over to sign me up. It took him something like 27 hours to get there. Not something you would do for someone that you had doubts about.

Yet the work permit blockages kept on coming. Had someone at Newcastle or Sunderland upset someone on the appeals panel? Was there a covert culture of xenophobia festering in the PFA I wondered? Don't forget, this was a trade union funded to date primarily by British players. Trade unions are there to protect their members and their interests. At the time, who could have foreseen the influx of foreign talent that was about to hit the Premier League? Trade unions in Britain have had a long history of resisting change and adopting restrictive practices. I wondered if perhaps this was the case. We will never know, but my arguments continued to fall on deaf ears and I know that the PFA were instrumental in the rejection of my appeals.

That was the stage where I determined that the appeals system was a waste of my time and would only frustrate me further. It was beyond my control. I knew what the rules were and I knew that my situation warranted a relaxing of the rules, but try as I might there was nothing I could do about it. So I had to look at what I could control and forget about what I couldn't.

So I thought to myself, What can I take control of here? I couldn't change the position of the Home Office on the criteria for non-EU footballers. I couldn't seem to sway the appeals panel, least of all the PFA. The only thing that was reasonably within my power was to change the policy of my international coach, and do what no American had ever done before – complete 75% of games. This was a big ask. I was at around 35% at the time.

Yet I was determined and I began to focus with an intensity that I had never known before. I decided that I must isolate all the possible reasons not to play me. Firstly, after spells with Brondby in Denmark and Galatasaray in Turkey, I secured a loan period at Columbus Crew in Major League Soccer. Effectively, I camped out on home base, so that being based in Europe was no longer a reason not to play me.

Miracle on 34th Street

So there I was, landing at John F Kennedy Airport, New York, with just four shopping days to go before Christmas. I just could not think about shopping. As I climbed out of the plane my mind was fixed on one thing and one thing only. I was picturing the offices of Major League Soccer in midtown Manhattan. They still held my registration, and I needed to convince them that they must release it right away if I was going to be eligible to play for Liverpool.

Their argument was this. I had signed for Liverpool and, subject to getting a work permit, it was agreed that the MLS would receive £1 million for my registration, and £300,000 on the basis of appearances. As my work permit had come through after appeal, the MLS argued that the contract that I had signed was invalid because it was contingent upon getting a work permit, but mentioned nothing about getting a permit through appeal. I believe they were game playing, hoping that by trying to block the move on the basis of a technicality, they could leverage more money out of Liverpool.

This was my life they were playing with. This was the culmination of a five-year battle, and I had a chance of winning against all the odds. I wasn't going to let MLS red tape and greed stand in my way. When I got to the MLS headquarters, all I was faced with was prevarication. I was like a freight train going in there. In retrospect, I regret some of the things that came out of my mouth. I threatened that I would never kick a ball for the USA or Columbus Crew again if they didn't let this transfer go through. Effectively I threatened to go on strike. I said things to Clark Hunt, the owner of Columbus Crew, which were personal and hurtful. I do regret this in particular because Clark was nothing but a gentleman, but this was my life, this was Liverpool Football Club, this was my dream – it was everything that I had worked so hard for. Nobody – nothing was going to get in my way.

After a day of argument and meetings behind closed doors of the MLS bigwigs, the registration was eventually released, and I stepped out into the street. Now I was calm enough to notice it was nearing Christmas time, and people were hurrying and scurrying along 34th Street doing their last-minute bits of shopping. It reminded me of that old Christmas time movie *Miracle on 34th Street*. I was on 34th Street and was heading for Liverpool and just for a moment I thought it felt like a miracle. Then I checked myself. This was no miracle. It was down to intense focus, the power of persistence and taking control of what I could take control of. It was down to me – a lesson that would stand me in good stead for the future.

The Anfield Living Football Museum

At long last the prospect of playing in the Premier League was no longer an interesting theory. Anfield beckoned. I was picked up at Manchester Airport by Norman Gard. He was the man entrusted to settle in all of Liverpool's foreign players. He dropped me off at the Woolton Redbourne Hotel in Liverpool and went about the business of sorting me out a car and arranging a bank account. In fact he did everything so that all I needed to do was concentrate upon what I came here for – to play football.

Just two days after that momentous phone call from my agent Paul Stretford, there I was in the changing room getting ready for my first training session with Liverpool. I was quite nervous and anxious. When I walked in I recognised a lot of the international players I'd played against, but I can't say that I knew any of them on a personal level. It's interesting that the first people to speak to me were the foreign contingent. One of the first people to approach me was the Norwegian Stig Bjornebye, who to this day remains a very good friend. Karl-Heinz Riedle was friendly and of course the goalkeepers Jurgen Nielsen and Tony Warner came over and introduced themselves.

The no. 1 goalkeeping choice, David James, didn't say a word to me, which seemed a bit strange really. It was a taste of things to come. David is a great goalkeeper, but I don't think he quite knew how to handle fresh competition for his slot. He had been no. 1 at Watford, begun to assert himself at Liverpool and become an England international. My arrival clearly made him uncomfortable. He saw me not as a team-mate but as a threat to his position.

What happened next was just unbelievable. Here I was at one of the biggest clubs in the world; the club structure and organisation were superb, the fans unbelievable, and I imagined that the training would be world-class too.

At the first training session we walked around the pitch twice.

I thought, OK. We did some stretches. I thought, *Hmmm*. Then we played five-a-side and went home. I thought that perhaps this was a one off. As the weeks went by, I began to realise that for the most part this was the preferred method of training at Liverpool. It was an era when football was becoming much more scientific, and here we were training like a team from the 1960s.

When I went over to the gym I was shocked. This may sound like an American bragging that my country's better than yours. I can assure you it is nothing of the sort. The plain truth of the matter is that a typical American high school would have better gym equipment than Liverpool Football Club had at the time. It was obsolete.

On top of this, the players seemed to rule the roost. If you didn't want to run, you didn't have to run. If you didn't want to play in a reserve game, you didn't have to. In truth, it was bordering on a living football museum.

I know I had not yet played in the Premier League, but I was an experienced international and regarded myself as a professional. I began to see why Liverpool was not the Liverpool of old. A lot of the players had quite a remarkable attitude. They tended to look out for themselves, and it was almost a case of it didn't matter too much if we lost as long as they as an individual felt they had played well. It was far from a cohesive unit. TV money was beginning to pour into the Premier League and other clubs were moving forward on all fronts. Liverpool was moving forward too, but on the footballing side seemed to be locked in some kind of suspended animation.

Of course, the great Bill Shankly had established a dynasty. He produced one fantastic team after another. Partly, it was because he established a system of doing things and built an unrivalled tradition. A tradition which instilled passion in the Liverpool way. Perhaps the greatest of all of his skills, though, was his ability to change and revitalise his teams before they tailed off. He kept the system of doing things much the same and skilfully changed the personnel just at the right time. The Anfield Boot Room was the place where the tacit learning about this method was passed on and, of course, the dynasty continued after

Shankly through to Bob Paisley, Ronnie Moran and Joe Fagan.

But every so often, perhaps once in a generation, changes occur in football which are of such magnitude that they demand a revolution in the way things are done, rather than a tinkering around at the edges. Some of the other clubs were in the throes of doing this. They were becoming more technical in their approach, more scientific, and were upgrading their training facilities. Liverpool, it seemed to me, was not. After all, the system laid down by Shankly had delivered the goods for decades. Perhaps this and the idea that it was irreverent to tinker with a system laid down by a footballing giant were holding Liverpool back. In their reverence for the great man they seemed to forget that Shankly was a master at anticipating change and taking action early. Liverpool seemed to have lost this which was perhaps the greatest of all his attributes.

The new money in the Premiership brought more intense competition and the search for ever higher standards of performance. The influx of foreign players served only to dilute one of the things that made Liverpool great – the passion brought about by a tradition that had been ingrained in many of its players from childhood. The foreign players knew about the tradition of course, but it didn't have quite the same effect upon them. For many of them, I'm sure, their interest in the traditions of Liverpool Football Club may have been on a par with a visit to an interesting museum or art gallery from where you come away with an understanding of the theme of the exhibition. Perhaps one or two pieces strike a chord with you and stay in your memory, maybe influence your thoughts and actions at times. However, for people like Steven Gerrard and many other Scousers before him, it had the effect of making them feel that they had Liverpool blood flowing through their veins. Now Liverpool was able to fall back on this tremendous passion less and less, and while the footballing world was changing, the great Liverpool FC was standing still.

Sprechen Sie Scouse?

To be brutally honest, I felt a little let down by the set-up at Liverpool. Yet it was still exciting and not without its funny moments. I remember being in a team talk. Roy Evans, the manager, was really having a go; his emotions were bubbling over. His Scouse accent became thick and rapid fire. I sat there totally bemused. I just could not understand a word he was saying. It was like a foreign language to me. When Robbie Fowler and Ronnie Moran chipped in I was totally baffled. There was a real language barrier for me. I seriously sat there and asked myself if they were speaking English. I struggled at first when Jamie Carragher spoke to me, I understood nothing; Steve McManaman – nothing. I tried to reconcile this. I'd been with my agent in Manchester and I could understand him. I'd been introduced to a Polish agent and I could understand him, and though I had struggled a bit with the Geordie accent when I was in Newcastle, when somebody said, 'Yupthetoontoneetbigmon,' I could just about get it. But this? This was just something else altogether.

Early on, one of the guys posed me a question: 'Ereyergoinfersumscran?' By the intonation I knew it was a question, but I didn't know how to answer; I thought that perhaps he had flipped into Gaelic or something. As time went by of course I came to terms with it, and I later understood that this was a polite invitation to go to lunch. As I settled in I really began to warm to Scousers. They are definitely a different breed of people. Totally unique. Even though there were problems in the city with crime and relative poverty, it was an exciting, fun place to be.

It was rumoured in the press that I would go straight into the team. That turned out not to be the case and I sat on the bench through January and well into February. David James kept his place but still continued to behave as if I didn't exist, as if I wasn't really there.

We were playing Everton at home and I was on the bench. I don't know if he was feeling his own self-imposed pressure, or what, but he was having a really shaky time that day. Jamo had conceded six goals in his previous two games, and we drew 1–1 in the derby thanks to a Paul Ince equaliser 11 minutes from time. Roy Evans had spotted Jamo's discomfort and turned to me in the dugout saying, 'You be ready for the next game.' That was one bit of Scouse that I had no problems understanding.

I had a few days to prepare myself. James was not told that I was going to be in the team, and I could hardly tell him since we weren't really talking. We stayed in a hotel near Birmingham in preparation for the next game at Villa Park. Just before we were leaving the hotel to get on the team bus, Roy Evans pulled him to one side and told him that he would be on the bench. You can imagine he was not happy. He felt insecure and all his worst fears were coming true.

Rather than seeing this as an opportunity to end the rift that he had created, he chose to go into an even deeper sulk about my presence. He didn't take to the pitch at Villa Park for the warm-up and didn't shake my hand or wish me luck before the game. This was a pattern that was to continue throughout our time together at Anfield. Even though we lost 2–1, I thought I played well on my debut. I never got to find out whether Jamo agreed.

Personally, despite his extraordinary behaviour, I've never had a problem with David James. I think he was and still is one of the best goalkeepers in the Premier League. The fact that he holds the record for Premier League clean sheets is not down to luck. It's made all the more admirable by the fact that he has achieved it while having moved clubs several times, and without the aid of some of the most solid defences in the league.

The thing I would say, and I know he can appreciate this now from a position of greater maturity, is that when another player comes in you have to be unselfish about it. By that I don't mean give up your place in the team, but it is not the other player's fault that he has been brought in. If you have a grievance about it, take it to the manager. To achieve real success in football you have to have a cohesive team and you have to, at times, let that rise above self-interest.

Years later, writing in the *Observer* newspaper, David described the feeling of losing his place to me as: 'One of the most profound moments of my career. I couldn't get over it.' He commented how he dreaded seeing me before a match and how childish the whole thing was.

Anyhow, at long last I had made my Premiership debut. Later, I'll come back to Liverpool to talk about my time there. I'm also going to look at team spirit, the dangers of cliques and how I learned to stop looking over my shoulder, worrying about what other people were thinking.

I mentioned that a lot had happened to me before I even got to Liverpool. I may not have played in the Premiership, but I was quite taken aback at what I have referred to as Liverpool's living football museum. I had been used to training in great facilities with some fantastic coaches who set high standards. It created a mindset which became part of me.

It was a mindset which began to develop almost the moment I stepped off that plane in Los Angeles bound for UCLA.

4

California Dreamin'

All the leaves are brown and the sky is grey
I went for a walk on a winter's day/
I'd be safe and warm if I was in LA
California dreamin' on such a winter's day

'California Dreamin'', The Mamas & the Papas

Swimming pools. Movie stars. Los Angeles could not have been further removed from my hometown of Bay Village in every possible sense. It was some three thousand miles away from home. It was enormous, it was glamorous and it was exciting.

For the small-town boy from Ohio, it was a journey that seemed little short of flying to the moon. Yet here I was arriving at the University of California, Los Angeles, and all I had to do was study and play soccer. It was as if I was dreaming, which in a way I was. I was California dreamin' . . .

U$LA

To say that the whole thing was incredible seems like a cliché. To say it was vast would be an understatement. To say it was exciting seems passé. To really get a sense of how I was feeling, you need to understand something of the scale of Los Angeles and the size and prestige of UCLA.

Take Los Angeles itself. It is a city of just less than four million people in an area of 500 square miles. It really is Tinseltown. Movies are being made on the streets and on the university campus; there are beautiful people at every turn and amazing surf beaches. I could quite easily run out of superlatives trying to describe Los Angeles.

Yet I need to hold some superlatives back because more are needed to describe UCLA itself. It is bounded by the prestigious neighbourhoods of Bel Air, Beverly Hills and Westwood. The student population is more than twice that of Bay Village, numbering 35,000. Faculty and staff add another 30,000 people. There is a major teaching hospital on campus, and facilities which are just unimaginable for anyone who has attended a European university, no matter how prestigious it may have been.

For example, in 2005, the average revenue for a soccer club in the English Championship was £13 million a year, or about $26 million, give or take. The athletics programme at UCLA typically has a revenue budget in the region of $60 million. Can you imagine that for a bunch of college teams?

That gives you some idea of the importance placed upon having a good sporting programme in US universities. In the UCLA athletics programme there are 200 coaches and staff, the athletic director is paid a quarter of a million dollars a year and success is not just something which is desirable. It is expected.

The business side of universities in the US is enormous. I would hazard a guess that it is second only to the Catholic Church. If you add up the land values, the annual revenues, the alumni associations and the commercial spin-offs, you are talking about an absolutely massive concern.

Take the alumni associations, for example. These seem to be on a bigger scale in the US than anywhere else in the world. UCLA does particularly well from its former students. Firstly, they establish a strong bond. You become part of the UCLA family. Secondly, donations to alumni foundations are tax deductible in America, so people have an incentive to donate to their alma mater. Thirdly, the whole of UCLA, whatever discipline you are studying, is geared for success. Invariably, people go on and do well. They want to donate and often they can afford to donate. It doesn't take a genius to figure out that if someone goes to UCLA and becomes a prominent actor, and they are living right next door in Beverly Hills, then encouraging them to donate and receive a tax break is not that hard. The Alumni Association has over 350,000 members worldwide and these days brings in more than $260 million a year in donations.

Then, of course, UCLA itself has become a global brand, and there is a department at the university which does nothing other than look after the licensing of the UCLA brand. It's a brand which stands for great sporting tradition and is synonymous with the laid-back California lifestyle. Since 1980, 15 stores selling UCLA-branded goods have opened in South Korea, five in China, and manufacturers have taken licences to produce UCLA goods in Singapore, Mexico and all over Europe. Licensing alone, forgetting about sales, brings in more than $400,000 a year in royalties.

The athletics programme keeps the university's profile high and provides a touchstone for the invaluable alumni. It is something that binds them together, not just while they are students, but for a lifetime. I could call up any one of my old friends from UCLA now, and they would know exactly how UCLA did last week in football. They will know where they will be ranked in basketball, who the draft places are going to, who's signed the letter of intent to come on a freshman scholarship like I did. It's incredible; it's all-encompassing.

Almost everyone who has an interest in sport in the US has their favourite college team. Many people would probably prefer to watch their college team over their favourite professional team. There is a certain air of purity about it. Nobody is taking any money.

Of course, in the US, universities are big businesses, and there is another incentive to have a successful athletics programme. In a good year, it doesn't cost you money – it can make you money. Here is how it works.

There is a pecking order in university sports. American football is the biggest draw, closely followed by basketball. These are televised events, and the TV rights can run into hundreds of millions of dollars. The big rivalry at UCLA is with University of Southern California (USC). The UCLA versus USC football game home fixture is played at the UCLA home stadium, the Pasadena Rose Bowl, which hosted the 1994 soccer World Cup final. The away fixture takes place at the LA Coliseum. It is not unusual to have 80,000 or more paying spectators for this annual fixture. In fact, I would bet that if you had a 200,000 seat stadium, you would fill it. This is the equivalent of Rangers vs Celtic, Everton vs Liverpool or Galatasaray vs Fenerbahce plus a little bit more. So you can begin to get a feel for the level of college sports in the US. It is beyond anything that you will find anywhere else in the world, both in scale and in its marketability.

Star-struck

I began to get a feel for this as soon as I arrived on campus. All around me were people who were stars and who were about to become even bigger stars. I'd walk into the athletics centre and there was Troy Aikman, the Bruins (that's the name given to all UCLA teams) quarterback who later won three Super Bowls with the Dallas Cowboys; I'd be lifting weights next to Jackie Joyner-Kersee who won three Olympic golds and four World Championships in heptathlon and long jump; Danny Everett had won Olympic gold in the 4x400 metres relay; and so I could go on and on.

It wasn't just sporting greats either. The basketball guys played their games at the 14,000-seater Pauley Pavilion, which is where our soccer changing rooms were. In their off season they would just have a bit of fun and have what we call a 'pick-up' game; the kind of thing where you call up a few mates and people rotate during play. We often went along to watch, and you would get people like Magic Johnson who was with the LA Lakers and all sorts of NBA stars just playing 'open gym'. One time I walked in and there was the movie star Kevin Bacon shooting hoops. He was preparing for a movie, *The Air Up There*, in which he plays a college basketball coach. At first it all seemed kind of surreal. I'd walk down the street and there would be Dan Aykroyd; you would walk to class and pass one Olympian after another. It was mesmerising. Day after day I was rubbing shoulders with people who were stars, something that just would not happen back home in Ohio.

Of course, soccer is fairly minor in the overall pecking order of the athletics programme. Luckily for me and the rest of the soccer team, the money generated by football and basketball helps to cross-subsidise the other sports. Soccer, on its own in the US college programme, would be a loss maker. Yet thanks to the amazing income streams, the whole set-up was as good as any professional team. We had our own place to play right on campus: the North Athletic Field. Today they have the Drake Stadium which has a capacity of nearly 12,000 spectators, making it bigger than the homes of some 35 English professional clubs. Everything was taken care of, and with Adidas as our kit sponsors we had all the equipment we could have wanted. We were able to fly to games all over the United States and stay as a team in good hotels. Our coaches were top class too. When I arrived the head coach was Sigi Schmid, who later became an assistant coach with the US national team and was no. 1 at LA Galaxy before taking over at Columbus Crew.

It really was just like being a professional. In terms of the academic side of things, we were treated more favourably than other students. We were given ready-made lecture notes and supplied with tutors, whereas other students would have to pay for these things. In my first year, I shared a room with Dan Beaney, who went on to play in the Major Indoor Soccer League with LA United. He was a defender from New Jersey.

Everything about UCLA seemed amazing, and it was. The place was huge. One thing that didn't have a superlative attached to it was our dorm accommodation. Huge was not a word that you could use to describe it. Our room was in total eight feet by twelve feet and in it were two iron beds. You have a choice about what to do: you can leave it as it is and spend a year banging into each other, you can make them into bunk beds, or you can go out and buy what they call a 'loft'. A loft is a small wooden platform on four stilts. You erect it in your room and put the beds on top, so that you can just about walk underneath them. We bought an old futon to sit on and put our little TV on top of a small fridge. Somehow, we squeezed in a desk for each of us. These things plus our very primitive built-in wardrobes represented home. UCLA does in fact have some of the best student accommodation, but even the best was at best pretty basic.

Even going to the first classes was amazing. Partly this was because the US system is quite flexible and you can experiment with a wide range of subjects before choosing your major subject after two years. So you can study all kinds of things as wide-ranging as astronomy, cooking, French, history – I took an interesting class on the history of the Ottoman Empire. Partly, the buzz of going to those early classes was about just looking around the room and seeing who was there.

So in my freshman class there was Joe-Max Moore, who went on to play for Everton; the women's volleyball team were absolute stars; there were people from the swim team who already had Olympic gold medals. So, it created an environment where success was regarded as the norm. The questions you would get were not of the type, 'Have you made the team yet?' People would casually ask you, 'So, when are you going to the Olympics?'

Redshirt in Tampa

Just being at UCLA kind of gave you a certain cachet. It got you noticed. I guess when national team coaches are looking for talent, then UCLA is one of the first places for them to look. At first they wouldn't have noticed me. In fact they couldn't have noticed me. I went to UCLA as what is known as a 'redshirt'. The way the system works is that you are eligible to play college soccer for four years. If you come in, as I did, as a redshirt, you can only train with the team for that first season – you are not eligible to play. However, after that redshirt season you still have four years of eligibility; even if you have graduated, you can play.

This enables a university to offer a scholarship to a player that they really want, but may not have an immediate need for. So I had to wait for the spring of the following year to make my full debut for UCLA.

You can imagine, with a place the size of the United States, and the number of universities with soccer teams, that having a conventional league structure would be impracticable. There are 23 'conferences' or groupings of teams, covering large geographical areas. At first, we didn't belong to a conference for soccer and so we organised our own independent schedule to pick up a record, to determine our national ranking. Just to confuse things even further, conferences also have divisions. So some of the schools could be in their Conference Division One for one sport and Division Three for another.

Anyhow, our coach Sigi Schmid drew up the most competitive independent schedule he could devise. As a result we were travelling the length and breadth of the US and this proved to be a great way of giving parents a chance to see us play. For most of our parents, California was a big trip, so Sigi's schedule meant that they could at least see one game by driving just a couple of hundred miles. We played in Akron, Ohio, for example, which gave Mom and Dad a chance to watch a game.

We played between 19 and 24 games a season through the summer to the end of the fall. The season culminated in December with the National Collegiate Athletics Association (NCAA) finals. This competition comprises the best teams from the 23 conferences, of which Pacific-10 is just one. Then, through a complex and varied system including the use of a mathematical formula called the 'Ratings Percentage Index', other teams may be invited to take part in the NCAA finals, so that there are 48 teams in all. The top seeded 16 teams receive a bye in the first round, while the other 32 play a knockout game based on geographical proximity, with the home team being the team seeded highest.

Eventually you would get down to the last four teams who would come together at a single venue to play in what they call the Final Four. Now you can see why it helps to have a university degree if you want to understand American sport! Yet this has to happen because of the vast distances involved. If it was a totally random draw like it is after the second round of the English FA Cup, you could see how you could begin the competition in December and still be playing the following Christmas.

Since the tournament began in 1959, UCLA had done really well. We had made the final four times, which, given the size of the competition, is an amazing achievement. We had lost out three times to St Louis in the final and won the NCAA only once. I got into the team in 1990 and we were beginning to gel into a strong team.

I find that people hear the words 'college soccer' and imagine that the quality of the players is of amateur standard. Well we were amateurs in the sense that we didn't get paid, but in terms of the standard, people are surprised when I tell them that the UCLA team would be the equivalent of a reserve team for a Premier League club. The standard was that high in those days. It has changed drastically now because, with Major League Soccer in existence, many of the best players go straight into the league. Pre-MLS, the top universities had a very high standard of players.

This is no idle boast. The evidence is there to support my claim. If you look at any Premier League reserve team, some players go on to make it to the top level and some don't. When I looked around at my 1990 team-mates, this is what I saw: Joe-Max Moore, who played for Nuremberg in Germany and for Everton in the Premier League before a knee injury ended his career (he played in an Olympic Games and three World Cups); Cobi Jones, who played Premier League soccer for Coventry and until recently still played for LA Galaxy at the age of 37, where he is now the first team coach under new manager Ruud Gullit; Mike Lapper played for Wolfsburg then Southend United before joining Columbus Crew; Chris Henderson had a great career in MLS and is now coach at Kansas City Wizards; Jorge Salcedo played in the MLS and is now head coach at UCLA; Paul Caligiuri played in Germany and, among many other clubs, LA Galaxy; and so I could go on.

These guys played in the Olympics and performed well against professional players – the likes of Cafu, Denilson, Roberto-

Carlos, Aldair – and went on to play in World Cups, so you can see that the standard was very high.

The one that got away was a guy called Ray Fernandez. He was a very good player and I think he could have gone on and done really well in the game. Somehow, and this happened to a lot of American players at the time, he did not see the game as a viable way of making a living and ended up playing semi-professional soccer in California.

As we began to gel as a team in my first full season, things really came together and we qualified for the NCAA finals, with a very strong defensive record. We received a bye into the last 16, where we faced San Diego. It was a close game which finished 1–1 after 90 minutes. Joe-Max Moore popped up to score a winner in extra time.

Next up were Southern Methodist University from Dallas, Texas. Our well drilled defence achieved a shutout and we scored twice to give us a 2–0 victory and send us to the Final Four.

The final stage of the NCAA championship was held in Tampa, Florida, and our semi-final opponents were North Carolina State. They were a powerful attacking team and had scored a very impressive 33 goals on their way to the semi-finals. We had to dig deep to contain them and our defence held firm. At 90 minutes it was 0–0. Two minutes into extra time Ray Fernandez was sent off and we were down to ten men. We felt that if we could hold onto the score line we would have done well. In an incredible effort, with only ten men we held the most potent strike force in the competition; it was 0–0 after extra time.

We went to a penalty shoot-out and scored our first three through Tim Gallegos, Joe-Max Moore and Sam George. I had had a busy day already, and couldn't get to their first three, so the scores were level at 3–3. Chris Henderson stepped up to make it 4–3. Scott Schweitzer came forward for Carolina; he would later play professionally in France and the US. After two hours of open play, maybe he was tiring a little. He hit a strong shot, but I managed to reach it and deflect it around the post. When our substitute, Mark Sharp, converted, there was no need for Carolina to take their fifth penalty. We were in the final.

Tampa's USF stadium was the venue for the final. We were to face one of the oldest educational institutions in America. With roots dating back to 1766, Rutgers, the State University of New Jersey, is steeped in tradition. In 1892, a legend was created when their star football player, Frank 'Pop' Grant, had his leg broken playing against Princeton. As he was carried from the field he is claimed to have said, 'I'll die for dear old Rutgers.' This had become something of a motto for the New Jersey boys, and we were expecting them to come at us with that old Rutgers fighting spirit.

They certainly did. Yet we had such a strong defence it was difficult for anyone to score against us. If you can keep a clean sheet, you always have a chance of winning the game. That's what we did. It was 0–0 at 90 minutes once again. Yet again, extra time was not enough to break the deadlock and we went into another penalty shoot-out.

The score was tied at 3–3 with just one kick remaining. We were one kick away from becoming champions. Jorge Salcedo was our final nominated penalty taker. Jorge was a very good player, yet he admitted that he had missed three times before when he had taken penalties.

This time, though, he had the advantage of watching the Rutgers keeper, Andracki, in penalty action. He had noticed Andracki's strategy was to try to anticipate which way the shot was going and to move early. Salcedo saw the goalkeeper commit and calmly placed the ball to his other side. In one kick he had broken his penalty jinx and confirmed us as 1990 NCAA champions.

Cuban Gold

We came home as champions and then had to sit on our hands for a while. Everything revolves around football and basketball, so, if you are a soccer team in college, you find yourself in a ludicrous situation. We would play no more than 24 games a season, and only from August to December, which is not enough to develop at the same rate as players from elsewhere in the world who were playing on a year-round basis. Then during the spring we were allowed to play friendlies, but there was a rule preventing us from playing more than eight times together. This is so as not to distract attention from your studies. To compete on a world stage you need to be playing at least ten months of the year.

This became a possibility for me when my coach Sigi Schmid got a call from the US national team Under 23s coach, Lothar Osiander, asking if there was anyone that Sigi thought he should take a look at. Sigi suggested he come and have a look at me. I'd never been called in anywhere for a national programme, then suddenly you start playing for UCLA and it's as if your stock goes up. It similar to what we see when players get signed by Manchester United or Arsenal; they seem to then automatically go into their national teams. It happened to Louis Saha, for example. He was on fire for Fulham, yet never got selected to play for France. He moved to Manchester United and almost immediately became a French international. That's sort of the way it was when you got into the UCLA team.

Lothar called me up for international duty, and I joined the Under 23 squad for the qualifying games for the 1992 Olympics. Now I was able to play all the year round and, in between my studies, playing for the UCLA team, I was beginning to travel and experience the world.

With the Under 23s side we had a couple of friendlies in Belgium and France. While in France, we went to watch Olympique Marseille playing Racing Club Paris at the Stade Vélodrome. You do not get those kinds of atmospheres in any American sport. You don't get the singing, the burning of flags, smoke and people going absolutely crazy about the game. In American football, for example, you get a huge roar when a touchdown is scored, but other than that if it wasn't for the cheerleaders it would be very quiet. It was this kind of experience that started me dreaming about maybe one day being able to play in Europe.

In the meantime, we had a hectic schedule if we wanted to qualify for the Olympics in Barcelona, and this, together with our friendly games, began to get me used to something which was later to become a big part of my life – long-haul travel. We went to Mexico, Guatemala, Honduras, Brazil, Argentina, Jamaica, Trinidad, Canada, Japan, Italy, Germany, Panama, Cuba and El Salvador.

The Cuba trip was an interesting one. It was the Pan American Games, and when we beat Mexico in the final, it was the first time a US soccer team had won gold in a FIFA-sanctioned event.

Winning was fantastic, and so too was the chance to experience this wonderful place that was Fidel Castro's Cuba. It is such a beautiful country with fine beaches, startling yet crumbling architecture and despite the real poverty, the people could not have been more friendly. Despite their reputed hatred of anything American, the Cubans were kind and welcoming. It taught me that even though countries may be political foes, the people of those countries are still able to get along as one human being to another.

We played our games in Santiago and then Havana. The Cubans had converted a rickety old baseball stadium for the soccer finals. Two makeshift villages were built for the athletes, yet things still had a primitive feel to them: the sewage system was poor and you had to place your toilet paper in a bin because otherwise it would block up the whole system. Little things like this help to build character and stop you from getting carried away with yourself.

Central America was always an interesting place to visit. El Salvador is crazy. Again, massive poverty and fantastic people who were always friendly – except on game day that is. Then they demonstrated their fervent passion and we were the enemy. They would throw rocks, spit on you and try to hit you with bags of urine. Then the next day, they were fine again.

What I will say about El Salvador and other countries that I have been to where there are similar financial constraints, is that a lot of those people who have gone the wrong way in life maybe have no choice in the matter. They either live in the streets with no roof over their heads or fight for survival; sometimes you have to tip your hat to certain people who find a way in life in difficult circumstances. I don't agree with the guns and the drugs but it is a tough road for some people so it's difficult for us to sit here and judge. We are not in that situation. We can't say what we might do if we were in their shoes.

That was the best thing about travelling at the age of 18 and 19. It sets you up for life. There is almost an obsession in the US about going to university. Although of course I will always be immensely grateful to UCLA for the scholarship and education that they gave me, in many ways, I feel that I learned more in the Third World countries than I did in any class at UCLA.

Playing soccer, although not at the top of the sporting food chain in college sports, was giving me a fascinating and exciting life. I was glad that I had turned down scholarships with other schools to play basketball and tennis. Soccer was for me, and it helped me gain a proper perspective on US sports. To me, at any rate, it seems that the complex rule-based systems have created a series of perverse incentives which are damaging sport and taking the excitement out of it.

Take the two big sports: American football and basketball. They work on a draft system, which on paper sounds fair and equitable. Players coming out of college go into the draft and the worst team has the first pick. On the face of it this is designed to maintain a sporting balance by making the weak stronger. How can you argue with that?

Well, I do. My argument is this. It creates a boring season. If you are not going to make the play-offs, you cannot be relegated so there is no incentive to go out and win. In fact there is a perverse incentive. At a certain point in the season, it's better to start losing because, as your record diminishes, your chances of pulling a big hitter out of the draft increase.

What you get in the Premier League is excitement from day one until the final whistle on the final day of the season. There is the fight among the elite to be champions. Half the league has a good chance of claiming a European spot, while the other half is either fighting relegation or fighting to steer clear of the dogfight. Everybody has something to play for pretty much all season. In addition, the bonus payments which increase according to your final position are usually shared among the players. People have said to me that an end-of-season game, say between the teams in 12th and 15th spots, is meaningless. Far from it, there could be an extra half a million pounds bonus associated with each place that a team moves up. There's also the pride factor. Unless you are fighting to avoid relegation, nobody wants to go for a summer break saying they have finished 16th.

Although people might argue that there is an untouchable elite emerging in the Premier League, I don't see it quite like that. Teams are very evenly matched on a game by game basis. The dominance of the big four is occurring because of their strength in depth. They are able to afford to keep effectively two and a half teams of Premier League standard players. They can ride out periods of injury or suspension more smoothly than the others. Yet week in, week out, the Premier League provides excitement, surprises and upsets which have been, to a large extent, smoothed out of American sports.

I also think that in the States business took over too much. The number of teams has increased and there has been a dilution of talent, with a concentration of the best players in perhaps three to five teams. Take the NBA, for example; when I was growing up, there were a lot of strong, evenly matched teams: the Knicks, the Bulls, the Pacers, the Pistons, the Lakers, the Spurs, the Celtics, the Rockets, the 76ers, the Hawks and so on.

A Taste of Fame

One area where American sport leads the world is in the maintenance of statistics. The stats are an obsession for the American sports fan, and with the Opta stats we now see this being replicated in soccer. When I look back over my career at UCLA, I know I can always refer to the incredibly detailed record books if I need to jog my memory. I get a tinge of satisfaction to see that I still hold the all-time UCLA career record for the 'goals against average' which is 0.6 goals a game. I've never played for individual records, but as I write this book, it is good to see that my name is still there.

In all of my time there we lost only seven games. Unfortunately, two of those defeats came in the NCAA championships. In 1991 we lost to Santa Clara 2–1 in the quarter-finals, and then in 1992 we again lost 2–1 to San Diego, going out in the second round.

Yet my final season at UCLA was a good one for me; despite being knocked out of the NCAA by San Diego, my season ended on a high.

I was invited to Baltimore to attend the annual end-of-season banquet organised to recognise America's top college soccer players. Receiving an invitation alone is an honour. It is the culmination of a process which begins at the start of the season. What happens is this. A committee puts forward a list of nominees for the best college soccer player in Division One teams across all 23 conferences in the US. Over the season as performances are monitored, the list is updated and eventually whittled down to 15 nominees. The list is sent to all Division One coaches who then vote, though they are able to vote for someone who is not on the nominee list if they wish. The top three are announced in November and invited to find out the overall winner. I was in good company. The other nominees were Claudio Reyna, who later played for Glasgow Rangers, Sunderland and Manchester City, along with Rob Ukrop who played as a US Under 23 international.

It was a fitting end to my time at UCLA when my name was called out. I was the winner of the prestigious Hermann Trophy, as the US college player of the year. It was an honour to add to my selection as an All-American in both 1991 and 1992.

It came just six months after the Olympics in Barcelona, which you will hear about shortly. It signalled a time when overseas interest in the young American keeper was hotting up. I had a choice to make. Should I stay or should I go? But more of that later too.

UCLA had gotten into my blood. It was an amazing time in an amazing place. I am and will always be UCLA. I am a proud member of the alumni and, in 2002, I was able to do my bit for my alma mater. Frank Marshall was the director of the movie *Arachnophobia* and produced or directed many others including

The Sixth Sense and *Raiders of the Lost Ark.* He has been nominated four times for an Academy Award. He was one of the players in one of UCLA's first soccer teams in the 1960s. Even though we have never met, he and I gifted the $232,000 for new floodlights at the Drake Stadium as part of a $1.5 million refurbishment.

In 2003, I received a great honour by being inducted into the UCLA Athletics Hall of Fame. The list of 179 members inducted before me reads like a 'who's who' of world-class athletes. Jimmy Connors and Arthur Ashe from tennis; Pooh Richardson and Don MacLean, two great basketballers; the great Jackie Joyner-Kersee and Danny Everret from athletics; and many, many more. Just a snapshot of the people who have made UCLA the most successful athletics university in the history of the whole NCAA.

It sure was just like a dream. A dream come true. Dreams don't have to end do they? Surely they can be stepping stones to new dreams. That's the way I prefer to look at it.

UCLA was a stepping stone to many amazing things. One of them was my dream to play in the Olympics.

I was California dreamin' my way ... to Barcelona.

5

Amigos Para Siempre

Citius, Altius, Fortius – Swifter, Higher, Stronger

The Olympic Motto, Baron de Coubertin

Americans are crazy about sports perhaps more than any other nation. They idolise their sports stars, particularly those at the peak of the main professional sports of gridiron, basketball, baseball and ice hockey. Yet for Americans there is nothing higher in the sporting pecking order than an Olympian. They are regarded as the absolute pinnacle, combining sporting excellence with something which is ingrained in the American psyche – patriotism. The Olympics are us against the world and it is a chance to showcase all that is good about the United States of America.

In 1992 the Olympics were to be held in Barcelona, Spain. For many commentators this was the greatest Olympic team the USA had ever assembled, and as an Under 23 international with the US national team, which had qualified for Barcelona, I prepared to take my place as something more than just a soccer player. I was to become an Olympian ...

The Road to Barcelona

I was just a college kid, and we had to do the same as every other team around the world that wanted to go to the Barcelona

Olympics. We first had to qualify, which turned out to be something of an education in itself.

In the first group stages we were up against Haiti and Panama. The home legs were very comfortable for us. We beat Haiti 9–0 and Panama 7–1. Surely the away legs would be a breeze. Yet we found it really difficult to play in those countries. We were young boys and had little idea of what to expect.

Haiti was probably the poorest and saddest place that I have ever been to in my life. What should have been an immensely beautiful place was decimated by incredible poverty. When we arrived we were the enemy. Everybody just wanted to beat the Americans.

The stadium was packed with 32,000 hostile Haitians, some literally hanging from the floodlights, and the only thing between them and us appeared to be little more than chicken wire. Beer bottles were being smashed against the fence and thrown into my goalmouth, so that my 18-yard box was covered in glass. The last thing that anyone would want to do is dive to make a save.

It was an incredibly electric, yet intimidating atmosphere. Even the security men tried to make us feel threatened. As the fans tried to break down our dressing room door at half-time and at the end of the game, the security guys did little to help. Despite the 9–0 walkover at home, it was all we could do to win 2–0 in the highly charged atmosphere of Haiti.

Although we had a police escort back to our hotel, rocks and stones were raining through the windows of our coach. We spent the journey lying flat on the floor, while the local driver ploughed on through, despite bleeding badly from a head wound after having been hit by a rock. You can imagine that this was an extraordinary situation for a university kid from a quiet Ohio village. I remember thinking, Whooah, what's all this about? Yet I also found the whole thing strangely exciting.

In the next qualifying stage we had to play against Honduras, Mexico and Canada. These were more restrained affairs, but we had assembled a really good young team, and came through the group, becoming the first US team ever to win in Mexico.

Just the run-up to the Olympics was a really exciting experience, which brought with it a nice surprise. Those of us who were still in college were given a $10,000 grant. This was for our living expenses and didn't compromise our amateur status. It meant that we could drop out of college for the period in the run-up to the Olympics and concentrate on preparing and playing.

I couldn't believe my luck. I was living out in Los Angeles, all expenses paid, simply keeping fit and going to Olympic training camps. It really was a magnificent period in my life, which helped prepare me for the cut-throat nature of sport. People would come into a 30-man squad, knowing that only 23 men could be selected. You never knew if you were going to make the cut. It was a good learning experience.

Training camps were usually held in Florida where you can play in good weather all the year round. At the final pre-Olympic training camp 30 players were called in and seven would go away disappointed. Every player was allotted an individual meeting with the coach, Lothar Osiander. This was an anxious time for pretty much everybody, but I felt OK about it. I had played in all of the qualifying games and Lothar had told me that I was his no. 1, so, barring injury, I knew that I would be going to Barcelona.

Shopping Trolley Olympians

The first thing that the layman sees of the Olympic Games is the television build-up and the spectacular opening ceremony. For athletes there is a stage before that. It is quite bizarre really and a little like an Olympian version of the TV show *Supermarket Sweep*.

The whole team and support staff were flown into Tampa, Florida. Each group of athletes would leave behind their personal belongings and take turns to go into a huge aircraft hangar type of building. In there each athlete was given a supersize shopping trolley, and as you wandered through the hangar you stated your size or personal details. The soccer team had a deal with Adidas, while the Olympic team was sponsored by Reebok at the time. So we had to have Adidas kit for playing and Reebok outfits for when we were not playing. Every Olympic sponsor wants to give you something, so you load your trolley up with whatever it is that the sponsors want to give you – leather jackets, rings, jewellery, tracksuits, shirts – all kinds of stuff really, and you come away with your supersize shopping trolley loaded up.

Rows of aeroplanes were on standby, and we flew out to Barcelona earlier than most because the soccer has to start a week before the opening ceremony in order for it to be completed by the close of the games. The only people who made their own way to Barcelona were the basketball guys. It was the first time that the NBA players had been able to get together and play together in the Olympics. They were more than just legendary, they made an awesome combination. In one team were three of the greatest players that have ever lived: Michael Jordan, Magic Johnson and Larry Bird.

To us college kids these guys were mega in every way. They were mega famous, mega wealthy, everything about them just seemed astounding. The USA team was assembled in a holding area deep in the bowels of Barcelona's Olympic stadium, awaiting the opening ceremony. As the 'Dream Team' arrived, the organisers inserted them into the assembled throng of athletes so that they were placed right in with the soccer team. There we were, amateurs from college teams, rubbing shoulders and interacting with people who we imagined inhabited a different planet in the sporting universe. Yet this is the power of the Olympic Games and, in truth, the power of sport which can strip away the veneer that we imagine is wrapped around other people by encouraging them to drop their façade and relate to each other, person to person. We were surrounded by greats wherever we looked, many of them from UCLA. Mark Knowles who played tennis for Bahamas introduced us to Jim Courier; then there were UCLA students like Steve Chambers the volleyball star, Carl Lewis and many, many others.

I'm not saying that we all became best pals, but we interacted on a daily basis as equals. These gods of the basketball court, track and tennis court related to us amateur college kids as teammates. That left a lasting impression upon me. The UCLA contingent alone was full of awesome athletes from all kinds of sports.

Someone once calculated that if UCLA was able to declare itself an independent country and compete in the Olympics on its own account, then this small community of 35,000 students would finish fourth or fifth in the Olympic medal table. It would be on a par with somewhere like Britain. That's the equivalent of somewhere like Liechtenstein or Patagonia outperforming major nations such as Germany and Australia.

The other thing you notice about the Olympics as an insider, but which you don't even think about as a spectator, is the tedium of the opening ceremony. Think about it. To get all of those athletes and officials parading around the stadium and assembled where they are supposed to be is a massive logistical task. You can't just turn up and walk in. So teams have to assemble, organise themselves, and then get themselves lined up in the right order long before the first team walks out into the stadium. So the spectacular ceremony and parade which you see on TV doesn't have the same impact for the athletes who may have spent a couple of hours waiting around, before emerging through the tunnel into the light. Of course then it gets exciting for the athletes as they parade into the stadium and begin to soak up the festival atmosphere. Then you take up your allotted place in the centre of the stadium and wait until the parade is complete and everybody is assembled.

It was night-time and the sky was dark as King Juan Carlos welcomed the world to Barcelona. Then the famous Olympic flame appeared through the tunnel and was carried around the track by an athlete who climbed step by step high up into the stadium, through the parting crowd. The flame was held aloft to great applause, and then there followed a dramatic moment of tension. The Paralympic archer Antonio Rebollo appeared. He thrust forward an arrow resting in a large bow that he was holding. The arrow touched the Olympic flame and was alight. Yet the Olympic tower which was to be lit by the flame for the duration of the games was some way away and high up in the night sky. Surely, he was not going to try to ignite the torch from a single arrow. What if he were to miss? There was palpable tension in the stadium as Robollo very slowly and deliberately took aim. He paused.

It was some dramatic pause and the whole stadium took a deep breath. He released the glowing arrow. It went high, much higher than the tower. It seemed to almost stand still in the sky for a moment, before plummeting down to light the Olympic torch as flames leapt into the blackness of the night. Everybody breathed again and the crowd absolutely erupted. The Games had officially started.

All of that waiting around was worth it. I was now truly an Olympian.

Boys Against Men

We had drawn a group comprising Italy, Poland and Kuwait. We had only two players who had any experience of professional football at any level. Steve Snow had played in Belgium for Standard Liège and Curt Onalfo had had a spell in the French Fifth Division. Other than that we were a team of college kids.

The Kuwaitis were not much different in that respect, but when you began to look at the Polish team and, significantly, the Italian team, you came across names like Albertini from AC Milan, Antonioli also of AC Milan and Dino Baggio from Inter Milan, who in later life I would play alongside at Blackburn Rovers. They were laced with Serie A players. Our manager went out and got a paper and in it were pictures of the whole Italian team. He cut them out and stuck them on a board, laying each player out in his respective position. Then he wrote against each name an approximate transfer value. He stuck this up on the wall so that we could all see it. That was some team that we were up against. College kids against top-class professionals, who were plying their trade in one of the toughest and most technical leagues in the world.

Even though it looked like boys against men, we had a very good standard of player. We had been playing for two and a half years in the run-up to the Olympics against professional standard opposition. The thought of facing the young stars of Serie A didn't daunt us one bit. In fact it was quite the opposite. We were all really excited by it. The thing that most of us had in our minds was that this was a fantastic opportunity to get seen and get noticed by being benchmarked against top-rate players. Most of the players had some thoughts about turning professional and the possibility of playing in Europe, so we were untroubled by the price tags that our manager had placed against the heads of the opposition.

Our first game was to be against Italy at Barcelona's magnificent Nou Camp, one the great stadiums of the world which is capable of accommodating almost 99,000 spectators, thus making it the largest stadium in the whole of Europe. On the day, some 15,000 spectators turned up, which gave this massive stadium something of an empty feeling, but the supporters were in high spirits and it was a big game for us.

My mom says that of all the things that have happened during my career, she will never forget that day. As the teams lined up for the national anthems she was overcome with a feeling of pride, and when we sang 'The Star-Spangled Banner' she says she felt the hairs on her neck stand on end. It was a great moment for us and for our families.

I don't know if the Italians underestimated us, but we gave them quite a surprise; we created one chance after another, and with the scores tied at 1–1 they managed to score the winner through a deflected shot which wrong-footed me.

Once the opening ceremony was over we then moved out to play our other group games inland in Saragossa. Funnily enough the biggest attendance was for our least glamorous game, against Kuwait. The La Romareda stadium in Saragossa has a capacity of about 34,000, and with some 25,000 spectators there it made for a great atmosphere. A large contingent of Kuwaitis came to the game to support their country, and incredibly to support us too. Kuwait had been invaded in 1990 by Saddam Hussein during the Gulf War and the Kuwaitis felt that they owed a debt of gratitude to the United States who led the coalition forces which expelled the Iraqi troops from Kuwait and liberated the country in 1991. Hence this was still fresh in the memories of the Kuwaitis and they were cheering both sets of players. They displayed banners saying 'Thank you America', and as the teams came out we joined together for a goodwill photograph with the players of both teams intermingled.

This was a bit of a strange feeling. You have got yourself psychologically prepared for the game and you are going out to be physical and with a determination to win, then you are involved in a friendly exchange and a group photo with the opposition almost in holiday pose. We beat the Kuwaitis quite easily, winning 3–1 and receiving fantastic applause from our own support and from the Kuwaiti fans. It was probably the only time in history that a set of supporters have celebrated a 1–3 defeat.

This was the first time that I had noticed the distractions that go along with competing in a major event. The Olympics is held in such high esteem in the USA that some people don't even realise that there is something even bigger for a soccer player and that is the World Cup. Really for a soccer player the Copa America, Asian Championships and European Championships are bigger as they are fully professional and open age, whereas the Olympics is restricted to Under 23s. Yet for the average American this was the big thing. As a result we took with us a large family and friends contingent. It's only natural that they would want to be part of something that for Americans is the top of the sporting tree.

The US Soccer Federation set up a family and friends programme which followed us wherever we went, and so we always had an entourage of some 150 people. The problem that this brings is that you cannot please all of the people all of the time, and if a decision is made on something, then the likelihood is that someone is going to be upset by it along the way.

This wasn't a problem for me; I was lucky and my family just got on with things in its own way. For some players it became a distraction, with family members complaining to players about all sorts of things from not being able to get ice in their drinks, to not being able to get food between 2 p.m. and 5 p.m. As if a player can get the Spanish to change the cultural norms that have been in place for thousands of years because a bunch of Americans have hit town!

Some parents behaved like the archetypal American abroad,

and this caused problems for certain players who really just wanted to concentrate on the purpose of our trip. We were there to win football matches, and some of the family and friends contingent forgot that that was what was important.

Although we were removed from the epicentre of Olympic activity over in Barcelona, there was an unusual situation in Saragossa that made this tournament seem a bit different from others. Normally, only one team stays in a hotel. Here we had all four teams staying in the hotel, mingling together and all eating together, creating something of an Olympic spirit which was great.

With three points on the board we had a chance of qualifying from our group. We needed to beat a very strong Polish side which was another team filled with full-time professionals. We ended up with a 2–2 draw, which was a creditable performance, but it was a game which on reflection we knew that we should have won. That put us out of the competition, which was a disappointment, there is no doubt about that, yet the Olympics were not over and we were given a choice as to what we would like to do.

Village People

United Airlines was one of the Olympic sponsors and they had flights in and out of Barcelona, so everyone in our team was offered a choice on an individual basis of going home right away, staying another seven days, or staying for two weeks until the end of the games.

Most of us, including me, opted for the seven-day stay, and we moved from Saragossa to the Olympic village in Barcelona. This was the most amazing experience. The village had been constructed by the sea and was built to house something in the region of 9,500 athletes from 169 different nations participating in 257 different events.

The atmosphere was amazing, with athletes mixing together regardless of their prowess or status in a real festival atmosphere. There were cafés, games rooms and each sponsor had built its own shop giving out whatever it was they were in business to do. This resulted in the bizarre situation of having a McDonald's restaurant available to the world's best athletes. It did get some use, but I know that the really top athletes gave it a wide berth. There were a lot of perks to being an Olympian. One of the sponsors, Supercuts, gave free haircuts for a whole year after the games. You could go to one of their branches anywhere and just produce your Olympian card, and you were pampered for free.

Around the village there were large TV areas where athletes would congregate and mingle with each other and there was a great spirit of friendly rivalry with everyone rooting for their country, whether the sport was coxless fours or kayaking or judo there was a fantastic atmosphere and a feeling of friendship towards each other.

It was strange to be watching someone win a gold medal on the big screen one moment and then just a few hours later be standing next to them in the line for the Olympic village cafeteria. Some athletes actually wore their medals around their necks in the village. I felt that some could carry this off, but for others it just looked like a show of arrogance.

There was a USA swimmer, Summer Sanders, who won two gold medals in the 200 metres butterfly and 4x100 metres freestyle; she wore both of them and it just looked right. She was young and cute and excited like a little kid. There were others who flaunted their medals, usually people who you would expect to win. You can understand it when they have just won, but four days afterwards? It started to look a bit showy with some of them.

We spent the next week watching as many events as we could, soaking up the amazing atmosphere and exploring the great city of Barcelona, which has a late night culture, so we would often get home at somewhere between 6 a.m. and 8 a.m. Well, we were out of the competition so it was a situation to be enjoyed to the full and that is what we did.

Then it was back to Los Angeles and after four days of recovery we went straight into pre-season training with UCLA, which the rest of the team had already begun about two weeks earlier. This I find is one of the great things about football. When a big event

The wonder years. Bay Village, Ohio – all white-picket fences and beautiful clapperboard houses. What better place to grow up? Unless you're an aspiring footballer that is… This is me holding a banner for my school's marching band – I'm the tall one.

UCLA first scouted me when I was 17. One year later they would be in need of a goal-keeper and I was awarded a scholarship.

In action for the USA in the 1992 Olympics in our close-fought game against Italy (*Getty*).

I've always believed in giving 100% at all times – at a cup final or in training (*Getty*).

Having visited Wembley with my Dad as a boy, I'd always dreamed of playing there. I finally got my chance in September 1994 (*PA photos*).

Brad Friedel
st Wishes,

Bill Clinton

was privileged enough to meet President Clinton with my fellow team-mates in 1995. A few
ears later, President Bush would be on the phone too wishing us luck against Mexico in the
econd round of the 2002 World Cup.

Me and my US team-mates before a 1998 World Cup qualifier against El Salvador in Boston (*J. Brett Whitesell/ISI International Sports Images*).

The 1998 World Cup squad including 18 Kasey Keller; 9 Joe-Max Moore; 21 Claudio Reyna; 6 John Harkes; 22 Alexi Lalas (*David Silverman*).

...n on the floor with the ball as Luis Roberto Alves jumps over me as the USA take on ...exico in the 1997 US Cup (*PA photos*).

Saving Lee Eul-Yong's penalty against South Korea in the 2002 World Cup was one of two penalties I saved in group play in a World Cup tournament (*Getty*).

is over, you don't really have time to sit back before you are straight into the next thing, which in this case was pre-season training. I'm a great believer in that as I don't think it's good to have too much time to develop an overinflated ego because you think you have done well, or conversely to dwell on mistakes because you have not. It's much better to keep active and to keep striving. That way you keep your feet well and truly planted on the ground.

Just a few days after arriving back in Los Angeles, I joined 1.2 billion other people and sat in front of the TV at home to watch the closing ceremony of the Olympic Games. The games that I had been a part of. The Unified Team comprising the countries which formerly made up the USSR finished top of the medal table with 45 gold medals. My team, the USA, came second, eight gold medals behind.

The closing song was sung by José Carreras and Sarah Brightman with music by Sir Andrew Lloyd Webber. It was called 'Amigos Para Siempre'. It means 'friends forever'. There is still an Olympic spirit which is special and which I am sure touched everybody who was involved in Barcelona 1992. We are all Olympians and in that sense we are indelibly linked. Most of us will never meet again, yet in some intangible way will remain *amigos para siempre*.

6

Bureaucrats 1 - Friedel 0

You were born to win, but to be a winner, you must plan to
win, prepare to win, and expect to win

Zig Ziglar

They say that in life you don't get what you deserve. You get what
you negotiate.

I'd never thought of myself as a negotiator, yet as I look back at
one particular phase in my life, I can see that is what I had to
learn to be. I've adopted a simple principle: decide what you
believe in and stand up and be counted. There will always be
people with opposing views. For a time, it seemed that almost
everybody thought differently from me. Yet the more I stood up
for what I believed in, the more opportunities opened up for me.

Then an immovable object came up against an unstoppable
force. It was British bureaucracy versus Brad Friedel. A game that
I had to win ...

The Art of Being 'One'

If you were to ask my mom what I was like as a little boy, she
would tell you that I was comfortable being around people, and I
was equally comfortable being on my own. I would sit for hours,
all alone playing with my toys. Being 'one' has never been a

problem for me, which probably goes some way to explaining why I don't fall in with the views of the majority or the authority just for the sake of it.

That's not to say that I am a rebel in any way. When it comes to affairs of the team I've always tried to be a true professional. I turn up on time, I follow the dress code and I carry out instructions to the best of my ability. As an individual, I have always been just that – an individual. I'll think about things and formulate my own opinion. If I believe in something I either want to follow through with it or defend it. Perhaps this is why people have at times branded me as stubborn or set in my ways.

I am in fact nothing more or less than a principled individual. This has meant that I have had to stand up against authority, go with less fashionable kit suppliers and risk never being able to play for my country again. Yet I am glad that I did these things. I learned that principles and determination can take you a long, long way. Without these things I could never have taken on my biggest battle. The battle with British bureaucracy.

All of the travelling that I was doing with the Olympic team, and the top-class players I was playing against, had got me thinking about the idea of becoming a professional soccer player. Whenever we went to play in France, a Frenchman called Eric Meter would take care of all the travel arrangements for the US team. When we were over there in 1990 Eric began talking to me about the chances of playing in France. He felt that he could help to set something up. At the time I was a young American player who was unknown and he thought that the best I could hope for was the Third Division of the French Football League. The view in France at that time seemed to be that American players were not that good. It didn't really appeal to me and I didn't take the discussions any further.

Then American players started moving over to England. Kasey Keller went to Millwall; John Harkes joined Sheffield Wednesday; Roy Wegerle was settling in at Queens Park Rangers and several others were going to European clubs.

At about this time, a British football agent called Graham Smith, along with former Arsenal defender Bob McNab, had begun poking around at UCLA. McNab had finished his career coaching in the National American Soccer League (NASL) and then moved to Los Angeles to become a property developer. Still, he just couldn't resist the lure of football; he and Smith came to watch a game and then would regularly come and watch me train.

When Graham Smith and Bob McNab started to talk to me, it was exciting because they were talking at a completely different level than Eric Meter had been. They had good connections with Premier League clubs. Bob, of course, had strong Arsenal connections, but with David Seaman established there was no way I was heading there. He also had good links with Nottingham Forest and Liverpool.

The Ottoman Empire vs Brian Clough & Robin Hood

In a roundabout way, it really all started when Graeme Souness was the boss at Liverpool. That was way back in 1991. Graeme had gone to Liverpool to try to transform the club. It was a tough time for him because he had Anfield legends such as Bruce Grobbelaar, John Barnes and Ian Rush coming to an age where he may have thought that their best years would soon be behind them. He was instead hoping to bring through the likes of Steve McManaman, Robbie Fowler and Jamie Redknapp. He liked to stamp his authority quickly, and inevitably his ideas were not popular, particularly among the 'old guard', one of whom, Phil Thompson, was fired. Meanwhile he was getting flak from the fans for selling the story of his heart bypass operation to the *Sun* which was a newspaper despised by many on Merseyside because of its inflammatory reporting of the Hillsborough disaster where 96 Liverpool fans died. Times were tough for him. In mid-1992 he had signed David James and I think he needed some goalkeeping competition for him so that he could move Grobbelaar out.

Some time later, there was a conversation between Bob McNab and Graeme Souness about me. Graeme was keen. He sent a scout over to have a look at me and it looked like it was all going to go forward, and that a move to Liverpool would be imminent.

The weeks passed with no contact from Liverpool. I don't know where you draw the line and imminent turns to improbable, but somewhere during the waiting period that's what happened.

With no word from Liverpool, Graham Smith and Bob McNab had managed to get me a trial at Premier League team Nottingham Forest. Having returned from the '92 Olympics I knew that I wanted to drop out of college and become a professional, and I told my coach Sigi Schmid who wished me well.

Not everybody felt the same. My trial was set for December 1992. At the time I had three classes going on in the university. I went to see each of the professors in turn, to see if I could take my finals early. My history professor said yes and I passed the paper on the Ottoman Empire; my literature professor said yes and I passed Russian literature; then my third professor who was running a prerequisite class declined to let me take the paper early. As I boarded the plane for England I decided that I should drop that class and would have to take it again sometime.

You can imagine, with my mom coming from a background in education, she was not very happy about me dropping my studies to play soccer. Yet by this time, even though I was still a young kid, I'd got used to making my own decisions. To pacify Mom and Dad, I said that I could always go back and finish my degree if things didn't work out.

The funny thing is that 17 years later that is still true. As I was awarded a scholarship, I still have the right to go back and carry on where I left off and pick up my scholarship grant for one more year, provided I am not under contract to any professional football club. I have a little over a year's study to complete and, who knows, I may just take the family to California for a year or so and do just that.

So I was a dropout, and Forest paid my expenses during the trial. They put me up at a hotel called the Windsor Lodge, which is quite close to the City Ground, and each day I went into training. I didn't see a great deal of the legendary manager Brian Clough, but he obviously made sure that he saw me. At the end of the ten-day trial, Forest had a contract waiting for me.

I thought that I had struck gold. The contract read like this. I was to get 50% of the £300,000 transfer fee, which would be £150,000; a signing-on bonus of £150,000 paid over three years; wages rising each year from £300 per week to £500 per week to £750 per week; plus bonuses.

In 1992 that was a heck of a lot of money for an American still in university. Of course this was all subject to the granting of a work permit. I was a young kid, I signed the contract and thought, Well, how hard can it be to get a work permit? I was about to find out.

To try to smooth the deal through, Forest asked me to sign for one day with the Dallas Sidekicks of the US Major Indoor Soccer League. Obviously, they thought that it would look better on the application if I was coming from a club rather than straight from college. Of course, this was all new to me and if I had known then what I know now, I would never have agreed to do it that way.

$35 a Day Keeper

The contract was signed, the work permit application had gone in and I flew home to be with Mom and Dad for Christmas. I got a call while I was at their house. It was Bora Milutinovic, the US national coach. He called me in to the national programme.

With no US professional league in existence, any players called into the national pool were all in residency in Southern California. It ran rather like a club team, and we would have 30–40 games a season from 1993 through to the summer of 1994. So with the permit still being considered I went to California and carried on training and playing with the national team.

This is where I began to feel compelled to stand up for what I thought was right. The US Soccer Federation wanted all the national pool players to sign contracts with them. They promised to pay you a monthly wage of about $2,500, but they ran the contract on a month-to-month basis, so they could just drop you as they felt like it. Also, they demanded to keep 90% of any transfer fee should you be signed by a professional club.

I didn't like the sound of this from the outset. At first I was able to say that I had a contract pending with Nottingham Forest, and they just had to agree. The contracted players had apartments, while I was put in a hotel. It was fine by me; they gave me $35 a day and free food.

At the end of January 1993, the first of many setbacks came. My work permit application had been rejected. Only then did I begin to look into the criteria and started to realise that I had chosen to try to play in the country that had the tightest of restrictions on foreign players. I realised that I was a college kid with one cap when you needed to have played 75% of your country's games; I was on a good wage but I was not going to be in the top 15% of Forest's wage earners – one of the permit criteria which was meant to demonstrate that you were a key player and not on the periphery – and, of course, realistically, in the world of soccer I was a virtual unknown. I hadn't had a clue about all this; the agents hadn't spelled it out to me.

Forest put in an appeal, but some six weeks later it was rejected. With the Forest contract now effectively void, the US Soccer Federation began to bang on my door telling me that I had to sign this contract of theirs. I refused calmly and politely, yet firmly. I explained what I had been offered at Forest and told them I just would not sign the contract.

Roughly the Forest contract had been worth $500,000 a year, and the Federation was offering $30,000 which they could terminate any time they wanted. I told them that the whole idea was ludicrous and that I was happy to continue on the $35 a day arrangement and be free to do my own thing.

They came back with a revised offer of $3,200 a month guaranteed until the 1994 World Cup. I said, 'No.' They said, 'Well, what do you want?'

My position was absolutely clear, which is why I was sticking to it. I wanted very much to play for my country, but I didn't want to have to sign a contract to play for my country. At the same time I wanted to carve out a good and long career for myself in Europe – to play for a club and for my country just like every other international player does. The Federation officials said they would go away and think about it, then get back to me.

A week later Bora sent for me. He had a grave look on his face as I walked into his office. As I sat down, he said, 'The Fed says you have to go home. I want to keep you here, but you won't sign their contract. I have to send you home.'

I said, 'Bora, let me ask you a question. How on earth is this a footballing decision?' Why would I have to sign a contract to play for my national team? It's not as though I could go off and play for Mexico or Brazil. I told him that if I were to get a contract with a team in Europe it could only benefit him. I would be getting better, playing in a good league against better players. I said that I could not believe that the national team manager was telling me that I couldn't come into camp because I wanted to better myself as a footballer and better myself for the national team.

Truly, this whole contract business was unnecessary. It was just the Federation's money-making scheme. They could see that a lot of the players had the potential to play in Europe and they wanted to rake in the transfer fees.

They threatened to kick me out five times, but I held my ground and they eventually backed off, leaving me on the $35 a day arrangement that I was happy with. My team-mate Mike Lapper had signed the Fed's contract and one day we happened to open our pay cheques together. He saw mine and I saw his. He was open-mouthed when he saw mine. There was very little difference at all. With my $35 a day plus game bonuses, I was making $2–300 less than the guys under contract.

I chose my own way and maintained my flexibility. I was beginning to get a reputation as someone who, though not a problem child, would stand up for what he believed in.

It happened again, when Adidas came calling. They had been the kit sponsors for UCLA so I'd played in their kit all through my college days. Maybe they thought that because I wasn't contracted to the Fed I was short of money. They offered me a kit deal in which I would get $25,000 a year. The lesser known Sondico came along and offered me four and a half times what Adidas had offered. Also, they asked me to design my own glove and goal-keeping apparel and gave me a royalty on sales. I thought about the pros and cons of each and I discussed it with my good friend and mentor Tim Harris. I chose Sondico. Not just because of the money – the whole thing was just more appealing to me.

Incredibly, this simple decision opened another can of worms. Bora took me to one side. He said, 'You don't sign for Adidas. Why?' I explained my reasoning at length. He looked at me and said, 'Bad decision.'

What? How on earth can the brand of glove that I'm wearing dictate what happens on the field? I'm thinking perhaps there is something else going on here. Anyhow, Sondico didn't do boots and Reebok didn't do gloves at that time, so I also signed a boot deal with Reebok worth $75,000. Therefore, just with my national team pay and my sponsorships I was making quite a good living.

My Name Is Milan Mandaric

Things took a more intriguing turn when Bob McNab asked me to come and meet someone: a prominent businessman from Northern California. My friend Tim Harris and I drove down to a Red Robin Restaurant in Orange County, Southern California, and Bob was there with an immaculately dressed gentleman. His name was Milan Mandaric.

He had grown up a Serb in communist Yugoslavia, and at 21 took over his father's machine shop. Five years later he had the largest business in the country making spares for the automotive industry. His success saw him branded a capitalist and, leaving most of his fortune behind, he headed for the United States. He created and built the Lika Corporation which manufactured computer components in the Silicon Valley boom era, and then sold the business to the Tandy Corporation. Other successful businesses followed and he began to invest in his first love – soccer. He had owned San Jose Earthquakes when George Best played there, and then went on to own Standard Liège in Belgium before taking over at Nice in France.

Why would this guy want to meet me? Bob introduced me and Tim, and we had a pleasant chat, before Milan put forward a proposition. He said, 'I will give you exactly the terms that Nottingham Forest offered you, but I will own you. If you sign a contract with a club, I take the transfer fee.'

Tim and I looked at each other. They say that when you are made an offer that sounds too good to be true – it probably is. We thought that there was something not quite right here. This guy would pay my transfer share, signing-on fee and wages? This sounded like a crazy proposition. We probably upset Milan a little because we stalled. We tried to find something wrong with this deal. We looked at it all ways to try to find a problem with it. We couldn't. What Milan was proposing was perfectly legal and above board. I signed a personal services contract, and Milan honoured the agreement, paying my signing-on bonus and wages exactly as in the Forest contract.

Of course anyone that follows English soccer will know that Milan subsequently bought Portsmouth and then Leicester City. He is a lovely man. He is the kind of guy with whom, once you become his friend, you are his friend for life. He is one of the three most influential people that have helped me in my career. I'm not sure that he even knows how influential he has been. He had tremendous faith in me and he placed his trust in me. He showed he wasn't afraid to put his money where his mouth is.

By not signing for the Federation, I now found myself earning a pretty decent six-figure sum without even having a club. I didn't make it public, there was no reason to. The big earners in the national team, guys like Tony Meola, were getting about $75,000 plus endorsements. I just kept it quiet. Bora got wind that there was something going on involving Milan, but he had no need to worry, all Milan wanted was for me to get the requisite number of caps so that I could get a work permit.

Milan liked Bob McNab a lot, but there were not a lot of clubs coming forward. Graeme Souness, who was still having a difficult time at Liverpool, began talking to us again. Then Liverpool hit a run of bad form and were not relishing a third round FA Cup tie at Ashton Gate, the home of lowly Bristol City. With the game poised at 1–1 and with Liverpool in the ascendancy, the floodlights failed. There was a second chance to finish off the minnows, but the replay ended 1–1 as well. Now, with the second replay at Anfield, surely this would provide some respite for the troubled team. It didn't. Grobbelaar was lucky not to be sent off and Tinnion scored the winner for Bristol.

It was January 1994 and it was a case of goodbye Graeme as Souness resigned shortly afterwards. With him went my prospective move to Liverpool.

Roy Wegerle had carved out a good career for himself in England and had introduced me to his agent, Paul Stretford. With little interest coming from England now that the Liverpool situation was unsettled, I switched agents and signed up with Paul. Milan was a little concerned about this. He liked to stay loyal and I think he felt that he was not totally in control of the situation. I reassured him and explained that I believed that Paul Stretford had my best interests at heart. Milan was worried that our agreement might be interfered with in some way, but I convinced him that Paul would not take him to the cleaners.

Keegan Is Confident

Paul Stretford was connected and influential and brought the former England captain and Newcastle United manager, Kevin Keegan, to the table. Newcastle put in a bid for me of £600,000. It was January 1994 and Bayern Munich were over in Cleveland, Ohio, in their winter break. I was there with the national team playing Bayern in a friendly and Paul came over with the Newcastle contract which I signed there and then and Milan sanctioned it. So it was all going ahead, contingent upon getting a work permit.

The difference was that I was no longer a one-cap wonder as I had been at Forest. I now had something like 40 caps. Tony Meola and I were alternating in games in a head-to-head competition to see who would be the no. 1 choice in the '94 World Cup. So with the best will in the world it was impossible for me to play 75% of my national team games. We were hoping that the work permit application would be resolved before the World Cup because there was the chance that I might not play. As it panned out, the

Home Office dragged out the permit application until after the World Cup. Of course Tony played all four games and was regarded as the no. 1 choice.

After the World Cup, I was officially at that time the US no. 2. The work permit application was again rejected. It was maddening because I felt that had I played in those World Cup games the outcome of the application would have been different.

After the World Cup I went back to California to collect my things, and Kevin Keegan told me to come over to Newcastle despite the work permit rejection. He sounded really confident that the permit could go through on appeal. He had Pavel Srnicek and Mike Hooper at the time but he wanted a new keeper.

I felt very optimistic when I got to Newcastle. Keegan's ebullient attitude made me think it was just a matter of time before they got the permit on appeal. It seemed like they had no doubts. They treated me like any new signing. I was put up at the Gosforth Park Hotel and given a club car. They searched for and found a house that I could move into, and I trained and travelled with the team, even though I couldn't play in a game.

There was a real buzz about the place. They started off the 1994–95 season with a bang, playing Keegan's swashbuckling brand of attacking football. It was a free-flowing team in a rich vein of form, including players like Barry Venison, Rob Lee, Andy Cole, Peter Beardsley, Ruel Fox, Scott Sellars, Darren Peacock, Malcolm Allen, Philippe Albert, Lee Clark and Steve Watson. On top of this, the Geordies were great fun, immensely passionate and very loud. It really was just a great place to be.

Of course, Kevin Keegan was a major reason why there was such a buzz on Tyneside at the time. He is a player's manager and another one who has a built-in winner's mentality. I thought back then, and it is probably still true today, that he had a particular skill as a manager. He was brilliant at making average players believe that they were better and he would get them to perform better. To this he added a mix of eccentricity, flair and goals through players like Beardsley, Cole and later on Asprilla and Shearer. Kevin is a really bubbly character and he tends to live on a high which players love, though because of his winning mentality he could quickly go the opposite way in defeat. While I was at Newcastle, they were absolutely flying; I don't think they had lost a game. Keegan created so much fun when he was winning that it was almost a carnival atmosphere and the players absolutely loved going into training. I was enjoying it for sure, but only from the sidelines.

Naturally people tend to think that the player applies for the work permit. This in fact is not the case. The work permit is granted to the club in respect of a particular player. I was with Newcastle for about ten weeks when the appeal was rejected. The PFA were heavily involved in advising the Home Office on appeals. I couldn't understand how some players with lesser credentials than me were getting through the work permit process. I wondered if there had perhaps been some bad blood between Newcastle United and the PFA.

Paul Stretford had good connections in Denmark through his colleague, the former Manchester United player Jesper Olsen. Brondby, one of Denmark's top teams, had an injury to one of their keepers. With my appeal rejected, I went over to Denmark during their winter break and signed a contract until the end of the season. In Denmark, you needed a work permit, but it was simply a matter of filling in a few forms. It was quite a different process from that in the UK.

Their no. 1 choice was Mogens Krogh, so I wasn't going to go straight into the team. The Danish Superliga has quite an unusual format. In 1994–95 there were ten teams in the Superliga and the season is divided into an autumn season and a spring season. At the end of the autumn season, Brondby stood at the top of the league. Then what happens is quite peculiar. The top eight teams split off from the other two and play each other in the spring season. The points that each team has won in the autumn season are then halved, so Brondby, having finished the autumn season with 27 points, began the spring season with 14. I came into the team and played ten reserve games out of the 14 spring season matches, but we were overhauled by a free-scoring Aalborg BK and finished the season as runners-up, just two points behind them. Still, it got me playing, albeit not at the level that I was striving to play at, and Brondby had achieved a UEFA Cup qualification.

While I was at Brondby, the national team were in the preparation phase for the 1995 Copa America to be played in Uruguay. I joined the team in Belgium, where we played a friendly, and in the crowd that night were Peter Reid, the Sunderland manager, and his assistant Paul Bracewell, who I'd met at Newcastle.

That summer I was in Paysandu, Uruguay, at the Copa America, when Sunderland matched the bid that Milan had accepted from Newcastle. Paul Bracewell showed dogged determination in his bid to get the contract signed. Paysandu is not the easiest place in the world to get to, so he had to endure a journey of something like 27 hours to get to me. We had a chat, I signed the contract and he got up and went home.

As a team we did well in the '95 Copa, getting knocked out in the semi-final by Brazil. I had played well too, and this is an important tournament, having the same status as the European Championships. So when Sunderland made a work permit application, I felt I had a very strong case. I had more caps; I'd just been the no. 1 in a top tournament; Peter Reid had made it clear that I was to come as Sunderland's no. 1 choice and that nobody else was going to play, and I was going to be in the top 15% of the club's wage earners. He laid out the case quite clearly.

The application went in and in August I was with the national team playing a friendly against Sweden in Norrköping. A journalist had somehow got hold of my hotel room number and rang me up. He introduced himself and then just came out with it: 'I understand your work permit has been denied again.' I could not believe it. I put the phone down and rang Paul Stretford, who confirmed the news that I didn't want to hear. Yet again I had hit a brick wall.

It was summer. I had no contract with Brondby. I believed I was going to Sunderland, and yet here I was with the season about to start and I didn't have a club. I had to ask myself what on earth was going on here. Was the PFA operating a policy of trying to protect its own, by opposing permits for foreign players?

Without a club, I went over to Denmark. A good friend of mine,

Mike Burns, was with Viborg and I trained with them just to keep myself fit.

In a rather poetic turn of events, the guy who began this whole merry-go-round by making initial enquiries about me, Graeme Souness, had taken over at Galatasaray in Turkey. He was allowed to have three foreign players, and his top priority had become finding a new goalkeeper. When Graeme knew I was available, Paul Stretford put together a deal which would take me to Galatasaray for $1.1 million and this was sanctioned by Milan Mandaric.

Throughout this crazy period of uncertainty, Milan had seen to it that I had security, and with all the problems I was coming up against, thanks to Milan, the one thing I didn't have to worry about was money. Milan took a calculated risk. He is a great guy, and I am pleased he got a good return for the faith and trust he placed in me. He is one of those guys who understands more than most that in life and in business you don't get what you deserve, you get what you negotiate.

7

Globetrotting Goalkeeper for Hire

Don't go around saying the world owes you a living. The
world owes you nothing. It was here first

Mark Twain

Welcome to Hell. This is the greeting that awaits all who come as
visitors to Galatasaray's Ali Sami Yen Stadium. The Turks are passionate, football crazy with a capital 'C', and they will scream,
shout, sing and occasionally go into a full-scale riot.

Life with Galatasaray was played out in a fever pitch, frenzied
atmosphere. It was exciting and rarely without incident. If you
were an opposition player or supporter, a visit to Galatasaray
could seem like Hell. Yet behind the match-day façade, I found
something that I was not expecting to find. Rather than Hell, in
Turkey and in the Turkish people, I found a little bit of Heaven ...

Turkish Delight

I left my training stint in Viborg in rather a hurry, boarding a
plane bound for Istanbul almost as soon as I got the call from
Paul Stretford saying that the Galatasaray deal was going to go
through.

When I got to Istanbul it was midnight, and as I approached
the passport control desk, I realised that I needed a visa to get

into Turkey. This was not such a big a deal as it sounds because people were buying them at passport control for £10 or $20. It only became a problem when I searched through my wallet and found that I was carrying only Danish krone, and credit cards were not accepted.

I knew Paul Streford was waiting for me behind two sliding doors beyond the customs area, so I implored the guards to slide open the doors and ask Paul to hand the money through. Eventually they agreed, and as they slid back the doors, I noticed an unusually large crowd of people who were waiting to meet passengers off the midnight flight.

I got my visa stamped, cleared customs and headed into the arrivals hall. As I did so I was hit by a barrage of flash bulbs as a horde of paparazzi headed in my direction. There were photographers everywhere, and I had not even signed a contract! I hadn't anticipated how big football is in Turkey and before my time was up I was going to spend an awful lot of time with these guys.

The former Liverpool defender Mike Marsh was on his way out of Galatasaray. He just hadn't been able to settle into the Turkish way of life, and Paul Stretford had to finalise Mike's deal first because of the limit on foreign players at Turkish clubs.

Even with Mike's deal finalised we waited until the last moment before signing, since there was a slim chance that Sunderland or Liverpool might come forward with some form of proposal. It didn't happen and I signed for Galatasaray amid an even bigger media scramble.

I began to get a feel for the immense passion of the Turks and their absolute obsession with football. When I turned up for the first training session, there were 2,000 people there who had come along just to watch. I would have felt flattered, except that it turned out that this happened all of the time. It was absolutely nothing to do with me.

Istanbul is a unique city. It is the only city in the world that is situated on two continents. Located on the Bosporus Strait, the city is divided either side of the magnificent natural harbour, the Golden Horn. On the one side is Europe, while the other side sits on the boundary of the Asian continent. At UCLA I had taken a class on the history of the Ottoman Empire, and now here I was living and working in the place captured by Sultan Mehmed II in 1453; the place that he declared to be the capital of the Ottoman Empire. It is an ethnic and cultural melting pot with a spectacular skyline of domes and minarets. I found the whole place so exciting. The other two foreign players in the team were Barry Venison, whom I'd met before at Newcastle, and Dean Saunders. Barry and Dean lived at Etiler where they had commanding views of the Bosporus. I made my home in Florya, close to our training ground and not far from the Black Sea.

I found it really great fun and very interesting as I immersed myself as best I could in the Turkish culture. I got myself a Turkish–English phrasebook, and subscribed to the satellite TV station Cine Besh. I would watch the movies and hear people speaking while looking down at the subtitles at the bottom of the screen. In time I could hold a reasonable conversation about football, talk to taxi drivers and be comfortable in restaurants, but if somebody wanted a debate about politics then I might struggle a bit.

It was proving to be a fascinating place to be, with extremes almost everywhere you looked. The northern side is very liberal, and even though it is a Muslim country very few of the women covered their head in a veil. There was a vibrant club scene, yet if you crossed the bridges and ventured south onto the Asian side it became much more traditional and more recognisably Muslim.

Man-to-Man Marking

The paparazzi were becoming my constant companions. There are specific football newspapers in Turkey, and the photographers are given targets for the number of pictures they have to get in a day. Journalists have a lot of space to fill, and inevitably the Istanbul-based football clubs are the focus for much of the TV coverage. So I got used to the situation where day after day I would walk the 50 yards from my home to the training ground with photographers waiting for me and as I walked they would take photographs of my head. The same head they had photographed a day or so ago. Then they would ask, 'Where are you going?' They awaited my reply as though we had never been through this ritual before. 'I'm going to the training ground.' Hardly a scoop, but the Turkish media is a relentless consumer of the minutiae surrounding football so they would follow you to the shops or the cinema or anywhere you happened to be going. The people are so in love with football that if there was a Hollywood actor or actress and a Galatasaray or Fenerbahce player walking down the road you could bet your house that everybody would know who the footballer was first.

Passion Explodes

I got used to being in the spotlight pretty much all of the time, but never more so than during games, when players became a target for more than just the occasional flashbulb. I made my debut at home against Genclerbirligi. It was an 8 p.m. kick-off, yet the stadium began to fill up at about 4 p.m. In Turkey, the 'foreplay' is all part of the experience of going to a game, and all four sides of the stadium would sing to each other in the run-up to the kick-off. Then during games all hell would break loose. Firecrackers, klaxons, drums, and a singing, chanting crowd which had worked itself up into a frenzy was the standard backdrop to a game. I had a good debut and I was quite happy with the way I played. We lost the game 1–0 and a goalkeeper was the star of the show. It just wasn't this goalkeeper. The thing I remember most about my debut is that the opposition goalkeeper had one of those days which we all dream of. He had an awful lot to do, but he was absolutely magnificent. Everything we threw at him, he managed to save. Still, I was encouraged. Here I was playing top-class first team football in the most amazing atmosphere and in a place that was both exciting and fascinating. Very quickly I began to feel right at home in Istanbul.

The away games were interesting. We had a tremendous support which followed us to the point where some of our away games felt almost as though we were playing at home. Yet the intimidation of the opposing fans often began before we had even entered the ground. When Barry Venison left, he was replaced by the Dutch defender Uli Van Gobbel, who was new to all of this when we headed off to Samsunspor to play in the quarter-finals of the Turkish Cup. The backup at Galatasaray was amazing. Everything was done for you. Your bag would be packed even down to the detail of your toothbrush. You had to do just one thing. Pick up your bag and take it into the stadium. When we arrived at Samsunspor we were met by an angry crowd which pushed up towards our team bus. They were being held back as we waited to collect our bags and take them into the stadium. Uli perhaps had not quite acclimatised to the strength of feeling that Turkish fans hold for their opponents, and quite nonchalantly swaggered over to retrieve his bag. As he bent over to grab the handles and lift it, a Samsunspor supporter broke through the cordon and launched an almighty drop kick, with Uli perfectly positioned to be on the receiving end. By the time Uli had recovered his composure the supporter had disappeared into the crowd. It was a rather undignified welcome to Turkish football.

Getting into the stadium was not without its hazards, but getting out on the pitch could be an altogether more dangerous ordeal. With the changing rooms situated underneath the stands, players have to walk up a staircase and come up pitchside through a kind of hatch. It is almost as though somebody gives a signal to let the opposition supporters know that the away team is coming out because a barrage of missiles, usually coins, begins to hurtle towards the tunnel hatch. Nobody takes their time getting onto the pitch in Turkey.

Throwing coins at the goalkeeper was such a common occurrence it almost had the status of a national pastime. It was an occupational hazard, and I would be smashed on the legs and hit all over the place. It was tough to maintain concentration in that sort of situation, but on the plus side, you realise that if you can concentrate under those conditions, you can concentrate virtually anywhere.

My mom always asked me if I felt threatened in this atmosphere. It was scintillating and at times dangerous, but I didn't feel threatened personally, and I found it all easier to accept because of some of the situations I had found myself in with the national team in places like El Salvador, Haiti and Costa Rica.

We progressed to the semi-finals of the Turkish Cup by beating Samsunspor; then we faced Besiktas in a two-legged semi-final. We triumphed and had made it to the final.

The draw had kept us apart from our greatest rivals, the famous Istanbul club, Fenerbahce. These two clubs have a rivalry which goes beyond the norm. In fact you might say that they have a mutual hatred for one another. This is a derby match on such a scale and of such intensity that it has to be one of the greatest derby matches in world football, certainly in terms of atmosphere. It is not uncommon for violence to erupt, before, during and after these games.

The Turkish Cup final is a two-legged affair, so our great rivals had to make the short trip across town for the first leg. In a tight, highly charged game we won and were able to take a 1–0 lead with us across to their home, the Sukru Saracoglu Stadium. At full time in the second leg it was 1–0 to Fener, making it 1–1 on aggregate. In extra time we pulled the scores level, giving us a 2–1 victory.

Souness's Last Stand

It was a dramatic game, but the real drama was yet to come. The manager, Graeme Souness, was delighted at the fantastic result, yet he had approached the game knowing in the back of his mind that his time at Galatasaray may be coming to an end, and through no fault of his own. In Turkey, as in many European countries, the club president is elected for a given term. As we were approaching the cup final the hype of prospective presidents was beginning to pick up a pace. Faruk Süren was a frontrunner for the presidency, and had made a pledge that if elected he would bring in Fatih Terim, the boss of the Turkish national team, who had the status of cult hero in Turkey. Graeme knew that, despite his success at Galatasaray, if Suren was elected then the writing was on the wall for him.

We were ecstatic at winning the Turkish Cup on Fenerbahce's

home ground and our fans were going wild as the podium was being erected for the presentation of medals and of course the cup. As we prepared to go and pick up the cup, Graeme got caught up in the emotion, and perhaps wanted to reinforce the message that he was committed to Galatasaray, even if the incoming president may not be committed to him.

Seeing a Galatasaray fan waving an enormous flag by the side of the pitch, he left the group of players who were patiently waiting to go up and lift the cup. Retrieving the flag from the ecstatic supporter somewhere near one of the corner flags, he rested the 12 foot flagpole on his shoulder, and ran towards the centre circle. Surrounded by smoke bombs, he skipped a few paces and rammed the flag into the centre spot. It didn't stick so he tried again, only for it to bounce out. He made no mistake on the third occasion and, putting the force of his whole body into it, he ceremoniously planted the flag of Galatasaray in the one place it had no right to be. The whole place erupted. Galatasaray fans were going wild celebrating the symbolism of Graeme's gesture. It was as if we had conquered and claimed their territory. If the Galatasaray fans were going wild, the Fenerbahce fans were wilder. Not only had they been beaten at home by their fiercest rivals, Graeme's gesture was rubbing their noses in it. It caused an absolute riot.

Fenerbahce fans began throwing anything they could get their hands on in our direction. Still we hadn't lifted the cup and a group of police officers rushed over and formed a protective circle of riot shields around us. We huddled together under the riot shields listening to the *thud, thud, thud* of one missile after another, watching the Galatasaray fans rejoicing and taunting their rivals about the flag which still stood in the centre of the pitch. We lifted the cup as the riot continued around us. Graeme, knowing that this might be his closing gesture as the manager of Galatasaray, savoured the moment, and as the Fenerbahce fans tried to climb the pitchside cages, swearing that they would kill him, he looked around and smiled as he walked down into the tunnel.

It was some time before we were able to properly celebrate the win. We spent the next three hours locked in the dressing room under police protection. Graeme was always very passionate about his football and dedicated to winning, having been brought up in winning environments. When you achieve a goal as a team and win a cup together that's a great feeling, and for someone like Graeme, even more satisfying if you have beaten your most intense rivals. While we were holed up in the changing room he was revelling in the atmosphere despite the rumblings which were going around about his future as manager. He had quite some time to soak up the elation of winning because there was no way we could have gone out into the streets until the rioting crowd had dispersed. When we did get out to our coach it soon became clear that the Fener fans were lying in wait. We had the curtains drawn on the coach and almost immediately began to hear the thuds against the side of the bus as it was battered by missiles. We all hit the deck and then a full bottle of Heineken smashed through the window. Graeme was still in his celebratory mood of defiance and he moved over to a window, slid his arm under the curtain and gave a clenched fist salute to the Fener fans. *Toooch, toooch, toooch* was the response as more missiles headed our way. Although I didn't see the papers the next day I understand that the picture of Graeme's clenched fist featured prominently. The picture of Graeme planting the Galatasaray flag in the centre circle has become an iconic image for the fans and for a long time it seemed like every Galatasaray fan had a T-shirt with that picture printed on it.

The rivalry between the two teams had never been so intense, but I did find that during my time in Turkey, apart from the match days, if you treat people as people they will respond. I had my difficulties with rival fans at times. There was one time when I went out and forgot to put down the shutters on the windows of my apartment. It was a day when we had won and Fenerbahce had lost. When I returned, there was a large rock lying in the middle of my living room floor and glass was everywhere. I looked at the rock and painted on the side was the word 'Fener'.

Their natural instinct is to hate you because you are Galatasaray. Locally, I found that if I was respectful, and talked to them when I was out, they began to warm to me a little bit, and their comments turned to friendly banter. They would laugh with me, and if we lost they would enjoy a laugh at my expense. It became good-natured rivalry, rather than the hatred that you would sometimes encounter.

Even walking into a shop could show up the divisions in the city. Once I went in and asked for a particular jumper that I wanted. I asked the assistant to get it. He looked at me and said, 'I am Fener.' I said, 'I don't care. I'd like that jumper over there please.' It was obvious I wasn't going to get it. I said, 'Thank you very much' and walked out. On the other side of the coin, a Galatasaray shop assistant would ask you which TV you wanted and implore you to take it free of charge.

With the exception of religion, I always tried to live my life as a normal Turkish person would. I shopped at the local fruit and vegetable market, I drank their chi and the strong Turkish coffee, and I hung out in local restaurants. I always tried to find friends who were Turkish; it gave me a great insight into their lives and I particularly enjoyed visiting their homes and seeing how they lived from day to day. I just loved learning about their lives and adapting to a culture which was completely different from my own.

Columbus Is Calling

During the close season I went back to the States to join up with the national team and begin preparation for the qualifying games for the 1998 World Cup. While I was there, the international fixture list came out and around about the same time Graeme Souness was sacked. He had brought the Turkish Cup to Galatasaray, and his flagplanting exploits had made him a legend among the Galatasaray fans. Yet nothing could save him. Faruk Süren had been elected president of the club and had kept his pledge of bringing in Fatih Terim as team manager.

At this time, individual football federations set their own international fixture dates. Our federation, CONCACAF, bore little resemblance to the fixture dates used by UEFA, which European leagues were bound to adhere to and accommodate appropriate slots into their domestic programmes. Our US international fixture programme scheduled 16 games of which 11 fell outside the UEFA international fixture dates.

Graeme Souness immediately fell into a job as manager of Southampton and had expressed an interest in taking me there, while Roy Evans was now the Liverpool manager and had rekindled Liverpool's interest, which had originally started with Graeme. This made me conscious that I had to do everything in my power to get my international caps up to the qualifying level for a UK work permit.

When I went into pre-season training with Galatasaray, I was really impressed with Fatih Terim, the new manager, and one of his first moves was to offer me a two-year contract. I had a big choice to make. Either stay in Turkey or focus on improving my chances of increasing my international appearances. I explained my thinking to Fatih. If I signed, the fixture list would mean that I would miss 11 of Galatasaray's games. That would be no good for the team or for me, and the amount of travelling I would be doing to make the international fixtures would inevitably take its toll. Fatih understood the situation, and Galatasaray agreed that I could go on loan to Major League Soccer (MLS) in the USA, which was in its inaugural season.

So that is what happened. I signed for the MLS on the understanding that I would play for my local club Columbus Crew. That's how the system works in the States. You sign for the league and arrangements are then made to allocate you to a club either through a loan or a payment. The MLS held my registration as a loan player and in due course made the move permanent by agreeing to pay Galatasaray in the region of $500,000. I had a clause inserted into the contract which said that if a big European club came in for me then they would allow me to go.

When I arrived at Columbus Crew, they were bottom of the league. I came in, several players including my old UCLA team-mate Paul Caligiuri got fit again and we went on an amazing run, winning nine games in succession and keeping seven or eight clean sheets. This run propelled us into the play-offs where we faced Tampa. The format was that the play-offs were a knockout competition, but it was the best of three games. We lost the first in Columbus, then went to Tampa and won, before losing the decider. This 'best of three' idea was just another attempt at the Americanisation of the great game of soccer. Thankfully these kinds of novelties are now being sidelined as the MLS is beginning to resemble the rest of the world, and as a result is gaining more credibility.

As I entered a second season with the Crew, I had a heavy schedule of international games and my percentage of caps was creeping up towards the magic 75%. Liverpool came in with an offer of about $1.5 million, subject to what had become the bane of my life, that is, getting a work permit. Liverpool put in the application and I gave my word that I would sign for them if it was approved. Shortly afterwards, Glasgow Rangers got in touch. Walter Smith was in charge and they sounded me out about a move, offering more money than Liverpool. I hadn't signed anything with Liverpool, but, more importantly, I had given them my word that I would sign if they could get the work permit. That meant more to me than the money. I had to do the right thing, and so I thanked Rangers for their interest and waited for news from Liverpool.

News came. I'd played 73% of international games and the bureaucrats were insisting on 75%. The work permit was rejected.

Welcome to Hell.

8

Gaffers in the Grey Area

I know where I'm going and I know the truth, and I don't have
to be what you want me to be. I'm free to be what I want

Muhammad Ali

Earlier I talked about my first impressions of Liverpool after my
permit came through on appeal. The cliques, the archaic training
methods and David James's self-imposed vow of silence. It was
not quite what I had expected as I had dreamed of playing in the
Premiership during those years battling for a work permit.

Yet I was playing and that's what mattered. Still there were
more struggles and more pantomime to come at Liverpool.
Having made my debut at Aston Villa, I prepared to walk out at
Anfield for the first time.

Trial by *Telegraph*

It was 7 March 1998 and Bolton Wanderers were the visitors. Alan
Thomson scored an absolute screamer against me, but thankfully Michael Owen and Paul Ince came up with the goods at the
other end to make sure it was a winning home debut.

Paul Stretford rang on the Monday morning. He said, 'Brad,
don't read the *Telegraph* this morning.' Well, I wouldn't have done
as a rule, but once he had said that, I couldn't resist going out and

getting a copy of the paper. A former Liverpool star had written a piece. No sooner had I made my first mistake, he was calling for Liverpool to sign a new goalkeeper. I had learned at Galatasaray that when you play for a big club you have to take these things, whether or not you think that they make any sense.

As far as football pundits are concerned, many of them like the pundit lifestyle, being negative without being accountable to anybody for anything. I don't think someone doing a negative article on a player is particularly ingenious or brave, especially when it is about a player at your 'beloved' club. I sincerely hope if ever I end up in that position after I finish playing, that I will try to back the players in a respectful manner. Point out mistakes, of course, that is a pundit's job, but getting personal is not a pundit's job.

Fortunately for me, my experience at Galatasaray had prepared me well for this sort of thing. Turkey is a big country, but for a footballer it is a goldfish bowl and you are permanently in the spotlight for better or worse. If it hadn't been for this experience, I don't know how I may have reacted to this particular pundit's negative outburst. Admittedly, I was not playing faultlessly. I needed to break out of my shell and be less insecure, but I think it is cowardly to sit in a chair and direct blame with no accountability. You don't hear current players, managers or coaches slagging off players publicly. They tend to smooth over the sharpness in their comments, aware that they may be making the same mistake next weekend. I think Andy Gray is excellent at this, and I think most players would agree. Even though he no longer plays and is neither a coach nor a manager, and therefore in that sense unaccountable, he points out mistakes in a more acceptable manner. I have no problem accepting blame where it is due, but a pundit, and a former player especially, should always try to show greater empathy.

What I had learned is that you have to live with this stuff and let it wash over you. Even learn to laugh at it if you can. If you can do this, as you get older you learn to be comfortable in the knowledge that what you are doing is good, correct and the right thing. Then people can say whatever they want to say if it helps them to earn a crust.

It's really a process of tuning things out. Almost as if you are in control of the tuning dial on a radio. You only have to hear what you want to hear. You have to do the same with the crowd as well. Take my first game in front of The Kop, for example. I found that I didn't take it in as much as I have when I have been back and played against Liverpool. You become so focused on the game that you don't notice the crowd, which is a good thing because as a goalkeeper you are quite close to the crowd throughout the match and if the team isn't doing the business, you can be a receptor for their negativity. During my time at Liverpool the crowd did turn a little negative. Whether it was due to the team having a bad patch or me as an individual, I don't know, and I did let that get to me a little bit. Now, I have learned to be able to tune out the crowd completely when I want to. If I feel that there is a time in a game when I can allow myself a little mental break, I'll sometimes tune in and have a listen to what's being said. Now that I'm totally in control of it, it's fun and I can enjoy the occasional banter that I get from away fans.

Despite the 1960s training regime and internal strife with Jamo, we were doing quite well. The young Michael Owen was emerging as a goalscoring force, and the squad was studded with great players: Robbie Fowler, Razor Ruddock, Jamie Carragher, Steve McManaman, Paul Ince, Karl-Heinz Riedle, Jamie Redknapp, Patrick Berger and, of course, David James among others.

Paul Ince was great to have around. He is a natural born winner. As a player he really enjoyed everything about his life to the maximum, on and off the pitch. He puts his all into everything. When Incey stepped on a pitch for a big game you knew that he would be one of the best two or three players there. That was him: a guy who always rose to the big occasion. This is true of all the managers I've had who were once successful players. They are used to winning and they can usually take their playing experiences and put things over to you. Sometimes that's difficult, especially when managing lesser players, because a manager can get frustrated and want to be out there. It's always easier playing, but as a manager Incey got Macclesfield Town out of jail, and took MK Dons to promotion, so it seems he is good at getting his message across.

The thing that stands out about Paul Ince is that he always takes the room. He has an aura about him, so that it doesn't matter who is in the room, his presence will take over.

Razor Ruddock, although he didn't feature that much in the team by the time I got there, was a top guy. He was hard on the pitch and yet gentle and easy-going off it. He had a great wit and loved being the social secretary. He was a great asset to the dressing room.

Michael Owen was perhaps at the other end of the spectrum. He was young, quiet and unassuming, but his massive talent earned him immediate respect and he slipped into the squad with ease. The guy was going places, but for me at that time I felt that Robbie Fowler was the better finisher. Michael had great pace and knew how to finish for sure, but Robbie seemed to have more of a special instinctive knack for finishing. He always seemed to know when to shoot, he could spot a goalkeeper wrong-footed or off-balance in a flash and somehow he always seemed to find the corner of the net, often without needing to put much power into his shots. He was outstanding, I thought, but not a disciplinarian's cup of tea. Robbie had a kind of English anti-authoritarian way about him. His attitude seemed to be: 'I'll play the games and I'll play them well, just let me do what I want to do'. He would take great delight in catching Phil Thompson off-guard at training and firing a ball with great accuracy so that it smacked him on the head. Things like that didn't endear Robbie to the management team.

Robbie's big mate was Steve MacManaman. Steve was a real nice fellow, a free spirit type, and I found him very welcoming. He and Robbie were actually very switched on and both have made some incredibly astute investments over the years.

The guy that seemed to have it all was Jamie Redknapp. He was good-looking, he married the beautiful Louise, was an England international and playing for Liverpool. What a combination! His career never quite reached the peaks it could have done because of injuries, which is a shame because I found him to be a good person from a good family. He could adapt to different situations. If there was a big social scene he could join in with that, if there was a clampdown on drinking he had no problems going along with it.

Anyway, we ended the season in third place behind Arsenal and Manchester United. We had secured a UEFA Cup place and I had managed to make 11 Premiership appearances. All in all, I was happy to be at Liverpool, thrilled to be doing what I wanted to do more than anything – play in the Premiership – and I was ready to make a mark during the 1998–99 season.

Houllier Parachutes in

When I returned from the 1998 World Cup, the most extraordinary thing occurred. Liverpool called a press conference to announce the arrival of Frenchman Gerard Houllier. Roy Evans was there believing that Houllier was to be the club technical director. To everyone's astonishment, especially Roy's, Houllier was introduced not as technical director but as joint manager. By all accounts this was the first that Roy had heard of this, and like the loyal professional that he is, he kept his own counsel in front of the press. I can only imagine what was said in the boardroom after the press had left.

Really, bringing in Houllier and his outstanding coach Patrice Berg was a move that had to happen. The whole club needed to be revamped from top to bottom if it was to have any chance of competing at the highest level. The way it was done, how it panned out and its conclusion struck me as an absolute disgrace. A loyal servant of Liverpool FC and a genuinely good human being, Roy Evans was treated diabolically.

None of us knew what to think about the joint manager situation. Who was in charge? Who should we call 'Gaffer'? Who did we go to if we had a question or a problem? None of this was made clear. In truth, I don't think anyone had thought through the implications of this bizarre situation. What tended to happen was that the guys who had been signed by Roy went to him and Houllier's signings went to him. The crazy thing was that they didn't need to give you an answer. When anyone raised an issue, invariably Gerard would say he needed to speak to Roy. Roy would say he needed to speak to Gerard. When you asked if you could meet them together it always seemed to turn out that one or the other was too busy to meet.

Rarely did we see them together. It was quite comical really. The one good thing about it was the introduction of Patrice Berg to coach the team. He was a revelation and of all the coaches I have worked with, Patrice is in the top two, along with Eddie Niedzwiecki. The whole approach was different. Patrice was much more scientific; he introduced heart-rate monitors. I can hear you laughing, but we didn't have things like this. We began position-specific training, he paid attention to detail in terms of diet, stretching methods and strength conditioning. He cleared out the old gym equipment and brought in all the latest Technogym equipment, so that all of us had a key containing our entire workout monitoring data.

Now we were being looked at as professional athletes and assets of the club. The whole approach was to try to improve the assets, both as people and as players. This was in stark contrast to the system that was in place when I arrived, which in crude terms I would sum up as: 'Let them play and hope they behave themselves'.

At first some of the players, the long-serving ones in particular, struggled to adapt to this new approach. Patrice came down hard on drinking schools, timekeeping and anything that he regarded as unprofessional. Then people began to accept the new regime in the way that other clubs were and a lot of the senior players in particular began to see that this was going to be of benefit to them. They became much better players because of it.

The management team had concerns that some players were not as conscious about their diets as you would expect professional footballers to be. In fact some players would have chicken and chips for their pre-match meal. Berg could not believe this. He took all the butter and the fatty foods away. They pulled some players who they felt had a weight problem and singled them out for special attention.

I didn't have a weight problem, but I did come under Houllier's gaze myself. At that time I would sometimes eat a chocolate bar before or after training, which I now know is not the best thing to do. Houllier pulled me to one side. 'You are always eating chocolate bars,' he said. I felt that it was giving me an energy boost and I explained this and he seemed OK, but obviously I know much more about nutrition today, partly thanks to the attention it was being given at that time.

Occasionally, Houllier would get a call or a letter from a member of the public saying that they had seen one player or another out late and drinking. I think that they found this behaviour to be unacceptable and at times maybe struggled a bit to come to terms with British culture. Yet Patrice did not rule out drinking altogether. As a Frenchman I guess that a glass of wine was more than just an alcoholic drink to him, it was part of his culture and an essential accompaniment to a meal. He deemed alcohol in excess to be a poison for the muscles, but was lenient towards players who wanted just one glass of red wine. He figured that the nutrient value in red wine outweighed the alcohol content.

I had already changed my diet before Houllier and Berg took over, but I have to be honest that I had grown up in a football culture where it was the thing to play a game and go out with your team-mates for a drink. I liked a beverage as much as anyone. For me that stopped in 1998. I wanted to be playing regularly for Liverpool and if that meant no drinking then I had no problems with that, and have remained that way ever since.

Houllier and Berg were astute observers of everything and were not afraid to confront problems of any sort that needed to be addressed. They would home in on individuals, groups, the team or wider issues in the club itself. They even felt the need to single out club captain Paul Ince, to the surprise of all of the players including me. Incey was made for the big occasion and always tended to perform on the big stage. For some reason Houllier and Patrice had a different view of Incey to that of the players. He was taken to task in front of the whole squad about something that had gone on in training.

We were taken aback by this. Incey was a great player and respected by all of the other players. I think that Houllier was trying to make a point, to demonstrate that he was the boss because at that time in Incey's career any manager would want a fully focused Paul Ince playing for them; yet before long he was on his way to Middlesbrough.

So things were changing. Houllier came with a clear agenda. The club desperately needed a revamp and he was a very smart strategist. He created a close relationship with the board, which loosened up funds for rebuilding the team and upgrading the training facilities. The pitches were always superb and Patrice brought a new and vital approach to training. Houllier was always looking out, trying to sign the next player who would add to the squad.

I prepared well and had a really strong pre-season. I was straight in the team for the first game of the season at Southampton. I was playing well and was looking forward to our meeting with Manchester United at Old Trafford. It was seven games into the season, I was feeling good and we were third in the league. A win in Manchester would really give momentum to our decent start.

I don't know what happened, but I ended up having a terrible first 20 minutes. I miskicked early on, and then a shot squirmed underneath me and went for a corner. When the corner came over, I punched the ball high into the air instead of long. It came down and hit Jason McAteer on the arm. The referee gave a penalty and Denis Irwin put it away. Things calmed down after that, but Paul Scholes added a second and we lost 2–0. Those 20 minutes gave Roy Evans the jitters and sowed a seed of doubt in Houllier's mind.

We went into training prior to our UEFA Cup game against the Slovakian team MFK Kosice. Nobody pulled me to one side to tell me I wasn't playing. The team was simply stuck up on the notice-board, and Jamo's name was where mine should have been. Of course, now he was back in the team he found me slightly more tolerable, but once he was out it was back to not speaking again.

While he was in the team, I had a difficult time with my

confidence at first. I played against Tottenham in the fourth round of the League Cup and had a nightmare first half. We were at home, and we had the players to win it. We lost 3–1 and I have no one to blame for two of their goals other than myself. I hadn't quite got my confidence back and I was looking over my shoulder too much.

Jamo was happy while he was playing, but as the season wore on I found myself back in the team for the final push. Jamo had a poor spell as the team slipped from fifth to tenth in the League, and he and Houllier were not seeing eye to eye.

Fudge & Tears

Nottingham Forest's great manager Brian Clough used to say, 'There can be no grey areas in football.' Despite the improvements which were emerging, the joint management approach left too many grey areas. Someone had to call the shots, and decisions were being fudged too often to try to maintain some kind of a consensus between Houllier and Evans.

Something had to give and, in November 1998, it did. It was Roy Evans. After 34 years at Anfield, Roy chose to resign rather than take on the back room role that was offered to him. It was a very sad day. This man had given his life to Liverpool Football Club. He loved Liverpool with a passion. Liverpool was not just a job to him, it was his whole life. His reason for being.

Roy came into the changing room to break the news to the players. It was very emotional for all of us and, in the course of his farewell, Roy broke down in tears. I really felt for him. I know football can be a macho sport with a 'big boys don't cry' attitude, but I do believe that every one of us could understand Roy's reaction. Quite a number of the players were fighting back the tears themselves. It was bad enough having to leave, but I felt the way it was done just stank.

I think that the whole Houllier affair was down to the 'powers that be' at Liverpool not being brave enough to make a difficult decision. In doing so they created a grey area that was more like a chasm, and a good man had to suffer. I think that they concluded that Roy's time was up but didn't tell him outright. It would have been tough to do that but far better than what they put him through. It is also my belief that Houllier knew when he came that Roy would soon be quietly moved upstairs.

In my own business dealings I've learned from this. If you have a difficult decision to make, it is better to make it rather than fudge it. Prevarication and uncertainty can make a situation ten times more difficult.

Roy inherited the hot seat at a time when things needed to change. He is a lovely guy and players wanted to play for him, but he was not a moderniser. Had he taken up the post ten years earlier, I am certain he would have been a great success and become an Anfield legend as a manager. Liverpool at this time needed a moderniser, a strategist with a new vision, and that is what they got in Houllier.

As one double act was beginning to unravel, another had begun. It was in some ways as unlikely a match as Houllier and Evans. Yet, unlike their combination, this was one that was really clicking.

As a goalkeeper, you get used to a degree of isolation and you learn to live with it. So much so that I hadn't even realised that there was something missing from my life. That is until I found it.

Pocket Dynamo

I wasn't even looking and quite by accident the most incredible thing happened. I found my alter ego, the yin to my yang, if you like. I scored a golden goal.

It was while I was in Denver, Colorado, with the USA team. We were preparing to play in the Confederations Cup in Guadalajara, Mexico, which is situated at high altitude some 1,600 metres above sea level. These are difficult playing conditions for anyone and we needed to acclimatise. Denver is set high up in the Rocky Mountains and some resorts are as high as 3,000 metres above sea level. So we set up our training camp there for three weeks and flew into Mexico for games.

It was the most amazing setting, and really great fun. I've never known anything like it. We went out every night, except before games of course, and funnily enough ended up playing some of our best football ever.

It was on one of these nights out that I met Tracy. This girl was unlike anyone I had ever met before. My being a footballer had no effect on her whatsoever. She knew only two words of football – Juventus and AC Milan – which she had picked up from Italian friends when she lived in New York. She knew nothing of the game, and didn't particularly want to.

They say that opposites attract, and we were total, complete opposites in every way, and yet something just clicked between us. I'm tall, placid and quite docile, really. Tracy is feisty, energetic and highly strung. She cannot sit still for a moment. If someone crosses her, emotions take over and she lets them know straight away. *Bam*. People love her or hate her for it. With me, if somebody crosses me and I don't think it's such a big deal, I'll just leave it. I'll let it scoot over my head.

I like Tracy's approach. There's a bit of me that sometimes would like to have that bite on occasions. Maybe that's what the attraction was. She came over to visit a couple of times and then came for good and we married. I thought, This is pretty good; the two of us make a great team. She looks after one part of our lives and I look after the other. Remember, this was a time when the media were starting to take an interest in footballers' wives and girlfriends.

Tracy is about as far from the stereotypical footballer's wife as you could get. Yes, she likes her diamonds and handbags, but that's as far as it goes. She's a bundle of energy, eclectic, different. She gets bored easily and has to be doing something all the time. I'm often saying, 'Whoa. Just sit down and relax for a moment.' She is her own person and can't settle for just being a footballer's wife. She has two degrees, one in business and one in psychology, as well a financial trading licence. She cannot stand a life of doing nothing, so she began to take over some of the property development work that I was involved in.

She is off the wall, and I wouldn't have it any other way. It has given me a totally new perspective on how relationships can be. Before, my relationships had been very structured, predictable, kind of small town Ohio. With Tracy, I never know what to expect. That's exciting.

Chinese Whispers

It was while I was playing in the Confederations Cup that I gave an interview and began to see Houllier's controlling nature about the media. I was approached by *Soccer365* to comment on the forthcoming season. Now Houllier had brought in a lot of players, something like 12 in his first term and then another 15 or so. Sometimes players click immediately, sometimes it takes a bit of time; I gave an interview which said something like, 'When you bring in a lot of players sometimes it can work, sometimes it's a shambles. I really hope it works for Liverpool.'

As I returned home, I was walking through passport control, and somebody said, 'Hey, you're in the paper.' Talk about Chinese whispers! The paper said, 'Houllier Shambles – Friedel' or some such nonsense. When Houllier had me in his office I explained what happened. He was beside himself, but I told him he could look at the interview online; I would never say negative things towards the team, especially when we were going into a new season and optimism needed to be high. When I turned up for training, the team photo had already been taken without me. He could have waited and I think he was giving me a message. He believed that I would have a go at him in the media and left me out of the first squad of the season. I had to get the interview transcripts to prove my innocence. It's not in my nature to be negative in that way. If I had a problem, I would ask to speak to the manager. Needless to say, I have never given another interview with that particular journalist.

With Houllier now calling the shots himself, David James was sold to Aston Villa and he brought in a new player. A goalkeeper, Sander Westerveld. He shelled out £4.5 million, which at the time was a lot of money for a goalkeeper. It meant only one thing: that I was not going to be Houllier's first choice. That's the way it turned out and I warmed the bench for much of the season. Yet Sander and I enjoyed a great relationship which was totally opposite from the one I had with David James. Tracy found a new friend, Judith Westerveld, and the four of us would often spend time together. Tracy's beautiful naivety and total lack of interest in soccer meant that she had no idea that Judith's husband had been brought in to take my place. As a result, we all struck up a valuable friendship.

I determined that I would be nothing other than a total professional all season. I gave Sander all the competition for his place that I could, and I genuinely wished him well when he was playing and I wasn't. But I needed to play. I hadn't fought a five-year work permit battle to warm the bench. Having spent £4.5 million on Sander, there was no way Houllier was not going to play him.

The guy that started the whole Liverpool merry-go-round, Graeme Souness, came in to bring it to a close. There was something quite poetic about that. Graeme was now managing Blackburn Rovers in the old First Division. It was a drop down from the Premiership, but I had been with Graeme at Galatasaray and I had faith in him. What's more, I would be playing regularly. I was available on a free transfer, with the proviso that Blackburn would take over the bonus payments due to the MLS. This was £300,000 (£100,000 every time I reached 100 appearances up to 300).

Everything was agreed and then Houllier sent for me. I still had a year left to run on my contract, and he sat me down and told me he would like to offer me a new contract. For me it was a non-starter. I just told him that I had to play and that I felt I could progress my career somewhere else at this time. Then he got a bit jittery. He said he wouldn't sanction anything if I went to the media. Perhaps he was thinking back on the 'shambles' episode a year earlier. He wanted me to sign some sort of declaration to say I wouldn't go to the media. It was all very odd, I don't know what he thought I might say. I said, 'Look, I'm not signing your piece of paper, I've got better things to do with my life than go to the media.' He backed down, and those were the last words we spoke.

In a short period I had been through the best of times and the worst of times. I'd found the person I wanted to spend the rest of my life with, and I had learned something about myself. At times at Anfield something was not quite clicking for me. I blame no one except myself. When I look back I realise that I often felt like I was looking over my shoulder, trying to impress somebody. When I played in the States I didn't care what anyone thought, I shook off my inhibitions and just went and played. That was how it was going to be in the future.

Whatever inhibitions I may have been carrying on my shoulders, I left them in the Anfield locker room. I'd been a roving goalkeeper making my home in cities across the world. Now I was heading for Blackburn – to be a Rover.

9

Four Thousand Holes

I have been a rover I have walked alone Hiked a hundred
highways Never found a home

'Love's Been Good to Me', Rod McKuen

There is an unforgettable line in a song made famous by The
Beatles, 'A Day in the Life' written by John Lennon and Paul
McCartney. The line goes, 'I read the news the other day oh
boy/Four thousand holes in Blackburn, Lancashire'.

As far as I knew, there were no holes in Blackburn, Lancashire.
Least of all in the Rovers defence. When Graeme Souness came in
for me, Blackburn Rovers already had not one, not two, but three
top-class goalkeepers. Why on earth would Graeme want another
one?

Some observers might have looked at my move to Blackburn
as an odd one. I was leaving a top Premiership team to play in the
First Division; I was going to be one of four people fighting for
one position and, to top it all, I was taking a 60% pay cut. It may
have looked as if I had taken leave of my senses. As if I had dug
one of those 4,000 holes for myself, into which I would sink, never
to be seen again.

Yet something about it felt right. I had a lot of faith in Graeme
Souness, who had been my boss at Galatasaray. Together we had
been successful, so I felt no reason to be anxious about holes in

Blackburn, Lancashire, imaginary or otherwise. I was on my way ...

Four Into One Won't Go

Graeme Souness and I had always enjoyed a very good working relationship. It was he, as manager of Liverpool, who made the initial enquiries that kicked off my five-year work permit battle. We never actually got to meet face to face when he was at Liverpool, though we did speak on the phone a couple of times.

The first time we met properly was when he signed me to play for Galatasaray. I think we developed a mutual respect. He knew that I always trained hard and did well for him on the pitch. I knew that as long as I did that he would always treat me well off the pitch. You cannot be best mates with your manager, but it is always better if you can have respect for each other.

Souness had taken over from Brian Kidd as manager of Blackburn Rovers in 1999–2000. Only five years earlier Rovers had been the Premiership Champions. Under new management they were languishing in fifteenth spot in the First Division, but under Souness's leadership were beginning to put a run of games together. Graeme and I spoke shortly after his arrival and the goalkeeping position was the last of his worries.

He had three excellent goalkeepers in Alan Kelly, John Filan and Alan Miller. He had a lot of players to clear out. This was not easy, as players had been bought when the transfer market was on a high and now it was on a bit of a slide. Blackburn had over-paid for some players, who then for one reason or another failed to perform to the level they had at their previous clubs. While in the Premier League, Blackburn had signed quite a number of players in the £2.5–£6 million bracket. When relegation to the First Division came, it proved difficult to move these players on for anything like the fees that had been paid.

So Graeme continued a costly clear-out and ended the season in the bottom half of the First Division. Blackburn seemed to be able to take the financial hit on these transfers thanks to the backing of the steel magnate and owner Jack Walker, and while I was at the Sydney Olympics with the USA in 2000, Graeme began rebuilding and contacted my agent about the possibility of me going to Blackburn.

I wanted to play more than anything, and I didn't think my prospects were too bright while Gerard Houllier was still at Liverpool, so work began on putting the deal together. It seemed that everything was going to go through, when Rovers were hit by devastating news. Jack Walker had suffered a heart attack and died. The Jersey-based multi-millionaire and local boy made good had pumped millions into the club, had catapulted Rovers to their Premiership success and supported the rebuilding that was now under way.

I thought the deal was dead as I flew back from Sydney, and I was getting ready to resume training at Liverpool when the call came to say that it was back on again. It was then that Houllier called me and offered me a new contract at Liverpool. Yet I wanted to play more than anything and while Blackburn waited for yet another work permit, I went over and trained with Everton for a couple of weeks, courtesy of the Everton manager of the time, Walter Smith, who remains a good friend.

This was another occasion when Graeme Souness did well for me off the field. I would be willing to bet that not one of the Rovers board wanted to sign me. They had three goalkeepers there already; they didn't want to pay the wages of another. Graeme went in all guns blazing and battled with the board to get my deal through. He was always very good at getting people to do what he perceived to be the right thing for the club, even when they disagreed with him.

Yet for me it was a risk. I saw it as a calculated risk. I took a 60% pay cut, but I still had some signing-on fees and loyalty bonuses to come from Liverpool, so I figured that, for the first year at least, I would be on the same money as I was on at Liverpool. When I looked at the team that Graeme had assembled, I immediately felt that we had a chance of getting promotion.

Mark Hughes had been signed, and others followed with Henning Berg, Marcus Bent, Alan Mahon and Stig Bjornebye. Already in place were the likes of Damien Duff, David Dunn, Matt

Jansen, Gary Flitcroft, Craig Short, Jason McAteer, Nathan Blake, Keith Gillespie and John Curtis. All of these were Premiership quality players.

By the time my permit came through the season was well under way, and my assessment of the quality of the squad was proving to be pretty accurate. They had started off well and gone on a run of eight or nine games unbeaten.

Upon my arrival, we travelled away to Barnsley. Graeme said to me that he could not put me in the team. John Filan was doing well, and we won 2–1 at Barnsley with a goal against us that no goalkeeper could have saved. Next, the team faltered slightly with a 2–2 draw against Portsmouth, yet neither of their goals could have been adjudged to have been Filan's fault.

I think Graeme was just waiting for an opportunity to put me in and, rightly or wrongly, he decided that the draw against Portsmouth gave him good reason, so he wrote my name on the team sheet for the next game against Wolves. I wouldn't say that Graeme was nervous before that game, but there was something about him. Though he didn't say anything to me, I could sense that there was a degree of apprehension. It was as if he was think-ing, You had better do well for me today. I was in for my Blackburn debut against Wolves and we came out 1–0 winners. I was up and running with a clean sheet. Graeme was suitably relieved.

Filo was not happy at all, and I knew exactly how he felt. I had been in the same position myself at Liverpool. He and Alan Kelly were both no. 1 keepers and had been for most of their careers. It's one of those hard facts of life that you have to learn to cope with as a goalkeeper. When a manager brings in another keeper, he is inevitably going to want to play him.

After I'd played a string of games in succession, Alan Kelly took me to one side. He said, 'Look. Whatever I do or say from here on in is nothing against you at all. It's against the manager, so I apo-logise in advance if anything offends you.' That was a nice touch.

These are the things that happen when you get a crazy situa-tion where four into one won't go. Both Filan and Kelly were excellent keepers and in the wings was another really good keeper in Alan Miller, but he didn't really get much of a chance to show it.

To their great credit, they were all absolutely and totally professional about the situation even though they may have felt frustrated at times. John Filan moved on and enjoyed two promotions with Wigan Athletic, while Alan Kelly remained and became a great no. 2.

I take my hat off to them. It was a difficult situation and they remained professional, they were great personalities and real fun to work with.

Turning the Corner at Turf Moor

Just eight miles separate the towns of Blackburn and Burnley. Both have similar industrial roots and both were among the original founders of the Football League. The rivalry between the towns and between their football clubs goes back over 100 years. What better place to gain the acceptance of the Blackburn supporters than Turf Moor, home of their bitter rivals Burnley?

I felt that I turned a corner in a match at Burnley. I could feel that I had won the approval and backing of the Blackburn fans. From that day on I felt that I have been on an upward trajectory as a goalkeeper.

During my time at Liverpool, I don't think I was operating at my peak mentally, and this was affecting my game. I spent too much time looking over my shoulder, worrying about what other people may be thinking. As I'd been in and out of the team at Liverpool, not that many people knew that much about me. The Rovers supporters found it hard to understand why I had been brought in when there were already three keepers at the club.

I'd started well in that we won against Wolves, but we went on to lose our next game. People were having their doubts. Then we went on a massive unbeaten run. We went to rivals Burnley and I know the fans were keyed up for this game much more than usual. Burnley came out strongly, and I found myself with a fair bit to do. They were a very physical side and I took a couple of knocks in the process of keeping a clean sheet. We scored twice and the fans were ecstatic. It wasn't an instant acceptance for me at Blackburn, but that was the day when I felt that they had understood why Graeme had signed me.

As we moved into the season, we, as a defence, were performing more solidly and the clean sheets became a regular occurrence. Coupled with the flair that we had in the team, we were marching towards the Premiership. With one game to go we were four points clear of our rivals Bolton Wanderers, meaning that our last game at Gillingham was a celebration; even though Fulham were champions by a clear ten points and broke the 100-point barrier, we were up.

The Ravanelli Roar

The risk I had taken in joining Blackburn, and the faith I had in Graeme, had paid off. I was back in the Premiership after just one season.

The promotion was a very big thing for the team. It was massive for me. My reputation at Liverpool had been dwindling as I wasn't getting games. Then, when I went to Blackburn people began to perceive me as a First Division player when I knew I wasn't. Being part of the promotion-winning team puts you back on people's radar screens. Now I wanted to play well in the Premier League. The perception of me was beginning to change from 'He failed at Liverpool' to 'I wonder what happened at Liverpool?'

As I've got older, I've found that the public perception matters less and less, but as a young man it can affect your confidence, so I was determined to show what I could really do in the Premier League. If you have good players and they have got into a winning habit, then that can be enough to carry you through the first half of your promotion season. That's about what happened to us.

Our first Premier League game that year was away at Derby. Foreign imports were in the headlines, and Derby themselves had invested in an Italian named Fabrizio Ravanelli. He was to become famous for spectacular free kicks, and he opened his account with a goal against me. The goal and the celebration meant that I would have the privilege of watching it over and over again in television reruns. We lost 2–1, but in our next game drew 2–2 with Manchester United. We didn't go into games thinking that we would be relegated; we felt that we could achieve a solid mid-table or higher position in our first season.

We were on course to do this, and playing quite well, until injuries and suspensions demonstrated the importance of strength in depth. We were consistently hard to beat, but went on a terrible run of 0–0s and 0–1s. We just could not score.

Graeme made a swoop for Manchester United's Andy Cole, paying £8 million, and slowly but surely the goals began to flow again, just in the nick of time too, as, despite our dip in the League, we were progressing well in the Worthington Cup.

We were delighted to be playing Tottenham Hotspur in the final at the Millennium Stadium in Cardiff, yet we could not ignore our precarious league position. We had dropped into the relegation zone. The only consolation was that we had three games in hand over our rivals.

In the run-up to the final the bookmakers had us beaten before we had even got on the bus. Spurs had big-name players, while we were suffering a catalogue of injuries and suspensions. Lucas Neill, Gary Flitcroft and Tugay were all missing. We put together a makeshift team, with Mark Hughes moving from striker to mid-field.

Teddy Sheringham and Les Ferdinand gave me a very busy Worthington Cup final. Spurs must have had a dozen good chances. With the score tied at 1–1, Andy Cole showed why he had been brought in by putting us 2–1 up in the 69th minute.

We had our share of luck too. It was late on in the game when Johannson upended Sheringham in our penalty area. The referee looked and declined the appeal for a penalty. When I look back I think it was a penalty, but the referee had made his decision, and we held on to win the cup and I ended up as man of the match.

The cup win revitalised us, and, despite our lowly position, we went on a run, winning six and drawing three of our last 12 games. That's top four form and we ended up in tenth place, which was quite a dramatic turnaround for a team that had been in free fall. We were established in the Premier League.

Wenger's Rule of Three

In our second Premiership season, we carried on where we had left off and things really began to click. We finished in sixth place which was a great achievement. Thanks to our Worthington Cup win, we had also secured ourselves a place in the UEFA Cup.

A first round victory against CSKA Sofia brought us a second trip to Europe – well to Scotland at any rate. We were to face Glasgow Celtic in the second round first leg at Celtic Park. Martin O'Neill was their manager at the time, and I feel sure that if you were to ask him, he will tell you that we absolutely battered them in the first leg. We totally played them off the park. Against the run of play, they scored the only goal of the game in the eighty-seventh minute. It was an injustice, but these things happen in football.

O'Neill must have given his players something of a pep talk because when they came to Ewood Park for the second leg, they totally played us off the park. There was no strange twist of fate to help us out; Celtic hammered home their superiority winning 2–0.

Our European adventure was over, and we'd hardly needed our passports. Yet we could be pleased with our League performance and the promise of great things to come.

For me personally though this second Premier League season ended on something of a high. Football is a team game and as such is all about the team. I don't play the game for my own personal glory. Yet each year, the Professional Footballers' Association invites all players to nominate their team of the year by way of a formal voting system. Players vote for who they think is the outstanding player in each position and that is how the team of the year gets assembled.

I felt particularly humble when at the end of the 2003 season I was included in the PFA Premier League team of the season as the outstanding goalkeeper that year. I don't get overexcited about awards, but this one was special because the result was determined by those who are in the best position to judge, that is, my peers and fellow professionals. Being adjudged to be consistently good over a whole season by players who are at the top of their profession is a great accolade and one that I was pleased to accept.

Arsene Wenger has become one the most successful managers ever and he has an intelligent way of looking at the game. You have to give his views respect. I heard him say something once, which makes a lot of sense to me. He said that if you change more than three players, it is a big risk because it can unbalance relationships between the players and therefore unbalance the team.

I've seen this first hand. After our great top six finish, I turned up for the 2003–04 season to find an incredible number of new faces in the squad, replacing quite a number of players who had moved on. I think that this is where things started to deteriorate for Blackburn Rovers. There was a huge exodus with players like Suker, Cole, Taylor, Bjornebye, Hignett, Mahon and Curtis all moving on. Other players moved too who were not necessarily first team regulars, but they were important to the dressing room. Some people with big personalities had gone and everyone had enjoyed the banter. Now we had a different team and a different atmosphere.

Graeme Souness's transfer policy was on the whole successful. Look at what he did: he got Morten Gamst Pedersen for £1.5 million. He must be worth ten times that today. He got Bjornebye for nothing; Henning Berg for a small fee; me for nothing. But three purchases really hurt him and Blackburn Rovers, and put a dent in what would have been a great transfer record.

Andrew Cole, who was signed for £8 million, was allowed to go to Fulham on a free. Cole was a total success on the pitch for Blackburn as well as being a great presence in the changing room. As a purchase it worked out. He had a brilliant relationship with the other players, yet Graeme fought with the board to sanction a free transfer, which represented a huge financial loss to the club.

Souness and Cole are two very, very strong characters. On a

personal level they clashed to the point where there had to be a parting of ways. It was an expensive parting of ways for Blackburn, and Cole has kept on scoring Premiership goals. Barry Ferguson was a great player who came down from Glasgow Rangers for £7 million. The funny thing about Barry's move was that I think he wanted to go home from minute one. You can call it homesickness or club sickness, whatever you like, but Barry seemed to want to go home straight away. He did, eventually, for £3 million. Bang went another £4 million.

The third of the trio was Corrado Grabbi, an Italian with an impressive goalscoring record who came in for a fee of £6.75 million. He scored only twice in his 30 appearances for Blackburn, yet he was not as bad a player as the fans may have perceived. He was a nice fellow, but again he had difficulty settling down. That happens with some players. He left on a free as well.

Though most of Souness's purchases worked out, these three seriously damaged the willingness of the club trustees to spend big money on purchases. The board became more cautious and would only sanction lower level deals.

With all these new players and the loss of some really good ones, we flirted with relegation that season, and a late turn-around got us up to 15th. There were a few fallings-out in the dressing room that season, and there was a sense that the board was becoming anxious. There were rumblings and the fixture list for the coming season gave us a difficult start to contend with.

5,000:1

The Premier League kicked off on 15 August 1992. Since that time more than 15,000 Premier League goals have been scored. In the all-time Premier League scoring chart, there are no fewer than three Blackburn Rovers Old Boys. Alan Shearer, part of the Premiership-winning Blackburn Rovers team, holds the top spot; in second place is the goal machine Andrew Cole; and in ninth place his former strike partner Dwight Yorke.

Statistically, there is a 0.02% probability of a goalkeeper scoring from open play. In fact the Premier League had been in existence nine years before any goalkeeper got onto the score sheet. Peter Schmeichel, then playing for Aston Villa, scored against Everton on 21 October 2001. Then there was a gap of only two and a half years before another goalkeeper scored. That was a goal I scored against Charlton Athletic in February 2004. Just over three years later Paul Robinson scored for Tottenham Hotspur against Watford from 83 yards.

So my goal was one of only three scored by goalkeepers, meaning that the odds of a keeper getting onto the score sheet are roughly 5000:1. It's interesting how since Schmeichel broke the duck they have been coming along at fairly even periods, roughly every three years. If you wanted to place a bet on a goalkeeper scoring from open play during a season, then the 2010–11 season might be as good a time as any.

I've hardly ever spoken of my goal. It was an evening game towards the end of February away at Charlton. The game was as dour as the weather, and we had a dismal first half. We got hit by two goals and then perhaps undeservedly managed to pull it back to 2–1.

It was looking bleak when in the 89th minute we got a corner. I thought, Well what have I got to lose? and I ran upfield and planted myself in the opposition's penalty area. It was a case of now or never for us. Thinking I might get a header in, I watched as the ball flew high into the box and over the top of my head. As I turned, Paul Gallagher struck the ball towards goal, and it ricocheted off a defender and into my path. It was a simple matter to tap it in with my left foot.

We were elated and there was great euphoria. We felt that we had 'nicked' a point that quite frankly we didn't deserve because we had been very poor. We were into injury time and Charlton hit a long ball downfield, which arrived at the feet of Claus Jensen, Charlton's Danish striker.

He hit a tremendous strike which bent, lifted over my head and even though I thought I may be able to get a hand to it the ball slammed into the top corner of my net. Euphoria dipped to despair in an instant. I've never really said much about my goal because the joy was so short-lived and we lost a game, when really we should have been able to hold on for a minute or two of injury time.

The things that are turning points in matches are of course goals. Every professional knows that you are at your most vulnerable during the four or five minutes after you have just scored. Often people aren't thinking straight when they have just scored and they can be caught up in the emotion and lose concentration.

I've noticed that the better footballers, the ones who stay at the top of their game for many years, are the ones that are able to maintain their concentration no matter what is thrown at them. You see players who have pretty decent professional careers, but they are never consistently at the top of their game. They have a problem concentrating for the full 90 minutes or for 38 games a season. They cannot concentrate consistently, so you know that at some point in the season they are going to have breakdowns – not because they are bad players but because of lapses in concentration.

Even though I was involved in a very rare event, a 5000:1 shot, a goalkeeper's goal, a lapse in concentration on our part meant that I've never really celebrated it apart from the time it took me to run back from the Charlton penalty area to my own.

By the Way, I'm off to Newcastle

We had a poor start to the 2004–05 season. It has been said that Souness had six to eight games to prove himself that year. That's a crazy thing about football. If you are going to fire someone, then fire them. Better to do it in the summer and have a pre-season with your new manager. I don't go with this idea of giving a manager a small number of games. Either get rid of him or give him a long stretch of games. You are only delaying the inevitable by taking the halfway house option.

We stuttered to a 1–1 draw with West Bromwich Albion on the opening day of the season. Then we had three difficult fixtures. Southampton away, which is never an easy place to go and win, Arsenal away and by way of respite a home game – against Manchester United.

We had chalked up just one point from three games when Manchester United came to Ewood Park and laid into us. Somehow we held them at bay, and were 1–0 up into the dying seconds of the game. Late on in the game they had a handball in the box which went unnoticed by the referee, yet they maintained their relentless pressure and scored an equaliser well into injury time.

We were in the relegation zone and Graeme is not stupid; I think he sensed that the writing was on the wall. After the United game there was a break for international matches, and I went into training. There were not that many players around and I was all alone walking down towards the changing room.

Graeme just happened to walk by. As I said, 'Good morning,' he looked up and did the same. As I moved closer he said, 'Oh, I should tell you. I'm on my way to Newcastle. It's a great opportunity and I've got to take it. Things here have not gone as I would have liked recently.'

I think he knew in his own mind that he had gone as far as he could go with Blackburn. I think he had a vision to get Blackburn promoted and solidified. That's what he did and won a trophy along the way. Nobody could look back and say that he was a failure, but unfortunately some people only seem to remember the last few months of his term or the last season when we were fighting relegation.

Overall, Graeme Souness was very good for Blackburn Rovers. He achieved his vision, and what maybe happened was that he required a £50 million cheque to take it to the next level. His management style is to buy in talent, to be a figurehead and disciplinarian. That's his style, and when he couldn't get the big cheque at Blackburn, maybe he thought he would get better access to resources at Newcastle.

Graeme may have been criticised in some quarters for making the decision that he did, yet I feel that he deserves to be given real credit for what he did at Blackburn over the period when he was the boss. I think Graeme has played a huge part in putting Blackburn Rovers where they are today, in a position where they are a well-established Premier League team capable of getting into Europe. It should be remembered that he masterminded Blackburn Rovers' ascent from the First Division to the Premier League, just at the time when the TV money was beginning to kick in. This was an extremely important time to consolidate in the Premier League because as each year has gone by it has become harder and harder for promoted teams to avoid the yo-yo syndrome. We won the League Cup under Graeme, had a top six finish and enjoyed the excitement of European encounters. He was a Liverpool and Scotland legend as a player, a Glasgow Rangers legend as a manager, and on balance I think that he deserves to be considered most certainly as one of the people who have been most influential at the club and as someone who did great things for Blackburn Rovers.

He has a particular view on the way he wants football to be played. He is not into the long ball game. He likes flowing passing and movement, midfield battles and quality runs. You can't always play like this when you are in relegation scraps.

Graeme left right away, leaving us to prepare for our next game – away to Newcastle. Under an agreement between the two clubs, he had to watch from the stands and could not take charge until after the game against us. They didn't need him. We lost 3–0.

Mentality, Mentality, Mentality

With players coming and going all the time in dressing rooms, you begin to notice something of the different mentalities that bounce around and in and out of clubs. Where Blackburn has benefited from changes in personnel has been on the occasions where they have gone out and recruited players with a certain kind of mentality – that is, a winning mentality. There was a time when people at Blackburn got used to the idea of losing. Losing is like an illness. I know Blackburn Rovers are a smaller club but you must hate losing. When we brought in the likes of Henning Berg, Andy Cole, Dwight Yorke, John Curtis from Manchester United, Stig Inge Bjornebye, myself, David Thompson, Steve Warnock from Liverpool, André Ooijer from PSV Eindhoven and Roque Santa Cruz from Bayern Munich, it always helped to change things. When players come in from a big club they come from a culture where winning is expected, a requirement of the job. When we were relegated it took a while to bring back the winning feeling and at times when we got back into the Premier League, we have needed the new signings from big clubs to instil a stronger winning attitude.

You have to get used to people coming and going, and over the years at times I've been saddened to see certain people leave, other times there have been player departures where I have been more than happy to see their backside as they left. All in all though I've enjoyed being with most of the players I've played with.

You get to find out what people are really like when you are together all the time, and often players are quite different from the perception that the media may have built for them. There can be no better example of this than my friend Robbie Savage. Robbie is regarded as something of a pantomime villain because of the nature of his play – he is an antagonist, a genuine *agent provocateur.* You may choose different words to describe him if he is playing against you rather than with you. He comes across as very loud both on and off the pitch. You certainly know when he is in the dressing room.

The thing that I have noticed about Robbie is that this is just a front. It is a cover for someone who can be quite shy really. Depending upon the circumstances he likes reminders that people are on his side. We are neighbours and I've spent a lot of time speaking to Robbie, particularly when we were Blackburn team mates, and I am glad that I could be there if he ever felt he needed advice.

He will have a big issue to deal with in his life at some stage, as indeed all footballers do. Football means everything to him. This was illustrated very dramatically in 2006–07. We were playing away at Watford when Robbie was involved, as he often is, in a crunching tackle. He was taken off with a broken leg.

It is only natural to be dejected and a little down, but I have never seen such a transformation in personality as I did with Robbie. He went from being the life and soul of the party to someone who was totally withdrawn. Football had been taken away from him, and even though it was only for a temporary period, it was as if his whole world had crumbled.

I have to give a lot of credit to the back room staff and the players at Blackburn. They all worked very, very hard to build Robbie's spirit back up. Coming back from a broken leg is bad enough, but the job with Robbie was to get him to rebuild his belief in himself. He was an empty shell, withdrawing from a world that he no longer felt a part of.

In particular, he was one of the players that I was sad to see walk through the door when he left to go to Derby. What came through was that his feelings of self-worth when in the football club were tightly bound up with being in the first team. Being out of the team does not sit well with most players, and when he was not the first choice perhaps he had a feeling of worthlessness. This is obviously not the case, and I know that he knows this now. Perhaps in a strange sort of way, the broken leg helped him to prepare better for a life after football.

Robbie Savage is a likeable lad who is nothing like the villain he is portrayed to be by the media. He had a big test in going to play for a struggling Derby team, but he was playing and that has always been his greatest desire. His biggest test is yet to come – how to create a fulfilling life for himself the day when the football stops.

This is something that footballers, and for that matter anyone in the public eye, have to be very careful about. It is so easy to lose sight of what is *really* important. Yes, our profession is a big part of life, and as professionals we should be passionate and gripped by it. Yet when you peel the skin off the banana you realise that things like respect, courage, loyalty, perseverance and positive mental attitude are far more important than any sport. What's more, you can take these things with you wherever you go, whether football is in your life or whether fate or age has seen you unceremoniously dumped, but knowing Robbie's character I'm sure that he will come through with flying colours.

In the modern game we have seen massive improvements in the past decade or so. Players are fitter, leaner, faster, stronger; they have good diets and for the most part control their alcohol intake. Yet if we want to talk about the characteristics of loyalty, perseverance and respect, we would do well to look backwards a couple of decades to some of the players who were around then. I have even seen a difference in player attitude just in the time that I have been in the UK. I'm all for player power, but at times I think that the balance of power has shifted too far in the direction of the players. It used to be that when a player was dropped or had a telling-off from the manager, it ignited some inner desire to get stuck in and prove the manager wrong. Today, contracts seem virtually meaningless, and there are players who will call their agents after a negative episode to try to orchestrate a move.

Too many players are looking for a way out when things don't go the way they want, when the place they should be looking is in the mirror. They should take a good look at themselves and tackle the issues head-on. I always think that it is interesting when a player knocks on a manager's door and asks the question, 'Where do I stand?' I tend to think to myself, Well. If you were in the starting XI that's where you stand; if you were on the substitutes' bench that's where you stand; if you weren't in the squad that's where you stand. Players need to face up to the realities of their situation more and ask themselves why they are in the position they are in, and what they are going to do about it. Too often these days their first answer is: 'I want to leave.' Sometimes, as at Liverpool, you have to leave to move on, but I'm comfortable with what I did because I behaved like a true professional by giving Sander Westerveld strong competition and I faced up to what I saw, I wasn't going to be Houllier's first choice. Leaving was my last resort, not my first.

Homespun Wisdom

One of the things I really liked about Blackburn Rovers was the close knit – almost family – feel of the place. This was illustrated after Graeme left for Newcastle. John Williams, the chief executive, came around to see some of the senior players. He discussed the shortlist that had been drawn up for the new manager's job.

Although, of course, he wasn't asking who we wanted to appoint, he asked which of them we knew personally, how they interacted with the players and how much they were respected.

They did a little more homework than an interview and a few calls. It was more inclusive as a process and I think it had a bearing on Mark Hughes getting the job.

Mark was the manager of Wales. I had known him well as a team-mate at Blackburn. We had won promotion and the Worthington Cup together. It was fun when he walked in on his first day in the manager's job. He was in the canteen wearing his suit, and I needed to ask him something. I walked over to him and I said, 'Hey, Sparky.' He just glared at me. I got it: 'Sorry, Gaffer,' I said.

Sparky or, as I got used to calling him, 'Gaffer' realised that he had to become detached the moment he became a manager. You simply have to.

As well as being team-mates we are also near neighbours and we used to go out for meals together. That had to stop too. It didn't mean that we disliked each other. It's an essential part of the process of switching from being a player to a manager. It is not appropriate for a player to have a drink or a meal with a manager, unless you are on official club business. It could cloud his judgement when picking a team. Mark is too professional a person to allow something to cloud his judgement and I respect him too much as a person and as a manager to even think about putting him in such a position.

As I get older I find that more and more of my friends are becoming coaches and managers. If it keeps up like this I'll have no one left to talk to.

Mark Hughes was one of those players who you always knew would become a manager. It was the way he thought about things which was impressive; he had a big name but didn't have the ego to match; he commanded respect; and he has a calmness about him. Sure he can become animated, but you don't see him ranting to the media. He tends to focus his energy where it can make a difference.

It's interesting to observe the contrast between Mark Hughes and Graeme Souness. Both are good managers, yet they are at different ends of the spectrum in terms of their style.

Mark is an 'improver', whereas Graeme is an 'importer'. Don't forget Mark's first taste of management was with the Welsh national team. With the greatest of respect to the Principality, it is not like managing Brazil or Argentina. You simply don't have the range of players to choose from. You have to work with what you have got and try to improve it. This is Mark's natural management instinct.

Graeme tended to assess players, and if he felt they were not good enough, he would move them out and try to bring someone else in. For the most part, he has a good track record of doing this, but there is only so far you can go with limited resources when using this approach. I have a lot of good things to say about Graeme Souness, even though his style is quite different from that of Mark Hughes. Graeme is good to play for when things are going well. He gets really excited and energised when you play well. He also has that ability that any good manager must have: he can come down very hard on people when he needs to.

I think that part of the success that Mark Hughes enjoyed at Blackburn was down to the team he put in place around him. Mark Bowen came in as his assistant manager, Eddie Niedzwiecki as first team coach, Kevin Hitchcock as goalkeeping coach and Glynn Hodges took over the reserve team. Together, they began this process of trying to make the squad better, while adding to it with astute purchases, rather than headline-grabbing transfers.

They introduced ProZone so that every aspect of our performance could be analysed in detail. Now all of the training sessions are filmed and analysed. Your heart rate is monitored from the very first to the very last second of training. Players cannot get away with coasting any more. Some players accepted these methods, whereas some were sceptical. Now it is just the way we do things.

In the old days, every club had someone who had a reputation for being the worst trainer. Once Mark arrived at Blackburn you could not identify the worst trainer. With him you are not allowed to be a bad trainer. The heart stats get put up in the ProZone room for everybody to see. Players do have a bit of banter about each other's results, but if someone falls behind, it is generally used as an incentive to get up to the required level.

The range of things we do these days in addition to football includes ice baths, cool downs, weights, stretching and massage. I've heard players in ice baths huffing and puffing saying, 'Is this really going to make me a better player?' The answer is no. It won't improve your touch or make you score more goals, but it will help you recover more quickly and perhaps give you that 1–2% advantage over your opponents that could make all the difference. It doesn't make you a better player, but it makes you a better professional.

If the gaffer makes you wear a heart monitor to ensure that you operate at 80% capacity for 30 minutes, it's not because he thinks it will make you score a hat-trick on Saturday. It's about mental and physical preparation for the whole season. If you can be fit for the whole season that benefits the team.

Really, we started to see improvements straight away. At the back end of the 2003–04 season we had started to leak goals. The new gaffer changed the formation and shored up the defence. We were down at the bottom and we had to get out of it. We were short on strikers for a while and were not scoring frequently, but by about December time, the fitness improvements were beginning to tell. We were hard and uncompromising, we had to be to survive, and that is how we were given the 'physical' tag which seems to have stuck to us. Clean sheets became something of a speciality, and that season we achieved 15, lifting ourselves from the bottom of the league and avoiding relegation by a clear margin of nine points. It was a tough season but progress was being made.

In 2005–06 we felt that we had something to build on. Craig Bellamy opted to join Blackburn, having had links with Mark Hughes when he was manager of Wales. Described by Sir Bobby Robson as 'A man who could start a fight in a lift', I really have little to say about Bellamy, except that he was a great goalscorer for us. In his first season at Blackburn he bagged 17 goals and took the pressure off lone striker Paul Dickov. These extra goals and our ability to keep a clean sheet – 16 shutouts this time – meant that, with few additions to the squad, we had gone from Premier League strugglers to finishing in sixth place and qualified for the UEFA Cup.

Bellamy left for Liverpool for £6.5 million after just 27 games and was replaced by Benni McCarthy, the South African striker who signed from Porto for £2.5 million. Mark Hughes had made a profit on Bellamy and used it to capture a striker who almost topped the Premiership scoring charts in his first season, coming in only two behind top scorer Didier Drogba's 20, with 18 Premiership goals and 24 in total. By anyone's standards, that has to go down as a remarkable piece of football business.

At the same time the gaffer and his team were working little by little on someone who looked like his future lay elsewhere. Morten Gamst Pedersen was a Souness signing but took a long time to get into the reckoning under Mark Hughes. His confidence was low, but Mark worked on it, doing little things on a one-to-one basis to build him up and get him to improve. At one point Morten was probably a month away from leaving the club, and probably would have gone given the chance. Then he scored in an FA Cup game at Cardiff, and suddenly began to blossom.

Can you imagine losing him and then having him play against you? The staff got the best of him just at the right time, and he has become a really influential player at Blackburn, attracting the interest of a lot of top clubs.

More recently the gaffer showed the value of the connections that he has built up with another inspired signing. Roque Santa Cruz was signed from Bayern Munich for £3.5 million. His scoring ratio wasn't that great at Bayern, where he was getting about one goal every five games. He scored his first goal for Blackburn after just three touches of the ball, when he came on as substitute for Benni McCarthy. Since then he has become a goalscoring machine, notching up a goal every two games. Other managers in the Premier League must be wondering how they failed to pick up such a talent at a bargain price.

I think that Mark Hughes has a couple of attributes which help him to do this kind of amazing business. One is that he has a tremendous network of contacts who feed him good intelligence. It is a world game now and plucking talent from under the noses of the world's top clubs is a talent in itself. Secondly, Mark is highly respected in the game. Players knew that they could become better by coming to Blackburn. They can probably match most clubs in terms of wages now, but they can't pay the crazy transfer fees.

He has built a well-deserved reputation as somebody who can find gems at bargain prices and improve what he has, while turning in a tidy profit in his transfer dealings. What more can you ask of a manager?

No wonder he was on everybody's radar screen, and knowing what I know about his back room staff, clubs looking for a manager would be fools not to have him on their shortlist, and that is why Manchester City came in for him over the summer.

You see a lot of managers who are regurgitated around the league. A lot of the same faces that sign a three-year deal, talk on TV, rant and rave on the sidelines and effectively do nothing which is proactive in terms of improving the club and its players. They get the sack, get a big pay-off and move on to the next club. It's a repetitive cycle.

Mark Hughes is not that kind of manager. It would have been difficult for him to always maintain a top six position for Blackburn because you can't just keep finding players who will score you 20-plus goals a season. Yet his teams will always be solid and play attractive football. Now, with a big chequebook at his disposal, with his philosophy, his staff and his aptitude for making good players better, he will undoubtedly be one of the best managers in the game.

10

The Cap Fits: International Duty

And so, my fellow Americans, ask not what your country can do for you; ask what you can do for your country

John F. Kennedy

In all of my time fighting the work permit battle, playing in Turkey and at Liverpool and Blackburn, international duty has been a big part of my life. It has been both an honour and an education. It has brought success and disappointment. It has opened my eyes to new cultures and allowed me to experience three distinctly different management styles.

As I grew as an international, I also grew as a person. Little did I know as I approached the final phase of my international career that the history books beckoned. Not the history books on the shelves of the UCLA library. I was to write myself into the history of the greatest show on earth, the World Cup ...

On the Radar Screen

When I'd arrived at UCLA I just wasn't even on the radar screen as far as any of the national programmes were concerned. It had never really occurred to me before how people progress in soccer in the States. I just played because I really enjoyed playing.

As I was growing up playing all these other sports, Mom and

Dad's financial situation meant that I could not always follow through. Sometimes I wanted to play ice hockey and basketball in the same year. I'd always make the state team and then I'd get selected for the regional team, but often I would not even go. Either we couldn't afford it all or I had too many other things going on. So as far as the national context goes, I had never really put myself in the shop window as a youngster in any of the sports that I was good at. Having so many sports in the US is a double-edged sword. It's great from the point of view of creating a well-rounded person, yet if you want to focus on a sport it can hinder your progress.

Soccer was not big in the public consciousness when I was in my early to mid-teens, and I really had no idea what the advanced stages were. There was certainly no professional league to think about. When I arrived at UCLA it began to dawn on me as I read the biographies of my new team-mates that many had been with the Under 20s national team already. They had been through the system of state, regional and national progression. It hit me that there was this development path and I just thought, Oh right, that's how it works.

What pleased me was that when I started playing with these Under 20 internationals and a couple of guys who were full internationals, I felt comfortable right away. That was nice to know.

I had not even made my UCLA debut, on account of being a redshirt, when my coach Sigi Schmid got a call from Lothar Osiander, the Under 23s national team coach, and Sigi suggested he come and take a look at me. Sigi called me to one side and said that Lothar was very, very big on first impressions. His preference was for big, tall, commanding goalkeepers so Sigi told me to go out and make a big first impression. That's what I did and before I had even saved a shot in anger for UCLA I was called up to the Under 23s squad to prepare for qualification for the Barcelona Olympics.

Now Sigi is German, Lothar is German and I have a German surname. It did cross my mind for a moment that maybe I was in the squad because of this. Maybe I was, but now the rest was up to me, and within a short time I had established myself as the

my home debut for Liverpool. years of effort to get a work permit had finally paid off (*photos*).

Saving from Tottenham Hotspur's Les Ferdinand in the 2002 Worthington Cup Final, a great moment for everyone associated with Blackburn Rovers Football Club … (*Action Images*).

…made even better by being fortunate enough to be awarded man of the match (*Action Images*).

My wife Tracy and me – one of those rare moments
when she is actually sitting still.

Me and my family and my two beautiful children, Izabella and Allegra.

...ocking an effort by Jimmy Floyd Hasselbaink at Stamford Bridge in 2003 which turned out ...• be a very good year for Blackburn Rovers, qualifying for the UEFA Cup (*PA photos*).

Up against former team-mate Michael Owen, who was one of those personalities who fitted straight into the team when he joined Liverpool as a teenager (*PA photos*).

...eme Souness, the man who started my European odyssey when he wanted to sign me for ...erpool, became my manager at Galatasaray and Blackburn Rovers and someone who I ...e a lot for giving me the opportunity to play football at the highest level (*PA photos*).

...he end of the 2002–03 season it was a nice honour to be recognised by my fellow players ...being chosen in the best 11 Premier League players for that season (*Action Images*).

Flying through the air to save a free kick by Arsenal's Thierry Henry. We went on to win the game 2-0 (*PA photos*).

But you can't win them all… In the 2003 FA Cup fourth round replay I failed to save Gavin McCann's winning penalty kick for Sunderland (*PA photos*).

Under 23s no. 1 choice, which resulted in that unforgettable trip to the Barcelona Olympics.

On our return from Barcelona, Sigi gave us a couple of weeks off and we joined pre-season training late. He had a strong voice within the US Soccer Federation and was keen to see his players progress. He made a strong case for myself and Joe-Max Moore to be considered for full international selection.

We had a gap in the UCLA schedule of about ten days, and one day during training Sigi came over and said, 'You are going to be getting a full national team call-up.' This is tremendous news for any player. When you are a kid still in college and you've just returned from the Olympics it is incredible news. I was both excited and a little nervous.

I really wanted a chance to impress the Serbian-born coach Bora Milutinovic. He had been a player for Partizan Belgrade, played in France and ended his career with Pumas UNAM in Mexico. Yet the end of his playing career was only the beginning for him. His real talent was as a coach. Before he took the job with the US national team he had already taken Mexico and Costa Rica to the World Cup finals. He eventually took the US national team to the 1994 World Cup and then he took Nigeria to the 1998 tournament. In 2002 he made history when he led out China in the World Cup (the fifth team he had taken charge of in the World Cup finals).

It was 3 September 1992 and at just 20 years of age I was about to make my debut for my country. We went up to a training camp in Bangor, Maine, and then took the short trip by coach across the Canadian border to Saint John, New Brunswick, for my induction against Canada.

The game went by in a blur as these important occasions so often do. Although I had pre-match nerves, I didn't doubt my ability. Having just come back from the Olympics, I knew I was capable of playing against full-time professionals. There were people playing against us in Barcelona that played for AC Milan and all the big European teams. When I looked out at our full national team, with the exception of myself and one or two other college boys, we were all professionals. By contrast, the Canadian team were not of the standard I had encountered in the Olympics, though anything can happen in a game, and I certainly had my blinkers on in the lead-up. Concentrating, trying to do the right things. The 3,500 people who turned up to witness my debut saw the US secure a 2–0 win.

It was a friendly game and, in the overall scheme of things, of little significance. Yet it was significant for me. I had done well in the game and achieved a clean sheet. I was now a full international and had got Bora's attention. One thing is for sure, if we had lost 4–0, Bora wouldn't have come looking for me again. So this blur of an evening in a remote northeastern Canadian Province represented progress. International progress.

Back to School

The next day was funny. I had to fly from Canada to Indiana to meet up with the UCLA team. I was an international goalkeeper one day, and then a college player the next. That kind of thing keeps your feet on the ground.

In any case, all I had achieved so far was having played one game for my country. The road to becoming the no. 1 choice was not going to be easy.

When you think of the size of the US and its population, it is an amazing fact that the number of soccer players it has produced is minuscule. Of those players, probably only about 50 have been good enough to play professional soccer in Europe. What is remarkable is that from this small pool of professionals in Europe, a large percentage of them have been goalkeepers.

I think there are two reasons for this. Firstly, soccer is the one major sport where the US has never achieved some form of dominance. It may be difficult, perhaps even threatening, for Europeans to accept that the US can produce soccer players to their standards. I think a lot of people do not consider goalkeepers to be pure footballers, so it is much easier for Europeans to accept an American goalkeeper over an outfielder. Secondly, we Americans tend to grow up doing a lot of different things with our hands and feet as far as sports are concerned. Bouncing, throwing, kicking, batting, skating, catching, running and so on. So we develop good coordination which makes us good raw material for the position of goalkeeper.

In the US national team there was competition for places everywhere, but none more so than in goal. If I was going to establish myself as an international, I was going to have to try to outshine three very, very good goalkeepers.

When I first broke into the international scene, Tony Meola was the first choice. Tony played just 11 games with Brighton and Hove Albion in England before returning to the US, playing for several teams and clocking up 125 games for Kansas City Wizards.

Tony liked to be in the spotlight on and off the field. He liked the limelight so much that he even gave up soccer at one period to star in the Broadway musical *Tony and Tina's Wedding*. He had a tryout as a kicker with NFL team New York Jets and for a while tried his hand at lower league baseball.

He was a very experienced international, and clocked up a phenomenal number of caps in an incredibly short period. This was because the US national team operated very much like a club team. With no professional league in the US, it was essential to keep the squad as sharp as possible, so that sometimes there would be 40 international games a season. Not surprisingly, in time, Tony became the first US goalkeeper to reach the 100-cap milestone.

Jurgen Sommer also had aspirations to be no. 1. He was of German descent and that made him eligible to play in Europe before any other US goalkeeper. He went over in 1991 to play for Luton Town in the old English First Division, then played for Queens Park Rangers and Torquay United before returning home to the MLS.

As if that were not enough competition, Kasey Keller was the second American goalkeeping export to England when he left Portland Timbers to join Milwall. He then gained profile and experience by playing in the English Premier League with Leicester City, followed by spells in Spain, four years at Tottenham Hotspur and a spell at Borussia Mönchengladbach, before returning to England with Fulham.

So I had experience, popularity, desire and tremendous ability standing in my way of becoming the no. 1 choice for the US.

The 'New Pelé' Syndrome

As I settled into the international set-up, I began to sense that Bora deep down didn't like Tony as a goalkeeper, even though he was captain. Comparatively, I think his work ethic dropped and he had a couple of tough years in 1992 and 1993, with the exception of an unbelievable performance against England in the 1993 US Cup, when the US won 2–0. By contrast, the other three of us all had aspirations to make it in Europe and, while we progressed, Tony stayed in US semi-pro soccer and began to slip back. Yet, perhaps because of his public persona, he enjoyed huge public backing. He was the media's boy back then.

In a way Tony suffered from the kind of American phenomenon that the young Freddie Adu has had to endure. The media pick a player who has something to offer outside the game and build up the hype whether or not he is performing on the field. Freddie Adu, for instance, played his first game for DC United at the age of 14 years and ten months. He was immediately hailed as the next superhero. Comparisons were made with Pelé. I've only met Freddie once and he seems like a nice boy. The truth is that the media hyped him in a way which suggested that he had already proved himself on the world stage. He was unable to maintain a first team place at DC United and was transferred to Real Salt Lake where he didn't make much of an impact before Benfica picked him up. After a small number of games he has been loaned out to AS Monaco. He is still very young. Freddie will hopefully make it in the game, and I hope that he will be able one day to live up to the hype that surrounded him from the moment he kicked a ball in US soccer. I can see Freddie doing really well in his career. It's not his fault that the US media feel the need to pick someone up and hype them before they are proven. I wish him all the best and hope that he has whatever success is due to him as he continues to grow into the sport.

Tony was a good goalkeeper who revelled in the publicity. He was the Freddie Adu of his day. I think it did him a disservice. He became satisfied and as the other keepers worked really hard, we caught him up and overtook him. In a completely selfish sense, I'm glad Tony did not go to Europe to play full-time. Ability wise he was good, but by not being able to sustain his performance mentally was good for the likes of myself, Kasey Keller, Jurgen Sommer and any other aspiring goalkeepers.

In Europe, both the media and the fans are more knowledge-able about the game. In the US the media tended to cover their lack of knowledge with an over-emphasis on the off-the-field issues. If you had a public persona you could play badly for ten or 20 games and still get a good game rating in the press. There were times when I almost felt that if you bumped into the sports reporters in the lobby and said, 'Hello,' they were going to mark you seven out of ten at least. If someone scored a goal yet played badly, they would get an even higher mark. There was a certain naivety in the press which drove this obsession with building people up.

For the moment, the US media have David Beckham. He is someone who is definitely able to deliver the goods on and off the pitch, so perhaps there is a chance for the next great American talent to grow and mature without feeling an impossible weight of expectation on his shoulders.

It is good that Beckham is keeping the spotlight on soccer in the US because if we are to grow as a soccer nation the job has to fall to somebody, and I think Beckham can handle it better than most. For a while, the spotlight fell on my buddy Alexi Lalas. He was an honest and very hard working defender who was built up by the US media to be the next Beckenbauer. The truth is that Alexi was an incredibly important player for the US, but the media's desperation to find a star meant that it was again hard for Alexi to live up to the billing that he had been given.

He's tall, he's ginger and he played with his long goatee beard in plaits. In addition he's passionate, he's emotional and at times he'd be all over the pitch. If he wasn't tackling someone he was trying to score. It's no wonder the media loved him. I think Tony Meola might even have been jealous of Alexi's popularity. I was

Alexi's room-mate when we were in LA and Alexi came in and said, 'I'm going on the *Letterman Show* tonight.' We were all elated. The *Letterman Show* is one of the biggest things in the US, and the idea that a soccer player was going to be on it was fantastic. It was bringing profile to the game. Tony had a different viewpoint. You could see that he was almost embarrassed by the news. He shrugged and said, 'Oh yeah. I got asked to go on that once.'

Alexi had more of the look of a rock musician than a soccer player, but he was a really cool guy and everybody loved him. He became a great focal point for US soccer because we didn't have one at the time, and even though there were better players, pretty much everyone was happy to see the media building up a good guy.

As for Kasey, he was always my main competition for the US no. 1 slot. I believe that we have a mutual respect for each other and we have both had long careers overseas. I think that we play the game for completely different reasons, but over the years he has been a huge motivator for me because I always had to try to compete against him and to try to be better. I'm sure it was just the same for him, and I have to say that over the years I have really enjoyed the competition.

World Cup USA Style

By the time the 1994 World Cup came around, Tony Meola was regarded as the no. 1 and I was seen as the no. 2. In the run-up to the tournament, roughly for every one game that I got, Tony would get two. As we got within a couple of months of the finals, it changed to a position where we were virtually alternating game by game. My hopes were rising.

There had been great controversy about holding the tournament in the USA, a country where soccer hardly registers on the sporting Richter scale. Naturally we qualified automatically as hosts and the pundits believed the tournament would flop. In fact, it broke all records with an average attendance of 70,000 per game.

Our opening game of the tournament was at the Pontiac Silverdome in Michigan, where we met Switzerland. It was another history-maker really, being the first World Cup game ever to be played indoors. The Silverdome is a roofed stadium and a natural grass surface which was laid onto wooden pallets was brought in. A crowd of 73,425 watched us tie 1–1 with the Swiss. Tony was selected and I sat on the bench.

Next we moved to the Pasadena Rose Bowl in California for the two remaining group games. The first against the highly rated Colombians, who, with players like Valderrama, Asprilla and Rincon, had qualified in spectacular fashion and before the tournament were tipped to win by none other than Pelé.

There were rumours that Colombian drugs cartels were exercising their influence over the Colombian team selection, and their 3–1 defeat to Romania in their first game came as a shock. Again, I watched from the bench as we ran out 2–1 winners, with one of our goals coming from Colombian defender Andrés Escobar. As he stretched to cut out a cross, he put the ball in the back of his own net.

The Colombians went home, knocked out of the tournament, and ten days later Escobar was dead. He was shot 12 times at point-blank range by a gunman who, according to police reports, shouted 'Goal' as he fired each shot. Nobody is sure if it was an irate fan acting on his own account or whether the murder was ordered by a gambling syndicate which had bet big money on Colombia to win.

Either way, it was a tragic waste of a life. An ugly outcome from the beautiful game.

With a win and a draw, we had every chance of progressing and Tony Meola again got the nod for the third group game against Romania. We lost 1–0, but we had already done enough, and headed to the Stanford Stadium in Palo Alto to face the mighty Brazil in the last 16 of the competition. It was 4 July, American Independence Day, a day that you would have imagined had been set up especially for the headline writers.

With Tony again in goal, we put up a valiant fight. Leonardo was sent off for fracturing the skull of Tab Ramos with his elbow.

Yet even with ten men Brazil are a handful, and Bebeto popped up in the 74th minute to give them a 1–0 victory. The Brazilians went on to win the tournament and with it their fourth World Cup.

I'd remained on the bench throughout, yet it had been a fantastic as well as a frustrating experience. It gave me a taste of what was to come.

Memories of Old London Town

The first game after the World Cup brought back a special memory for me. It took me back to the time my dad had taken me on that rickety old London Underground train to watch my first big soccer game: Liverpool versus West Ham at Wembley Stadium. One of my goals had been to one day play at Wembley, and I started the game against England, splitting it with Jurgen Sommer. We lost the game 2–0, in front of a fairly sparse crowd for Wembley, but it was another milestone in what was still a fledgling career.

Bora Milutinovic resigned as US coach shortly after the '94 World Cup, and his assistant Steve Sampson was put in as interim coach at first. His position was made permanent after a good showing at the Copa America in 1995, where the USA and Mexico had been invited to join the ten qualifying South American nations in a competition which has the same status as the European Championships.

Leading up to the tournament Steve Sampson had adopted this policy of alternating goalkeepers game by game. We were based in Paysandu, Uruguay's third largest city. The coach came to me with an intriguing proposition. He offered me a choice. I could play in two of the three group games and miss out on the quarter-finals, or I could opt to play one group game, giving two to Kasey Keller, and then play in the last eight matches.

So what do you do? The bird in the hand or the two in the bush? Suppose that we didn't qualify and there were no knockout games to be played?

I thought about this, and opted to take a risk. So Kasey played against Chile and we won 2–1. I then came in against Bolivia where we lost 1–0. Our future in the knockout stages depended on beating Argentina, and it was Kasey's turn to occupy the no. 1 spot. We produced the result of the tournament, beating the Argentineans 3–0. My strategy had paid off, we were in the knock-out stages and I was lined up to play.

Our quarter-final game was against Mexico. I kept a clean sheet as the teams reached a stalemate after 90 minutes. At the end of extra time the score was still 0–0, and so it was to be a penalty shoot-out.

Wynalda scored our first, and then Garcia returned the compliment. Joe-Max Moore put away our second. When one of Mexico's all-time top scorers, Hermosillo, stepped up, I saved; we were 2–1 up. Caliguari scored again for us. Here was a chance to progress to the semis as Alberto Coyote came up to take their third. I saved again, and when we scored our fourth we were through to face – you guessed it – Brazil.

Steve Sampson was true to his word, and having made my choice to opt for only one group game, I was given the nod for the semi-final.

The game was played in a small town in the south of Uruguay called Maldonado, and unlike our World Cup clash in '94, which was played in front of a huge crowd, only 8,000 people attended. It didn't matter; we were in great company as Brazil's team included Aldair, Ronaldo, Dunga, Roberto Carlos, Juninho, Leonardo, Edmundo and Zinho to name just a few. We lost 1–0 again, this time to a goal by Aldair. Still, we had done well to make it to the semi-finals.

French Farce

Kasey Keller and I continuing splitting games between us pretty much 50:50. By the time 1998 came around – another World Cup year – I had been on an extended run of internationals, and then in February Kasey was brought back in and we beat Brazil for the first time ever in Los Angeles. He stayed in right up until France '98, and was first choice for our opening game of the tournament against Germany. Now, Germany are always a force to be reckoned with, but in this World Cup they were regarded as no great shakes. We lost 2–0, which normally is nothing to be ashamed of. It was the manner of our defeat which was unacceptable. We didn't record a single shot on goal. We moved on to Lyon, where Iran beat us 2–1. At least we scored a goal this time, but with Kasey still in the team, I was beginning to feel that I was going to be a World Cup spectator a second time.

That was not to be. Some of the players went straight to the press after the Iran game and absolutely annihilated coach Steve Sampson. Perhaps feeling the pressure, when we moved to Nantes for our final game he put me in the team. We lost our last game too, by a 1–0 margin. At last I had tasted the experience of playing in a World Cup. At least that was one positive thing I could draw from it. As a team we had finished 32nd out of 32. That was totally unacceptable.

How had this happened? We had a lot of the players that did well in '94 who now had four years more experience. A lot of them were now playing professionally in Europe. We got to the semi-finals of the Copa America and we had a crop of young players coming through. We were in the last 16 in '94, there was no way we should have been worse in '98.

I think the responsibility lies fairly and squarely on the shoulders of the players. A lot of players took liberties and then blamed the manager. I'm not saying that the manager was without fault, as there were all kinds of issues there. But when you go to a World Cup, you have to set that to one side and play for your country and your team-mates.

The problems really started when Steve Sampson was appointed as coach. He went in way over his previous experience. He had only ever been a college coach, and Bora Milutinovic had him brought in as his assistant and translator. When Bora was fired, other likely candidates had jobs and so Steve Sampson got hired as the best they could find at the time. He brought in Clive Charles as his assistant and, to be fair, Clive helped to keep things on an even keel for as long as he could. Clive took the training while Sampson just sat back and let things transpire at first.

At first the players loved this. Bora's sessions were very long and monotonous. You would often be training for two and a half hours and then have meetings which would make you go brain-dead. Yet Bora showed that his approach, mind-numbing as it was, consistently brought teams together and got them winning games.

Although I didn't like Bora's sessions, there was a purpose to them and he got damn good results. With some of the players that he had available, you have to say that he got results which on paper we should never have got.

Steve had never run a professional team before; he had never been around professional players.

What professional players can detect is inconsistency. Maybe this is down to nerves, a lack of knowledge or confidence, but players can and will see through it. On top of that they can see if people in positions of power hide their lack of confidence by seeming arrogant. That's what I thought Steve did.

Players who may have revelled in the relaxed style at first began to see this as a lack of authority. For example, Steve would run a training session and shout, 'Stop. This is what I want you to do.' A player could say, 'No. That's not right.' Then a discussion might ensue, and it was possible to talk him out of something that he was certain about only a few minutes earlier.

If anyone had tried that under Bora, he would have kept you out on that training ground for four hours until he had convinced you that he was right. He was consistent, decisive, tenacious and authoritarian. You knew 100% that he was the boss. Whether he was right or wrong, whether you loved him or you hated him, when he was there, he had control of the room. Steve had some guys looking into spaces and asking, 'How is he here?'

When it came to the World Cup in '98, there were a lot of things which didn't feel right, and they were not all down to the manager. You can say that there were bad choices made about the hotel, the family programme, the training, the media relations – all sorts of things. Yet the players were out there on the pitch, and we underperformed. We have to take personal and collective responsibility for what we did or did not do. Player for player we were better in France '98 than in USA '94 and we finished last.

Whatever my views of Steve Sampson may be, players have to look at themselves if they cannot perform and motivate themselves in World Cup finals.

The media at home were baying for blood and it was no surprise when Steve Sampson was relieved of his duties. His replacement was Bruce Arena, the guy with the best win record in US soccer, who until recently had been the coach at New York Red Bulls.

Bruce came in right away with a very confident attitude. It was a case of 'I'm the boss and I'm here. If you want to mess with me then there you go – down the road'. As a senior player, I found that I could have differences of opinion with Bruce. He could have an argument behind closed doors with people like me and Kasey and Claudio Reyna. He might not always agree, but he could handle different opinions from senior players in the right setting.

So here was a third kind of management style. Bora had been the perfectionist, a master tactician; Steve was promoted above his level of experience; and Bruce had the credentials, could take in other views, but left you in no doubt that he was the boss. Just watching this was in itself a great education.

Though the media came down hard on us after the '98 World Cup, and you can't blame them, the US fans will always support you during a game. The official supporters' club, Sam's Army, is a smaller set-up than what European countries have, and they always try to make a lot of noise. They will pack a stadium for World Cup qualifiers, but there is a difference between an American crowd and a European crowd. An American crowd tends to make a noise when something good happens, whereas in Europe you tend to have more chanting and singing together with a constant noise level that changes volume with the ebb and flow of the game.

Having said that, the US fans are the most patriotic in the world. They will support you 100%. They would never boo off a US national team. You are representing your country and you receive applause whether you win or lose. Even after our horrendous performance against Germany in the '98 World Cup, we were not booed off.

I find the situation in England strange. There is a different kind of relationship between the national team and the fans. Frank Lampard is a very, very good player. He's one of England's greatest assets, yet he gets booed when he touches the ball. That's outrageous. From my perspective I tend to wonder if the fans actually want the national team to win or whether they enjoy living in their own misery.

I don't understand why they do that. I don't know if it's a jealousy issue because he's got a bit of money and he's done well for himself or because he happens to play for Chelsea. It's crazy that when Steve McClaren was in charge, his name was mentioned and people booed. If you don't like him don't go to the game. Have an opinion by all means, but don't go to the game to vent your frustrations on the team. It's almost as if in England people like it when the national team fails so that they can say, 'I would have done this or he should have done that.'

The Germans have a word, Schadenfreude, which means taking pleasure in other people's misfortune. It would be better if England fans rediscovered their patriotism and passion and dropped the Schadenfreude.

Jorge Campos Wears Turtleneck

Great supporters can be a great advantage. The thing I realised from playing internationals is that countries do all sorts of things to play to their advantages. Years ago the US Soccer Federation decided to play internationals where they would be most viable. If you played a Central American team like Mexico or Costa Rica in a place like Southern California, Texas or Florida, you could bet you would be playing with an away crowd even though you were at home. If there were 100,000 tickets for a game against Mexico, somehow, some way, 90,000 of those tickets would end up in the hands of Mexicans. It makes for a tremendous atmosphere, but you have lost the best part of the home advantage.

When you play these teams away, they take you to high altitude or play in blazing heat. Maybe they don't arrange for there to be an intimidating atmosphere, but there sure is one. They take you out of your comfort zone to ensure an added advantage for themselves, and then they try to take the game.

The US Soccer Federation now sees the economics of qualifying games as a secondary concern. They use all of America's attributes to give their teams better home advantage. If you are playing Canada, you can take them to Southern California and you will have a home crowd.

When playing Mexico in an important World Cup qualifier, as we did in 2001, we took them up to Columbus, Ohio, in the winter. The temperature was –5ºC at one point, and the pitch had to be heated to make it playable. As we lined up in the tunnel ready to go out into this bitter cold, I was kitted out as usual. I had my shirt and shorts on just as I always do. I'd had a good warm-up out on the pitch and felt fine. As the Mexican team lined up beside us, I looked over to their diminutive and eccentric keeper Jorge Campos. He was wearing a turtleneck sweater, over which he had another shirt; he had liner gloves to go inside his goalkeeping gloves; his ears were covered with earmuffs and he was in long trousers. He waddled up to the side of me like some kind of marshmallow man. He almost shivered as he said to me, 'What are we doing playing here?' I smiled courteously and said, 'We wanted to show you how lovely Columbus can be in the winter.'

The Mexicans froze. They hadn't even been on the pitch for a warm-up; they stayed in the locker room and did some stretches. They were just not in the game and the 2–0 scoreline in our favour does not nearly represent what a one-sided game it was.

When we did the same to El Salvador in Foxborough, they didn't even want to line up for the national anthems because they were so cold; they just wanted to get the game going.

History Maker

We used all of our advantages to qualify for the 2002 World Cup in Korea/Japan. This was the first time the tournament had ever been held in Asia. It was to be my third World Cup and, as we moved into 2002, we had an international schedule of 14 games before the tournament. My club commitments obviously meant that it was out of the question for me to play in all of them. As the tournament dawned, Kasey had played eight full games and two halves; Tim Howard had played one; Tony Meola had played one; while I had managed two and two halves.

Despite Kasey having more starts than me in the year, I felt that this was my big chance. I had solidified myself at club level, and I was as fit as I had ever been in my life. The opening game was against Portugal in Suwon, South Korea.

Bruce Arena named me in the starting line-up. I was in, and we made a dream start, scoring after just four minutes from John O'Brien. With just over half an hour gone, we were 3–0 up. The Portuguese rallied to stage a recovery and bring the score back to 3–2, but that's how it stayed. We had won our opening game.

Then it was on to the Munhak Stadium in Incheon to face the Korean Republic. As far as I was concerned at the time, I was just going about my business – we were winning 1–0. The Koreans were awarded a penalty. This could ruin our perfect start to the tournament. Lee Eul-Yong stepped up to take it. My thoughts and my sights were directed only towards the shooter. That's all. He was a left footer, and I saw a look in his eyes that said that he was not confident. In a big game, a penalty taker who lacks confidence will usually open his body and side-foot the ball to his stronger side. He did. As the shot came in I dived to my right and parried it away, but the ball stayed in play and came out to a waiting Kim, who could only shoot the rebound wide of the goal. I made the save and we came away with a very valuable point.

Everything was going great in our camp, until a mad first five minutes in our final group game against Poland. I was again the first choice. The Poles got into gear quickly and we were 2–0 down after just five minutes. Then something happened which in the first instance was annoying; then it became a piece of work that I had to concentrate upon; then just seconds later it became part of my own and World Cup history.

The Poles were awarded a penalty. Maciej Zurawski stepped up to take it. My thoughts this time were only on trying to stop it and saving the embarrassment of a very large scoreline against us. That's all. As the shot came in I dived to my left and not only got my hands to it, but was able to firmly hold onto the ball. It was a satisfying moment, but that's all. We were still behind in a game which we would eventually lose 3–1.

Later, I was told that no goalkeeper had ever saved two penalties in open play during a World Cup.

We had four points and South Korea had to face Portugal in a game that the Koreans had no need to win as they had already done enough to qualify. Yet the Koreans performed diligently to turn over the Portuguese, who finished the game with just nine men. The Koreans scored their vital winner just ten minutes from time, producing a result that got us into the next stage, and drawing some criticism of us from the US media who branded us as 'lucky'. We had been fortunate, but there was no doubt about it; we were in the last 16 in the World Cup finals.

We faced Mexico in the knockout stages; a rivalry similar to England vs Germany. For 46 years the USA had lived in Mexico's shadow as a footballing nation. We were without a win against Mexico between 1934 and 1980, during which time we played 24 times, winning none, losing 21 and drawing three. Then we beat them 2–1 in 1981, and things could not have been more evenly matched since. Between 1981 and the 2002 World Cup we had each won eight times and drawn six times. This game was going to be balanced on a knife-edge.

Just before the game we were asked to assemble as a group in our hotel and get ready to receive a conference call. The guy on the other end of the line was none other than the President of the United States of America, George Bush Junior.

I'd been lucky enough to have been invited to the White House with the national team some years earlier, when it was a great privilege to meet President Clinton and, although we weren't meeting President Bush face to face, it was a great moment when he called up to speak to us.

He wished us all good luck for the forthcoming game against Mexico, and told us that he had telephoned his opposite number, President Vicente Fox of Mexico. He was quite open in admitting that he told President Fox that he knew very little about soccer, but he said, 'I told him we are going to win.'

It was only months earlier, following the 9/11 attacks on New York City, that President Bush had described Korea as part of 'the axis of evil'. Without wanting to be political, I can only assume that he was referring to North Korea. While we were in South Korea we found it to be an extremely friendly and sporting nation even when we played against them. Either way, what was clearly apparent was that the security arrangements for our visit to this tournament were different from the usual arrangements. When I had been to tournaments before, the US always had decent security arrangements. In the run-up to a tournament, a small group of people would typically get together for the security briefing. I understand that for the 2002 World Cup security briefing there were more than 100 people present.

The extent of the security arrangements became apparent as soon as we arrived. We were ushered from our plane straight onto a coach. As the coach drove along the route to our hotel we were accompanied by no less than four helicopters. In front of our bus was a fully armed SWAT team. Following our bus was a fully armed SWAT team. This was the arrangement every time we left our hotel.

At our training ground, a gentleman from the CIA had set himself up with a little monitor. This was a chemical weapons detector and carried out a reading every 15 seconds. If there was trouble, there was a little bunker that we were to take refuge in.

Back at our hotel, we occupied a whole floor. The floors below us and above us had to remain empty, while only a single lift was allowed to stop at our floor. All other lifts had been reprogrammed so that they missed out our floor. All in all, there must have been 20 or so security men looking after us that we knew of. Apparently there was also a lot of undercover security, so that if we went to the shopping mall next to our hotel, we would be shadowed without even being aware of it. After a while it just became the routine and we didn't let it affect our preparation.

When the game against Mexico came around, we went into it determined to be strong at the back, to try to break up the Mexican rhythm and to get them on the counter-attack. Our plan was executed to perfection. We caught them with counter-attacks on two occasions and produced the shock of the tournament. We were in the quarter-finals, on equal terms among the best eight teams in the world.

Suddenly, soccer was big news in the United States, prompting President George Bush to admit that before our game with Mexico he knew nothing at all about soccer. Something he said he had in common with the average American, yet suddenly we were up there with the best and everybody at home was taking notice. For all of his lack of knowledge of the game the President proved to be an accurate tipster when he told President Fox of Mexico that we were going to win. Meanwhile, the same media people who branded us as 'lucky' were now proclaiming us as heroes. That's football.

I had played four games in the World Cup, written myself into its history, and thanks to our strong start we were going into the quarter-finals to face Germany; further than any US team had ever been before.

Our game against Germany in France '98, regardless of the result, remained a blot on our copybook. We had not performed. We did ourselves and our country a disservice. This time, whatever the result against Germany, we were determined that there would be no repeat of that powder puff performance in France. In fact, we were beginning to feel that we had a good chance of progressing to the semis.

Sometimes in soccer, you get one of those inexplicable games. Ulsan, South Korea, was the venue for our World Cup quarter-final against Germany, and the venue for one of those games that just don't add up. It was one in which we played Germany off the park, yet could not score. We didn't just hang on against one of soccer's superpowers. The Germans were bigger, stronger and vastly more experienced than us as a team, yet we outshot them by 11:6, and five excellent scoring chances evaded us. Michael Ballack outjumped two defenders to head home a free kick in the 39th minute, and although we dominated play, we just could not get the ball to go in the net. With about 15 minutes to go there was a clear handball in the German box which the referee chose to ignore, and the Germans hung on with their trademark gritty determination. At the final whistle both sets of players sank to the ground exhausted. Then the chants began to ring out from our fans. Not chants of derision because we had lost, but a chant of pride at the way we had played and how far we had progressed. '*U-S-A! U-S-A!*' Our captain Claudio Reyna went over to our fans and unfurled the Stars and Stripes. The USA was no longer an outlier in world soccer; we were there competing on equal terms with the best that the world had to offer.

We had got to the last eight in a competition involving 194 nations and had done better than France, Argentina, Italy and Uruguay, four of the seven nations that have won the World Cup, and equalled the performance of a fifth member of the exclusive World Cup winners club, England.

As for the Germans, they beat South Korea in the semi-finals before being beaten by Brazil in the final.

We had achieved more than any US team before us, yet I think we deserved to beat Germany and we could have beaten Korea. The impact on soccer in the US would have been unimaginable had we gone all the way to the final.

The 2002 World Cup took the profile of soccer in the USA to another level. It got onto people's radar screens and was noticed by the dyed-in-the-wool US sports fans who still regard it as a minority sport. Though now it is a minority sport worth taking note of because we are recognised as being somewhere up there with the best and a nation to be reckoned with.

I'm pleased to have made some contribution towards raising the profile of soccer in the American psyche. It is now the second largest participation sport in the US, with 18 million people playing on a regular basis. I believe that the success of our national team has played some part in that growth.

In professional terms, though, Major League Soccer is still in the early days of once again trying to win a foothold for the professional game in a sports-mad nation, with a lot of traditional indigenous sports and sporting heroes competing for airtime. These other sports are high profile, glamorous, home-grown and, importantly, have a history. In a country where the timeline of history is short, it is our sporting heroes in our traditional games who provide a tangible link with our past. Relatively speaking, soccer is the new kid on the block.

I think soccer in the US will continue to build on the foundations that are being laid in the MLS. The move to bring David Beckham into the MLS with LA Galaxy was an interesting one. It was a deal worth a reputed $250 million to Beckham over five years, and he announced his intention to raise the status of soccer in the US.

Regardless of what the media or anyone else may say or think, I know something from my own experience. Of all the players in the game today, David Beckham is one of the best passers of the ball; one of the best free kick specialists; and is a fantastic provider of assists, mainly through his tremendous crossing ability.

Yet soccer is a team sport, and we know that David is a team player who has always had the good fortune of being surrounded by outstanding players at two of the world's greatest clubs. That is a winning formula. That's what makes David Beckham a valuable asset: his ability to combine with and add value to other great players.

Without wishing to be disrespectful, I think it is fair to say that LA Galaxy is a very ordinary team when compared to the teams that Beckham has been a part of. It will be difficult for David to shine in the way that people expect him to, in particular as much of his game is about helping the team to succeed. It is not like being a striker, where the fans know if you are a success based on whether you score a lot of goals or not. The success factors for Beckham are more subtle, less immediate and dependent upon others to be able to capitalise on his natural talents.

At the end of the day, Americans love winners. LA Galaxy will need to have a very strong and successful second season with Beckham, otherwise I believe that the five-year plan to raise the profile of soccer through the 'Beckham effect' will be seriously in danger of dissipating and disappearing with a whimper.

I want to see the MLS go from strength to strength. I'd love to see the 'Beckham effect' have a real impact. My considered analysis is that, in my lifetime, soccer can and will progress in the US at a very steady rate. I don't think it will be able to overtake football, basketball or baseball at the professional level any time soon. I do think it has the potential to take over from ice hockey though, and that would be progress.

You have to remember that in England the game has had some 130 years to build up, with the competitor sports of cricket and rugby growing alongside. Soccer in the US has a big job to establish itself alongside our traditional sports. It is not a five-year job. It is not even a 20-year job. Most likely it will take more than 100 years of development. Nobody will acknowledge this because it is outside the timescales that corporations work on, and so executives may deny it and claim it is a five-year job, but all the evidence suggests otherwise.

Nevertheless, soccer in the US progressed because of the 2002 World Cup. History may show that it was a small upward blip on a 100-year journey, but without doubt 2002 was a real highlight in my career. I felt that I had at last got an elephant off my back. At last I was recognised as the no. 1 keeper in the US. It always irked me a little that in England I was more highly regarded as a goalkeeper, but less so in the States. Now that had changed and I was a history maker but, more importantly, the US came home from this tournament as a team to be reckoned with.

I have a permanent reminder of that great period in my life. It sits in front of me in my study at home. I met Barry Venison in 1994 at Newcastle United and we played together in Turkey, before subsequently becoming business partners. He had pictures of both my World Cup penalty saves framed. Above them is a caption which simply says 'History maker'. A fantastic gesture and a reminder of a fantastic time.

After 82 full internationals, I had a lot of things going on in my life, and I decided it was time to concentrate fully on them. I played my last game against Poland – and kept a clean sheet. A great way to finish an international career.

In all other countries that I know of, international footballers are presented after every game with a cap, beautifully embroidered with the country emblem and the details of the game. In the US there is no such tradition. Although the term 'caps' is used to denote the number of games you play, you don't physically get given a cap. After 50 caps you get a certificate and after 100 caps you get a gift like a Rolex watch.

Perhaps it doesn't have the romance of having a cap. Yet, I love the US and I am as proud as I can possibly be to say that I have had the honour to represent my country, to have given my all and to have achieved, in no less than two Olympic Games and three World Cups.

The cap fits for sure – even if it is only a metaphorical one.

11

Up for the Cup

Think enthusiastically about everything; but especially about your job. If you do, you'll put a touch of glory in your life. If you love your job with enthusiasm, you'll shake it to pieces. You'll love it into greatness

Norman Vincent Peale, US clergyman (1898–1993)

Playing football and being paid for it is an amazing privilege. It means that you are among the lucky few who can say that they earn their living by doing what they love. You could just do it for the love of it, except that as a professional you want even more than that – you want to be a winner. You want to taste glory, fleeting as it may be …

Penalty King

In 1890, in a place called Milford in County Armagh, Northern Ireland, Mr William McCrum devised the notion of a penalty kick to penalise foul play around the goalmouth. This innovation caused outrage among the English Victorian establishment who ran the game. The English FA could not understand the need for such a rule, arguing that football was a gentlemen's game and gentlemen would not commit a deliberate foul. The press went even further. They referred to the penalty kick as 'the Irishman's motion' and declared that it represented a 'death sentence' for the game. Nevertheless, it eventually became officially adopted.

Times have changed an awful lot since then, yet the penalty kick continues to cause as much controversy today as it did then. I mentioned before the odds of a goalkeeper scoring a goal as being in the region of 5,000:1. The issue that preoccupies goalkeepers, though, is how to stop them and, during the course of a career, every goalkeeper finds himself in a situation where the odds are stacked against him – that dreaded penalty kick. The penalty taker always has the advantage. He has a statistical advantage since many more penalties are scored than are saved. Secondly, he has a timing advantage since a goalkeeper has only between 300 and 600 milliseconds to react once the ball is kicked. Needless to say penalties are not a goalkeeper's favourite event, but they are part of the job and as a professional you have to do everything in your power to even up the odds a little.

I seem to have developed something of an aptitude for saving penalties. I made history by saving two penalties in open play during the 2002 World Cup. While at Blackburn, I faced 26 penalties and saved eight, which means that I stopped almost one in three. This really is a way that a goalkeeper can have a very big influence on the game because not only have you kept the score down – either maintained your lead or prevented your team from going behind – but you have also had a psychological impact. Your own team-mates are given a boost, while the opposition can become frustrated at the miss, maybe even start to think that this is just not going to be their day. The penalty taker may lose confidence. Thus you have taken a situation where the odds are stacked against you and possibly turned them in favour of your own team if you can make that save.

In 2006 I entered the Blackburn Rovers record books when I had a remarkable spell saving three penalties out of three in just four Premiership games. This included two penalty saves in a game of three penalties and no goals, away at Sheffield United. We had a Lucas Neill penalty saved by the United goalkeeper Paddy Kenny.

For my part, I had to save a penalty from David Unsworth and then, in the dying minutes of the game, a second one from Rob Hulse. It enabled us to come away with a valuable point in the early stages of the season.

People have asked me what the secret to the penalty save is. Well, there is no clear-cut formula that has me diving one way or another. Sometimes it's an intuitive feeling, sometimes it is something in the way they run up. In fact there is very little guessing. I look out for how the penalty taker lines himself up; what his run-up is like, whether it is short or long; I look at which way the body is positioned and I'll watch the planting foot to see which way the ball's going to be directed. The best penalty takers don't give you any clue at all, and then you have to wait a split second longer. Frank Lampard took a very good penalty against me because he hit it hard and kept it low. If it's in the air I have a better chance of saving it.

Researchers in Israel did a study which reckons that you have a one in eight chance of saving a penalty if you dive to the left or right, and a one in three chance if you don't move. This assumes, though, that all goalkeepers are equal and reckons without the advantage that I believe watching for the visual cues gives me. I like my approach to penalty saving. Statistically it is very, very effective and I will only be staying still if all the visual clues that I pick up tell me that that is what I should be doing in order to make a save. In fact, another scientific study done in Italy in 2003 videoed a sequence of penalties and suggested that goalkeepers can improve their performance by learning to spot the visual clues given out by the kicker, which is exactly what I try to do.

As for the two penalties at Sheffield United, I've been up against David Unsworth before, I've played against him for many years and I knew what he was capable of. I used his run-up to try to detect what he would do, and I got it right that time. Rob Hulse was a new situation altogether. I'd never faced him before, so I tried to read him the best way that I could.

Making two penalty saves in one game gave me an amazing feeling. The fact that the second was in the dying minutes of the game and secured a point made me absolutely elated. When the final whistle blew I travelled the length of the pitch, congratulating Paddy Kenny on his save along the way. I knew that my wife Tracy, who was pregnant with our second child Allegra at the time, was sitting in the Blackburn end with the rest of the Blackburn supporters as she always did at away games. In my elation I reached over to embrace Tracy, leaving the stewards unsure about what action they should take. I think they under-stood how I was feeling and stood back so that I was able to share a celebratory kiss with Tracy.

I'd had a great day at the office, but I have to say I will always do my homework before a game. I go through the players that take the penalties with the scouting team, using data from ProZone. With this system, you can review the videos of penalties taken over the past few years. So a couple of days before a game I go down and see what I can detect. Sometimes I can pick up something in a player's style which will allow me to have a better chance of making a save if I come up against him. Sometimes I will watch the video 20 times over, other times I will watch it only once. There are certain players who are so good that they offer no clues about what they are going to do.

I try my best not to guess because that way you are probably lowering the odds to less than the 33% chance that I have now, so I try to read them in order to increase my chances of making a save. I find that the bigger the game, the easier it is to save a penalty because the onus and all the pressure are on the striker to score.

Obviously, I'd much rather I didn't have penalties to deal with, but I have no fear of them and, just like anything else: the more you practise, the better you prepare, the better you can become.

Semi-sational

There are people who say that the worst thing in football is to lose in a semi-final of a cup competition and that it is worse than los-ing in the final itself. Having played in four semi-finals with Blackburn Rovers, I'm not sure that I would agree with this.

What I can say is that all the semi-finals I've played in have left me with different feelings. The thing I do know is that I would much rather get knocked out in a semi-final than feel the disappointment and embarrassment that Blackburn Rovers felt in 2008 when we were dumped out of the cup in the third round, being beaten at home 1–4 by Coventry City. With all due respect to Coventry City and their players, that hurts. Coventry City are where they are for a reason and Blackburn Rovers are where they are for a reason, and we should not have let that happen; yet that is the magic of the cup I suppose.

At least when you get knocked out in a semi-final, disappointing as it is, you have some measure of success to reflect upon and to build upon.

Our 2002 Worthington Cup semi-final was against Sheffield Wednesday who were a division below us at the time. It was a really good feeling when we beat them over two legs, but perhaps not the feeling that you would expect.

We played the away leg first at Hillsborough on a very difficult pitch, and came away having done a professional job. We won the game 2–1 so, as well as taking an advantage to Ewood Park, we had the insurance policy of two away goals. So to be fair, we were expected to go through to the final when Wednesday came over to Ewood Park for the second leg. We started well, and despite having a man sent off, we finished with a 4–2 victory, making it 6–3 on aggregate.

Rather than the absolute elation which you associate with getting to a final, our feeling was not one of great delight, but more of a job well done. It was a tie that we should have won and we did. For Blackburn Rovers it meant the club's first visit to a cup final in 42 years, so there was a lot of satisfaction in that too.

The Worthington Cup got rebranded as the Carling Cup and we had another good run in 2006, reaching another two-legged semi-final against Manchester United. We performed very well over both legs. The first leg at Ewood Park ended 1–1, and we went into the second leg at Old Trafford as underdogs but feeling that we had done well and knowing that we had already beaten United at their place in the Premier League that season.

It was a finely balanced game as we went into the second leg, but we had an early setback when Van Nistelrooy scored for

United after eight minutes. Steven Reid brought the scores level just after the half-hour, and soon afterwards there was a very harsh penalty decision in which the referee adjudged our defender Khizanishvili to have committed a handball. It felt like a major injustice as Van Nistelrooy stepped up to the penalty spot. Justice was restored though as I saved the penalty kick and kept the scores level at half-time.

In the second half we continued to play well, but Louis Saha spooned in a volley from a Rooney cross and that goal took United to the final and dumped us out of the semi. That was a really disappointing result because we matched United and it was a really passionate semi-final. But it was again a two-legged game, which kind of spreads the tension of the occasion out a little bit.

Single match semi-finals like the FA Cup semi-final condense the drama, the tension and the anticipation of reaching the final into one small stretch of time. I've reached two FA Cup semi-finals with Blackburn Rovers and have different feelings about each of them.

In 2005 Arsenal made the FA Cup semi-finals for a record fifth consecutive year. It was our misfortune to be drawn against them. This was the year in which Chelsea manager José Mourinho had tagged us as 'bully boys', saying that we did nothing but kick people. The truth of it was that we had a lot of very good footballers at that time and we were at the stage where we were becoming solidified as a team under Mark Hughes.

We were one game from the final and up against a team that has all the 'bells and whistles'. We always give 110% and that day was no exception. It's just that every so often you come up against a team that are just better on the day. On that particular day, not only did Arsenal have all the 'bells and whistles', they were chiming and tooting together in some form of footballing three-part harmony. They were awesome on that day, and though we managed to harness them for half an hour, we were outplayed. Van Persie, Pires and Vieira were just outstanding.

I'm not sure that we even had a proper shot on target, and Arsenal kept me busy for the whole game which we lost 3–0. We were happy to be in the semi-final and disappointed to lose, but on the day they were a better team. They were just on fire, and we had to take the disappointment and walk away with our heads held high knowing that we had given it all that we had.

There is an old saying in English football: 'Sometimes your name is on the cup'. When a team continues to overcome massive obstacles to progress in the tournament, it can feel almost as though it was meant to be and that by some strange quirk of fate you are destined to win the cup.

In the FA Cup 2006–07, Blackburn Rovers fans could have been forgiven for believing that our name was on the cup that year. The road to the FA Cup doesn't come much harder. Each round brought with it a stiff challenge. In the third round we got a very tough draw: Everton at Goodison Park from which we came away with a tremendous 4–1 victory.

Next, another away fixture and a tricky one at that. It was against Luton Town on a very awkward pitch. We scored four again and kept a clean sheet. Surely we were due for a home draw. No such luck; it was away again. Worse still it was against the mighty Arsenal. There are obstacles and there are obstacles. Arsenal away in the fifth round of the cup is what you call a massive obstacle. We drew at Arsenal, and at last enjoyed home advantage in the replay which we won 1–0. On paper Plymouth Argyle and Watford would have been the easiest draws in the quarter-finals, but this year was just not going to be easy for Blackburn Rovers. We had a home draw at last against Manchester City. Our 2–0 victory put us into yet another semi-final.

With a cup run as tough as that we went into the semi-final absolutely believing that we could win even though we had been drawn against the mighty Chelsea. We all knew we were in for another tough game, but there was not one person in the dressing room who did not believe that we could win.

In contrast to the 2005 semi, the 2007 FA Cup semi-final held at Old Trafford was a different matter. It was a game which reminded me in many ways of the USA's 2002 World Cup quarter-final defeat against Germany when we dominated the game.

In the end we lost to a single goal scored by Michael Ballack.

Just as the US team had done in the World Cup, we took hold of our semi-final against the high-flying and much fancied Chelsea team. They had the better of the opening exchanges, but we gradually came into the game and then Frank Lampard opened the scoring, leaving us 1–0 down at half-time. In the second half Petr Cech had a busy time. David Dunn cracked a 20-yard shot which Cech pushed around the post. Christopher Samba got in a header from the resulting corner, before Jason Roberts forced Cech to save again. Morten Gamst Pedersen hit the post before the pressure finally told and Jason Roberts equalised from ten yards.

Chelsea were not off the hook yet, and Cech saved the blushes of his skipper, John Terry, when he prevented a certain own goal at full stretch. With the scores tied at 1–1 the game went into extra time.

I mentioned that the game reminded me of our loss to Germany. This was because of the chances that we had to win the game. Then there was another reminder. Michael Ballack, whose goal had knocked the USA out of the 2002 World Cup, again popped up to score in the 109th minute and knock Blackburn out of the 2007 FA Cup.

It was a gut-wrenching moment when Ballack scored. We were in the ascendancy, and I was thinking that if this game were to go to penalties then we would have the advantage. We were the underdog and we had the momentum.

This was the most memorable of all the semi-finals so far. It was also the most disappointing. It was a game that we could have won. Thankfully, it was a short journey home from Old Trafford and I was able to get back in time to see my kids before they went to bed. It's always nice to do that after a loss. I find that I am able to shake off the disappointment of losing much better now that I am older. In my younger days if I made a mistake during a defeat I would allow it to fester for days afterwards.

After the Chelsea defeat I was able to deal with my disappointment by analysing the situation. I asked myself, 'Did we play well?' The answer was, 'Yes we did.' I asked, 'Did we have a great cup run in the most difficult circumstances?' The answer was, 'Yes we did.' I asked, 'Will we let it affect our next game in a negative sense?' The answer was, 'No. We are going to take the positives from the semi-final and try to play the same way. If we play like that, then nine times out of ten we will win.'

With that, it was time to play with the kids.

Asian Eye

Blackburn is a relatively small town to have a Premier League club, with a population of just under 140,000. In fact, according to an analysis by Blackburn Rovers fan and local Member of Parliament, the Right Honourable Jack Straw, it is the smallest conurbation by far which is able to sustain a Premier League club.

Their gates may appear small when compared to Arsenal or Manchester United, but considering the population that they have to draw from and the existence of nearby clubs, with an average of 23,500 they do very well in the circumstances. Blackburn is a very community-based football club and, whereas Arsenal have a standard ticket price of £46 per head, Blackburn have kept theirs to £15 a head and used some of the TV money to reduce the season ticket prices. When you think of it this way, Arsenal has three times Blackburn Rovers' average gate, and three times the ticket price. They have a ninefold advantage in gate receipts alone. It is amazing that a team like Blackburn Rovers can compete with them on even terms, and a great credit to the Rovers board that they do it remaining true to their community.

The Blackburn community has other interesting characteristics other than being small and tight-knit. After the Second World War, the economy began to pick up, and many local people saw this as an opportunity to get out of the cotton mills. Manning the night shifts became difficult and recruiters were sent out to India and Pakistan to find workers.

Over the years Indian and Pakistani people have built a life for themselves in Blackburn and now some 20% of the population is of Indo-Asian origin. There has been a lot of discussion about why there has not been an emergence of football players coming through our clubs with origins in the Indian subcontinent. Relative to the population they are undoubtedly under-repre-sented and less than a handful have made first team appearances at any level in the English professional leagues.

It is hard to say why this is. I don't believe that it is due to dis-crimination. I think that it is more of a cultural issue. In India and Pakistan, cricket is the be-all and end-all of sports. It is quite nat-ural that people hold onto their cultural and sporting roots in some way. If we brought the population of Bay Village, Ohio, to live in Blackburn could we really expect them to drop all of their interest in American football?

It's not about people from India and Pakistan not wanting to play football, but it has everything to do with not having a deep love for football and having one for cricket. If you look at some of the great cricketers that they produce, they are big, powerful and strong. Cricket, culturally, is their first sport and they naturally address their talents towards it just as many Americans will do towards football, basketball and baseball, and as the English will do towards soccer, rugby and cricket.

With India at 145 in the FIFA World Football Rankings and Pakistan at 164, you don't have to be a genius to work out that football hardly features on their radar screens. The best athletes are gravitating towards cricket in India and Pakistan just as the better Indo-Asian athletes are here.

It will take time for a player with Indian or Pakistani ethnic ori-gins to come through big in the Premier League, but sooner or later it will happen. Then football might have a chance of tapping into a pool of sporting talent which is on its doorstep – especial-ly in Blackburn.

I Have Been a Rover

After all the years of moving around the world, I felt that I had finally found my footballing home in Blackburn. There were great times, achievements and disappointments, but that is what foot-ball is all about, isn't it?

Nobody can have been more delighted than I was when I signed a contract with Blackburn which would keep me there until 2010. I had clearly demonstrated my loyalty to the club when I renewed my contract before the 2002 World Cup. Loyalty has always been a big thing for me.

Yet something was happening behind the scenes which brought about a totally unexpected turn of events. Later, I'll talk about the choices that unfolded before me in the summer of 2008. But first, I wanted to take you behind the scenes of top flight football for a moment to look at some of the things that go on, the characters that you meet and what you can learn by looking at it with a goalkeeper's view of the world.

12

Hocus Pocus Focus

Ability is what you're capable of doing. Motivation determines what you do. Attitude determines how well you do it

Lou Holtz

Ever since people grouped together in tribes for safety and economic security the question of what makes one group or another successful has been thought about and debated. Why do some tribes survive even though they may not be the strongest? How is it that throughout the centuries armies have created great empires in the face of resistance? Why do some teams just sort of click and others which may have a plentiful supply of talent fizzle out?

These are all questions of leadership, team spirit and mental attitude. Those things which are intangible and which seem to spring up almost spontaneously in some places at a particular time and not in others. The things that are as crucial for football teams as they are for tribes, armies and office workers.

It's interesting that during my time at Liverpool we had a star-studded squad with incredible talent and, though we threatened to achieve, we tended to stutter. Whilst at Blackburn, I watched as players came and went. Though we had a few ups and downs, I feel that I can say that we pretty consistently were a team which punched above its weight. We had great talent, of course, but not the talent in depth of the big four teams. Regardless of that and our relatively limited resources we managed to remain up there and competitive.

What is it that helps teams to do this? Talent of course. Application for sure. I think also that there is a lot to be said for team spirit. But what is team spirit?

Scrambled Ego

In the 1980s, after years of research in industry, Dr Meredith Belbin put forward his theory that high-performing management teams tend to be made up of nine different types of people. His proposition is that really great teams have a mixture of characters who are valued for their particular strengths and whose weaknesses are understood by the other team members, tolerated and often compensated for by them, as they strive towards common goals.

I can't claim to be an expert on this, but when I think about my experiences in football changing rooms, training grounds and out on the pitch, I can appreciate that I have drawn much the same conclusions as Belbin in respect of football teams. You need a different mix of talents and characters. I'd tend to put it like this. There are three elements to great team spirit – ego, respect and camaraderie.

I've often thought that team spirit – that elusive thing that is difficult to describe and put your finger on – is about egos, what Belbin calls personality types. I don't mean big egos. To have a great team spirit you have to have the full range. People with big egos add something to the atmosphere and you need people with relatively small egos who can compensate for them.

Another element that binds teams together is genuine mutual respect across the full spectrum of the ego types. I always think that you have got something special when your match-winning players show respect to everybody, right down to the young kid who may be in the squad for the first time. If these big match-winners start hammering people all the time, team spirit can dissipate very quickly. Team spirit can be fragile and can take years to build up and moments to lose.

Then the third element is camaraderie. Maybe that's the mistake some teams make. They believe that team spirit is all about camaraderie. It is an important factor, but alone it is not enough. It also has a dangerous side as far as team spirit is concerned. If you are not careful, it can create groups within groups which become cliques. When this happens teams can stutter, regardless of how much talent they have. You can have situations where people feel 'in' one moment and 'out' another, and others may feel excluded or on the margins. This can happen in a situation where, to the outside observer at least, great camaraderie exists.

It was a bit like that at Liverpool, where there was already an established clique when I arrived. Everybody could see that Michael Owen was going places. Even though he was only about seventeen at the time and a quiet lad, the rest of the lads, both English and foreigners, took to him straight away and he slid effortlessly into the squad. Things should have been done for each player in order to develop a team spirit, but that simply wasn't the case all of the time.

As Gerard Houllier brought more and more foreign players into the squad, you gradually saw not so much a division as such, but there was clearly a British group and the rest. There were other groups within the squad as well. It can be hard to come into a situation where there are established cliques, especially as many of the foreign players didn't conform to the cultural norms of certain cliques, which in those days tended to include drinking or gambling. Some of the British players seemed to want to prove to the foreign group that you could drink, eat poorly and still be a good footballer. The fact is that you can, but not for as long as you can if you look after yourself properly.

Foreign players were coming in with the notion that to be a good professional you play your game and look after yourself. At that time, this was not the norm for the main Liverpool clique.

Today I think things are a lot different. Take the 2007/08 Blackburn Rovers squad for example. There was a lot of camaraderie between the players as well as a lot of mutual respect. You don't always have to be going out together to achieve this, or even like someone necessarily, but you do need to have respect for them. Though I think it does help when players do socialise together, my team-mates know my position. Firstly, at my age I don't feel that my body will allow me to go out that much. Secondly, as I tell them, I want to spend time with my wife and kids. The younger lads love that one. 'What? You want to spend time with your wife?' We laugh about it because it's done in a friendly, humorous way and camaraderie can come out of acknowledging the differences between us and having fun with them.

At Blackburn Rovers, inevitably some of the guys hang out with each other more than others. There are groups of mates but they are not divisive in the way that cliques can be. One of the things that exists in that squad is that a lot of the lads have the ability to poke fun at themselves more than at others, and with this approach you can get a tremendous team spirit going.

On Being the New Boy

I mentioned earlier how Michael Owen's outstanding natural ability saw him shepherded into the dominant group despite his quiet, unassuming demeanour. I've always found it interesting to observe the different ways in which people fit into a squad when they first arrive.

For example, I had only ever played against Robbie Savage before he arrived at Blackburn, never with him. If you've only ever played against Robbie and don't know him as a person, your feeling will be that you don't really like him. Yet he can enamour himself to a new group of players instantaneously. I remember when he walked in on his first day at Blackburn. It took him approximately three and a half seconds to have everyone laughing. That's the way he is; he bounces into a room with a smile on his face and a joke ready to roll off his tongue. He's a player that you would rather be playing with than against, and definitely a player who really brings something to the dressing room. He's eccentric, has a sharp wit and once you get to know him as a person rather than as a footballer you cannot help but like him.

Roque Santa Cruz came in differently, but was accepted from

minute one as well. The thing that comes over with Roque is that he is so mellow, placid and totally inoffensive. He's a really friendly guy, who likes to laugh at the jokes and enjoys going out to dinner with the lads. He was accepted immediately but in a different way to Robbie, because he was gentle, cordial and polite.

These two added to the team spirit because of their likeability. I'll never forget the impact that Andy Cole made when he joined. It was different. We were in desperate need of goals at the time, and Andy had delivered the goods on the biggest stage; he was a big money signing from Manchester United. Andy stamped his personality on the squad very early on. He was relatively quiet and then you began to realise out on the training pitch why he has been consistently successful. Even on the training pitch Andy will not take any nonsense from anyone. He had come from a particular school of football which had given him an unrelenting winning mentality.

In training he wanted everything done properly and professionally and he wanted to win. He took it very seriously and in his early sessions there were a couple of altercations with other players. I forget the exact incidents, but it was of the nature that if he lost a game in training he would make his displeasure known to other players right away. This ruffled a few feathers, but his attitude was that he had come with a big reputation and he had come to score goals. People saw that he wasn't being cocky. He was a serious professional who would have an altercation one day and come in the next day having forgotten all about it. Of course he did what he always has done: he began to bang in the goals and he gained the respect of the team. He was very good for team spirit in a different sort of way than Michael Owen was at Liverpool or Roque and Sav have been at Blackburn. He had higher expectations and he raised the bar for everyone. He wasn't the kind of guy to go around hugging everyone but he did a lot for the younger players; he brought a new intensity to training and with his winning mentality he raised team spirit by helping to raise people's sights.

These three players all had a positive effect on the squad in different ways. Of course you sometimes get players who come in and have a negative effect. They will try to take advantage of the system and managers have to be careful with these types because if they are seen to get preferential treatment they can really cause unrest within the group.

A lot of the time though, dressing rooms are a bit like neighbourhoods, in that they are self regulating. If somebody steps too far out of line he may come into conflict with the senior players or the manager and often this has the effect of settling things down.

You don't have to like a person but you do have to be able to respect each other as players. I once played with a guy who turned up late for training and landed in a helicopter on the training pitch. He was playing very well at the time and knew that the manager had little option but to use him. I understand that there may have been extenuating circumstances behind his lateness, but the nature of his arrival rubbed a few of the players up the wrong way. It was detrimental to the morale of the squad. We all held the manager in the highest regard and this was downright disrespectful.

When I was at Galatasaray, two players had links with the media which were just too close. We would find that our team meetings were being reported almost word for word in the press the next morning. Again this caused a big division which was unnecessary.

I have my own way of coming into a squad. There are people who can bound into the room and their natural wit and charisma can carry them through. That's not really my style. I tend to go in and just maintain an even keel. I'll keep fairly quiet and concentrate on my job. I prefer to try to win the respect of the group through my performances and then build my relationships after that.

I can see now that this was one of the issues that made it difficult for me to settle at Liverpool. When I first arrived I wasn't in the team so it was difficult for me to win respect based on my performances. When I did get into the team, I have to admit that I was up, down, here, there and everywhere. So I found that I would gain respect from some players for my performances some times and not others. I found myself searching for my place within the cliques on a year-round basis. I'd think, It's here, then over there and then, oh no it's over here. At times I'd think, Hey, I've had four good games in a row and everyone's talking to me. Then I'd have a bad game and it felt like people weren't talking any more. Having these little groups can unsettle you when you are trying to adapt to a new team environment.

That's how it goes when you have those doubts in the back of your mind and you are not sure where you fit. It's easier to come in if you are charismatic. Yet I took those experiences with me to Blackburn. I didn't change my approach to coming into a new squad but I was able to stop looking around for my place in the groups and concentrate on winning respect by performing well.

Laughter Is the Best Medicine

Some managers try to do things to maintain and boost team spirit. Sometimes they can be quite artificial and sometimes these things can backfire. Yet if team spirit was as simple as running a few team-building exercises, every dressing room would be walking on air all of the time and that simply is not the case.

In fact, when I was at Liverpool, there were a couple of occasions when we got bound together quite by accident, and rather than being because of the management team it was at the expense of the management team. I guess it's the same in any situation where there are authority figures; there is always something of a 'them and us' situation – just like being at school in a way. This slight tension between the two parties has the knack of occasionally throwing up situations which bond the team together even though they are not meant to.

One day at Liverpool, Houllier called a meeting in the dressing room. He wanted to express his concern that he felt discipline was slipping. He was reeling off a list of things he was not happy with. He cited players who were turning up late for training and so on. Then he turned to the subject of mobile phones. Just as he did so the muffled sound of a mobile phone in somebody's pocket could be heard. He paused; we all looked over at Michael Owen because it seemed to be coming from above his head, but the phone stopped and the boss carried on. The caller had left a message and the phone rang out again and again. Each time it rang Houllier continued, until Phil Thompson interrupted him and shouted across the room, 'Michael will you turn off your phone?'. Michael looked innocent and said, 'It's not mine, that's not my ring.' Thompson was having none of it. 'It is. Now get up and turn it off.'

Ever the diplomat, Michael again insisted that it wasn't his phone but he said, 'If you like, I'll go and look for it for you.'

At this point David Thompson, who was always a very funny lad, joined in. It was curious because David always sat next to Michael in the changing room and for some reason on this day was sitting next to Patrick Berger a few places away from his usual spot. We all had our squad numbers written above our places, so everybody knew whose pockets Michael was rummaging in to try to find this phone.

As Michael was searching for the phone, David feigned frustration. 'Come on lads, whose phone is it?' When Michael eventually retrieved the offending phone he realised that it had been David's phone that was ringing. The exchange of looks between them gave away what had happened.

When the staff left there was silence for a moment and then an almighty outburst of laughter from everybody. The whole dressing room was hysterical. It's ironic really that the management team were trying to get more from the squad by instilling more discipline, but that this 'off the wall' moment perhaps did more to bring the squad together than any management intervention. As I recall we won our next game.

There was another slightly 'off the wall' incident at Liverpool that had a similar effect. We were playing West Ham at Anfield and I was on the bench along with Karl-Heinz Riedle, Patrick Berger, Steve Harkness and Michael Owen. Paul Ince was there because he was either injured or suspended.

At Anfield the opposing benches were really close together and so the West Ham bench, which had Neil Ruddock and Ian Wright among their group, was right next to us.

Throughout the game there was a constant stream of comments going back and forth between Ian Wright on the West Ham bench and the animated Phil Thompson who was up and down in front of ours. I think Ian Wright must have been getting to him a bit because when we scored the first goal Phil Thompson stood up, turned round to Wright and with a clenched fist salute screamed, 'Yeeeessss geeeerrrinnnn.'

When West Ham scored some time later, Ian revelled in the opportunity to give Phil some more stick and began mocking him quite openly. As the game progressed other West Ham players joined in the discourse between Thompson and Wright. Some of it was not so nice but some of it was funny and at times we found ourselves laughing about it a bit.

The next day, we were called in to the office. Somebody had called in to complain saying that Karl-Heinz Reidle was the only professional on the bench that day because he had not joined in the laughter. The fact was that we were not howling with laughter in a way that was disrespectful to the club; we just found it amazing that an assistant manager could get so distracted during a match and that Ian Wright was able to get under his skin to such an extent.

Phil Thompson wanted Ian Wright to apologise and maybe that's fair enough. He wanted us to apologise too, which we thought was a bit strange – a grown man who had allowed himself to get so wound up by a member of the opposition wanted us to apologise for somebody else making fun of him.

The effect that this had was that everybody had a story to tell from their perspective and it caused a lot of camaraderie among the whole squad. It was a team-building event that occurred without a team-building event. I know that we were laughing at somebody else's expense, but it had the effect of bringing the squad closer together.

So there are these random, unplanned events that affect team spirit. Yet managers can and should work on it as well and my experience is that some do it better than others.

Mind Games

The other thing that can sometimes have an effect on players is the mind games. Sometimes these are self-made, sometimes others try to instil ideas within you which will affect your game.

A lot of players have superstitions. As it happens I'm very superstitious myself but, illogical as it may sound, I'm superstitious only in a positive sense.

For example, about eight years ago for my pre-match meal I had a bowl of cereal followed by scrambled egg and a poached egg – two eggs done in different ways. I can't even remember what happened after that, maybe we won or I signed a new contract or both perhaps, I don't know. Yet I have built within my own mind some sort of positive association with this particular pre-match meal and I have had it ever since.

We have lost games since then so it is not as though it is some magic potion. If we were on the road and the hotel ran out of eggs, I would simply have something else. Yet if I can have that particular meal I will have it. It makes absolutely no sense at all; it is just something that I like to do. So, you see, I am only positively superstitious. If I can follow my routine it makes me feel good, if I can't I don't see it as a negative thing or an omen. I would simply do something else.

I think that most people have little rituals like this that they go through. David Bentley would not wear his tracksuit when we travelled to away games at Blackburn. We lost once when he did that and afterwards he always wore his club suit. We still lost games, of course, but, as I say, there is no rhyme nor reason to it; people develop their own little habits.

My goalkeeping gloves are another example. If we lose I don't want to see the gloves that I wore ever again, not even in training. They get taken away from me and sent off to a charity or given to one of the younger lads. They are gone and out of my life for ever. If I were being totally logical then when we go on a winning streak I shouldn't change my gloves until we next lose, yet I do. Sometimes they can tear so I will change them and it does not affect me at all. Try to get me to wear gloves that we lost in for a second time though and I just won't entertain it. Mad; crazy; stupid. Call it what you will that's just the way it is.

Of course football is a game which can be influenced by your mental state, and these superstitions are really simple psycholo gical anchors which can help to get you in the right state. I hear that Petr Cech has taken to wearing an orange strip based on some research that says that when the eye encounters an orange object it appears bigger than it actually is. I've heard this kind of thing over the past 15–20 years. My view is that as a goalkeeper you play in whatever makes you feel comfortable. I've worn every colour going, including orange, and they all make me feel the same way. If orange could make a substantial difference to your performance then I think every team in the world would be playing in orange. Yet if Petr feels comfortable in orange and it gives him some mental edge, real or imagined, then it is no different to having two eggs cooked differently, so who am I to argue with him?

As far as colours go, personally I feel no effect. Whatever kit our sponsor provides is the kit that I'm going to wear. Often sponsors have asked me if I had a preference and I'd suggest one, but I don't think I ever got the colour that I asked for so now I've just stopped expressing any preference. It is not something that matters to me.

Away from the worlds of superstition and academic research there are much more direct and often less subtle ways that people use to try to influence the performance of others. The mind games. The things that players say to each other during play.

Personally I'm not a 'trash talker', that is, the type of person who will say things to try to put another player off his game. A lot of people have tried to do it to me over the years and I still hear a lot of it today.

I remember a time when Blackburn played Newcastle one season when Craig Bellamy was a Newcastle player and up against our defender Craig Short. Bellamy, who has blistering pace, came over to Shorty and said, 'I'm going to end your career today. I'm going to leave you for dead so many times you'll want to quit.' It really wound Craig up. It's bad enough having to try to contain Bellamy without having self-doubt in the back of your mind.

Graeme Souness told me how he used to be physical with players in order to gain his space. He would threaten to kick seven shades out of players, but he found that Bryan Robson was one player who could not be bullied and the two relished the intense physical battles that they fought. Bullying has always been part of the game and just occasionally you see a player shrink in the face of it.

Then there's a bit of a fad going around at the moment where a player will stand facing the goalkeeper as a free kick is about to be taken. They do things like wink at you and move their arms around. I asked the referee Mike Riley about this before a game with Manchester United. He said that if a player is moving around in an offside position then he is impeding the keeper and offside will be given. If he is doing it from an onside position, then there is nothing you can do but try to deal with it.

There was just one time when I had to ask a few questions of myself when somebody said something to me. I was with Blackburn and, being a former Liverpool player playing against Everton at Goodison Park, I was ready for the banter and usually it is good banter.

I heard a voice in the crowd behind me. He was shouting something absolutely vile about my mom which I could not repeat. He had never met my mom and I found it completely demeaning and uneducated coming from an adult.

If you have a problem like this you are supposed to report it to a steward. So as I retrieved the ball to take a goal kick, I said to the steward, 'Am I supposed to stand here and not say a word?' He was abusive to me and said, 'Just get the ball and take the goal kick.'

I turned to the guy in the crowd and I said, 'Look. If you want to you can call me a bald so and so; a red-nosed Yank; try some banter or say something clever, that's fine. You can say whatever you want, but don't talk about my mom like that.'

I took the kick and the funny thing was it didn't put me off; instead it created a quiet anger which I channelled into my game. It made me even more determined to do well. As it happens we won 1–0 away from home. Then I did something I've never done before or since and at the final whistle I ran the length of the pitch right up to this guy. I told him in language that I thought he would understand exactly where I thought he should go and what I thought he should do. I always get stick at Everton, I enjoy it and I thrive on it, but on that particular day, I wasn't having my mom disrespected like that.

The crowd will always try to get under your skin and I have occasionally seen players go into their shell when the crowd is on their back. It's even harder to ignore when a player tries to get under your skin. Way back, players would tell an opponent that they would be waiting for them outside the ground to sort them out. In my early days in the Premiership the threat would be, 'I'll see you in the tunnel.' Even this one is dying out now as cameras are everywhere you look.

One time with Liverpool when we were playing Chelsea at Anfield, I was on the bench. There was an altercation on the pitch between Liverpool's keeper David James and two Chelsea players Marcel Desailly and Franck Leboeuf. Now Jamo against Desailly would have been quite a tussle because they are both big fellas. As we went up the tunnel at the end of the game, they were bursting to get to one another and then the cameras appeared. Both players were restrained and angry words were exchanged but that's all. What else could they do? They would have been banned for a string of games for fighting. So now, even the threat of seeing you in the tunnel after the game is a pretty hollow one.

Robbie Savage told me of a bizarre incident that he was involved in when he played at Leicester. He and team-mate Gerry Taggart, who was a hard player, were involved in a disagreement during a game. Sometimes you see this happen and Robbie put forward his point of view, at which point Taggart did something that you don't normally see happen. He walked over, slapped him and said, 'I'll see you in the dressing room after the game.' Remember these were team-mates sharing the same dressing room. Robbie laughs now as he recalls his strategy for dealing with an irate Gerry Taggart when confronted in the Leicester City dressing room. It went something like, 'Sorry, Tag. Sorry. Sorry, honestly I'm really sorry.'

I think this story sort of sums up the reality of much of the on-field talk that you get in the Premier League. People say things on the pitch but in no way does this mean that it is going to turn into a fight. Years ago, sometimes things would end in punches being thrown, but this is rare these days. If it came to the crunch most players I think would rather take a punch than back down. In reality if anything like that happens, other players dive in and it would be little short of a miracle if a punch were to land. Despite the on-field talk, the gesturing and the bravado, at Premier League level actual violent confrontations between players are very rare.

The Referee's a ... Human

I feel sorry for referees. They have a very difficult job to do. I know that when I referee five-a-side games between 12-year-olds, I am getting it wrong all of the time and they want to tear my head off. So I can empathise with Premiership referees. I think that the standard of refereeing has improved since referees became professional, but against this the game has become faster, technology enables intense scrutiny of every incident and the law-makers add to the confusion, particularly with the latest interpretation of the offside rule, which I have to confess I don't fully understand.

So taking all of these things into account I try the very best I can not to be too harsh or critical. Sometimes I have to admit that can be a very, very hard thing to do, but I do try.

There was an incident towards the end of the 2006–07 season when Blackburn were playing at home against West Ham. We were 1–0 up through Christopher Samba when Carlos Tevez equalised through a dubious penalty decision. That was bad enough, but four minutes later Bobby Zamora had a shot at goal which eluded me, but TV replays clearly showed that the ball hit Carlos Tevez who was standing on the goal line and bounced away from the goal. Instead, the goal was given. We are not allowed to speak to the referee until 30 minutes after the game. The managers and assistants will go down and knock on his door to discuss various incidents. We are not really supposed to go down, but we can and on this occasion I went to see Howard Webb. I explained my view of the incident that led to the goal. He said, 'Brad, if I got it wrong I apologise. It's not something I would do on purpose. I'll go away and look at it.' To be honest I think Howard was misled by the linesman, but he calls the shots and he carries the can. All professionals make mistakes and what I admired was that he wasn't trying to hide from his error.

We felt hard done-by about conceding a goal that wasn't a goal. As it happens, after that game West Ham, who seemed marooned in the relegation zone, began a surge which saw them secure survival on the last day of the season at the expense of Sheffield United, so on reflection I'm sure that the goal hurt everyone associated with Sheffield United as much as it did me. The way the game has gone now means that these mistakes influence more than just a single result; they can have multi-million-pound implications and this puts yet more pressure on referees.

I think every manager and most players would tell you that there is always a certain referee or referees that seem to bring out a bad result for your team or you seem to suffer as a result of harsh decisions. For my part, I tend to feel that this is nothing more than coincidence, but sometimes when you believe something you reinforce your belief by looking for more evidence and filtering out things that go against your belief. So if a referee has had a couple of games where he has given harsh decisions against you, maybe you start to notice all the things that go against you when he is in charge and skip over the rest.

Maybe if players feel this way about a referee they may be less tolerant of his decisions and this can backfire. I know that their job is to be impartial, but one referee put it to me like this. He said, 'We are human beings. If players are constantly abusing you and shouting profanities at you it is going to wear on you. It's more likely that fifty-fifty decisions will go against you.'

So perhaps it is a self-perpetuating cycle that teams get themselves into with certain refs. They have a bad experience or two; they create a belief that this ref is against them; they filter what they see and reinforce their belief; their tolerance of this ref is lower and certain players may systematically abuse him. As a consequence 50:50 decisions go against them and the whole cycle begins again.

You may be thinking that if a referee is being systematically abused why doesn't he just send the player off? I have thought the same thing myself. The truth is that even though it is an offence to abuse the referee, it goes on all of the time. You don't need me to tell you that as it's easy to lip-read what some players are saying. If referees applied the letter of law, I don't exaggerate when I say that the way things are at the moment we would end up playing five-a-side every week.

In one game I was right there as a very high-profile player abused the referee in the crudest possible terms right to his face. Not once but about ten times. He was already on a booking and he should have been sent off. As I watched this I politely asked the ref, 'So, are you allowed to swear now?' He looked at me and said, 'Brad, come on …' I said, 'It's just a question. He's on a yellow card already and if you book him you will have to send him off. I don't care whether he stays on or not, that's not the issue. He's such a star that if you send him off it will be pored over by the media for weeks. If that was a Blackburn Rovers player he would be off and it would be reported and forgotten.' He replied, 'Brad, you don't want every player off the pitch, do you?' I said, 'Of course not. I'm just asking you the question.'

I think that they all have a very difficult job. There cannot be many jobs where you are under such intense scrutiny, where everybody knows better than you and where 'experts' rip you apart with the benefit of hindsight and technology which is not available to you. I admire them all; it takes courage to put your neck on the line the way they do every week. I think there are certain refs that make their difficult job more difficult because of the way they relate to players and those that do the opposite. Mike Riley, for example, is an out-and-out gentleman and I think players respond to that. Mark Clattenburg will allow you to have a chat with him about certain issues which helps matters on the pitch. I can't understand why refs adopt the attitude of telling players to go away all of the time. Sometimes you have to, but not all the time.

So all sorts of things can influence what happens off and on the pitch: from leadership to team spirit, mind games of your own and mind games that other people play, through to the fact that we sometimes forget that referees are human beings too, just like you and me. All of this is part of the game and part of what makes it endlessly fascinating. For me there is only one thing you can do to get beyond the random things that happen, the mind games and the superstition, and that is to intensify your focus on what you are trying to achieve and to try to help your team-mates to do the same.

Hocus, pocus … focus.

13

One Million Miles: A Goalkeeper's View of the World

Millions saw the apple fall, but Newton was the one who
asked why   *Bernard M. Baruch*

When you add it all up I certainly have been a globetrotting goal-keeper: two Olympic Games; three World Cups; Pan American Games; Copa America; 82 full internationals; UEFA Cup games; spells in Denmark, Turkey, USA and England.

All in all that is a lot of miles covered. Sometimes I would travel 12,000 miles just to play an international game – and that was a home game. In truth, I don't know how many miles I've covered over the years in the course of my international career and during the time that I moved around like a hobo trying to get my work permit. If I guessed that it would be one million miles, I don't think that I would be too far off the mark. That's a lot of miles by anyone's standards. It's a lot of moving around. It represents a lot of energy being consumed.

There are moments. Moments of stillness, when I sit back and reflect on all that moving around and ask myself what it was all about. What was it all for?

I'm reminded what it was all for every day. Whether I am going into training, stepping out to play against the best football players in the world or spending quality time with my family. That is what it was all for on the face of it.

Yet as I reflect on the people I've met and the situations I've encountered in the course of one million miles, I can see now that it was more than just an amazing experience. It was in fact the most remarkable education anyone could have asked for.

It's given me insights which I can take with me for the rest of my life, wherever I may go, whatever I may do. Insights which I can use in good times and bad, during the highs as well as the lows. Insights which have been valuable to me in the past, which I can continue to use today and which will really come into play in the future.

My interest is both in the now and in the future. The one thing that I can be absolutely sure of is that my life as a professional footballer will come to an end. It is an inevitability that many players try to ignore.

While I enjoy every moment of the life that I am privileged to lead, I know that I will one day have to reinvent myself. I'm filled with excitement about this because by looking at the world through the eyes of a goalkeeper I've developed a set of principles which I know will continue to stand me in good stead. These are principles which I have gleaned by being close to the great and the not so great and reflecting on the situations I have faced, both the good and the not so good.

So here they are: a bunch of stories illustrating principles which are important to me. The 'Gospel according to the goalkeeper'.

Goals, Goals, Goals

As a goalkeeper defending my territory, there are no grey areas. There is no room for ambiguity. I have to stand up and be counted in defence of what is important to me.

Life however is not so clear-cut. In fact it can be as chaotic and frantic as any goalmouth scramble. It's not surprising that sometimes people lose track of what is important to them. I've met many successful people from all walks of life, and this has reaffirmed to me the importance of something I already knew. To get anywhere in life, you have to create your own goals.

If you know what is important to you it will help you to address all your energies and efforts towards achieving your goals and standing up for what you believe in. It is how great players and great people progress. Yet if it was as easy as that everybody would be doing it, and clearly everybody is not.

Setting the right sort of goals; breaking them down; measuring your progress and striving for goals which will challenge you are all part of the process. A process which, whatever you do in life, will ensure that you at least know where you are going. It will give you a kind of track. This is important because we all come off the rails sometimes. If you have a track at least you can get back on it if you come off. Sometimes we can learn more from our mistakes than our successes.

The greatest thing about having goals is that they give you a chance to feel and appreciate success, at whatever level you are, no matter what you do in life. These small successes create belief so that we set even higher goals, achieve greater things and have at least a chance of experiencing greater success.

Setting and striving for goals are ways of putting quality into your life.

My Quality Goals

You can imagine that having played in two Olympic Games, three World Cups and top-level soccer all around the world, I have rubbed shoulders with some of the all-time great athletes. Soccer legends such as Maradona and Ronaldinho; Magic Johnson, Larry Bird and Michael Jordan, basketball's 'Dream Team'; not to mention FloJo and Steve Lewis who were amazing athletes and the great gridiron quarterback Troy Aikman.

I say this not to be a name-dropping big-time Charlie. I say it as a prelude to something that I have thought about a lot over my life. If you were to ask me who my sporting hero was, I would be able to answer you without hesitation. I would have no need to sift through the names of the greats that I have encountered. I know who my sporting hero is. Unless you are an avid follower of US college soccer or have an encyclopaedic knowledge of the short-lived Major Indoor Soccer League (MISL), the chances are you will never have heard of him.

His name is Tim Harris, and a big part of who I am today, as a player and as a person, is down to him.

Tim was an All-American goalkeeper who played for UCLA before I did, and went on to play indoor soccer for Los Angeles Lazers. He was the goalkeeping coach when I arrived at UCLA and he took me under his wing, but he turned out to be much more than just a great goalkeeping coach. He became my mentor.

He'd been in a relationship with a volleyball player called Judy Bellomo. Tragically, Judy was taken ill and died following an operation. Tim was left with a void in his life and I guess that coaching and advising me helped him to fill that void.

We would train at 6 a.m. at a place called Live Oak Park, so that I could later get to classes. Now that Judy had gone, I had become the centre of his attention, the recipient of his focus and the beneficiary of his advice. I was just a young kid, yet he taught me something that proved more valuable than any of my academic courses at UCLA. He taught me about goals.

One day, he gave me something written on a scrap of paper. I still have that scrap of paper today. It is at home in my office. It introduced me to the concept of goal setting. He said, 'If you want to be a great goalkeeper, you need QUALITY.' I looked down onto the piece of paper and in large black letters Tim had written the word 'quality'.

It turned out to be an acronym for all the characteristics that a great goalkeeper should aspire to have. It helped me to break down the art and science for being a goalkeeper, and to set myself demanding targets against each attribute. It went like this …

Quickness
Upstanding
Agility
Loudness
Instinct
Technique
Yell to organise

So we began to work with tremendous focus on all of these things, arranging drills and training regimes to improve each one. We set goals for each attribute and on a periodic basis would do tests to see if there had been the level of improvement we were looking for.

So I'd say to myself, 'OK. Quickness. Do I need to work on it? Absolutely.' I'd measure myself on things like how quickly I could get up and down, and how fast I was over short sprints. Tim would set up daily training programmes for me and I had a gym programme too.

For 'upstanding' we would judge it on the timing. You have to stand up and not dive too early. Good players can put the ball either side of you, so it is important to be upstanding until the last possible moment.

Agility is about being a good athlete and looking after yourself. There are lots of ways you can measure your agility. We would use repetition to develop an instinct for what may happen. Loudness is something that goalkeepers must develop even if it doesn't come naturally; and technique is something that you acquire through guidance and practice and continue to do so throughout your career. Finally, a great goalkeeper knows when it is time to 'yell to organise' and take control of a situation.

Whatever your goals are, you can break them down and measure your progress.

Pavlov's Dog – Hard-wire Your Good Habits

When you are heading towards your goals, you are still going to make mistakes, have setbacks and sometimes be up against things that are beyond your control. I know that this happens to me, and it certainly did in my early years.

I remember being in a psychology course where we studied the famous Pavlov's Dog experiment. Pavlov noted that dogs always salivated before food was presented. He began ringing a bell before presenting the food. In time the dogs began to become conditioned to salivate upon hearing a bell. Their brains had been reprogrammed or hard-wired to associate food with the bell.

In my approach to achieving my goals, I realised that I was a little bit like one of Pavlov's dogs. If I made a mistake in a game, I would go to the training ground every single day and work on what I should have done, until I had performed it correctly 50 times in succession. In this way the manoeuvre became hard-wired into my brain, so that, just like Pavlov's dogs, when that stimulus or incident arose again, I reacted without thinking. I would get myself to the point where I didn't want to make a mistake like that again, partly because I wouldn't be heading towards my goals, and partly because I didn't want to have to do the damn thing 50 times again. It created a dual incentive to improve. A positive one and a negative one.

Dick Scott was the assistant basketball coach in my high school. He used to say, 'Practice doesn't make perfect. Perfect practice makes perfect.' You can practise all day long, but if you are practising the wrong things, then all you are going to do is become a master in the art of doing the wrong things.

The reason some people are outstanding at what they do is no secret. David Beckham is not just great at free kicks simply because he is. Michael Jordan was not an unbelievable shooter because he was lucky. Both understood that you have to practise, and practise perfect.

I would watch my Blackburn Rovers colleague Morten Gamst Pedersen. He stayed behind at training all of the time, practising free kicks over and over and over again. Is it any wonder he is very good at it? Talented players, talented people will never become great unless they practise perfect.

Set Demanding Goals

This is where it can be useful to have a mentor, particularly when you first set out striving for goals. It would be all too easy to keep on setting goals that you could achieve easily, and then tell yourself how good you are.

These are 'fools' goals'. At best you will stand still. More likely you will slip back. Tim Harris, my coach, set goals which stretched me. When I achieved them I felt a sense of satisfaction.

He was my mentor, who taught me how to live my life so that I had a better chance of achieving my goals. Because of this I found that I wanted to do well for myself, but I also found that I wanted to do well for Tim.

I set goals for my soccer and also for my college work. You can set them for your business and your family life. It gives you a focus, and there is an old adage, 'What you focus on tends to happen.' Tim was always mindful that he had to set demanding goals for me, and he did it in different ways. Sometimes he could be quite subtle. At UCLA there was an outstanding volleyball player called Karch Kiraly. He was absolutely tremendous and in time would go on to win three Olympic Golds and a World Championship. Tim came over to me one day and pointed to Karch. He said, 'You know what? He does five hundred fingertip press-ups and a thousand sit-ups every day.' He just looked at me and walked away.

I think he knew that he had instilled in me an idea, a new goal, a standard to be achieved. It was crazy, but at 19 years old, I was there doing my 1,000 sit-ups before I could go out at night. Often my friends would have started their evening and I'd be doing footwork drills in the dark. When I'd achieved my goals, I'd go back and shower and then go and meet up with my friends.

Reward Yourself

Find some way to reward yourself for achieving your goals. You have to decide what an appropriate reward is for yourself. For me, I don't want a reward which will hinder me in achieving my next set of goals. These days, I just get a deeper sense of satisfaction, a kind of contentment. This is enough for me.

If I don't quite achieve my goals in a season, I have one week off. I will try to relax. If I do achieve or even exceed my goals in a season, I have one week off. I will try to relax. You may ask, what is the difference? The difference is that when I have achieved I feel a greater sense of satisfaction and contentment during my week off.

This drives my wife Tracy mad. She will say, 'We are on holiday.

Why don't you come out and have a drink with me?' I just answer, 'Well of course I will come out with you. I just won't have a drink.'

If I don't reach one of my goals I will either reset for the next season until I can achieve it, or I will re-evaluate the situation. Perhaps the goal may have been too lofty in its aspiration in the first place. There has to be an end to it. Either through redoubling my efforts to get there or reassessing what I am aiming for.

Consistently paying attention to demanding goals, breaking them down, measuring myself and striving to be better has given me a lifestyle I could not even have imagined. It has opened up a world of opportunity and possibility in so many facets of our lives. Isn't that reward enough?

It all began with one man. He is my sporting hero, Tim Harris, the man who brought goals into my life. He was a goalkeeper himself, and would always tell me how much better than me he was. After I had been playing in the Premier League for a number of seasons, Tim, now vice-president of operations at LA Lakers, called me up. He said, 'Brad, I've been meaning to tell you some- thing. It's very hard for me to tell you.' He paused for a moment and said, 'I no longer think I'm a better goalkeeper than you.'

Without even realising it, I had achieved one of my greatest goals.

The Luck Factor

Football is a game where luck plays a part. Life is like that too. Some teams are branded as 'lucky', managers curse the fact that Lady Luck may have deserted them this week, while players and fans alike have their rituals which they believe will bring them luck. But can it be that some people enjoy more good fortune than others? Studies have shown that people who believe they are destined for great things persevere in the face of failure, have a positive effect on the attitudes and behaviours of people around them, expect positive interactions with others and look for the positives in the face of adversity. These are all things that will help their belief in good fortune become a self-fulfilling prophecy.

Everybody in their sport and in their life is going to have their share of ups and downs. There is nothing to be gained by thinking negatively. There is nothing wrong in aspiring for greater things and adopting a positive attitude about making it happen.

Often people don't do this because they are fearful that they will become jinxed, or may face humiliation should they falter in their attempts to achieve things. When people say they are going to do this or that or the other, and they don't, it's not because of some hocus-pocus jinx. More likely you will find that they had the aspiration, but didn't follow it through with positive beliefs, attitudes and behaviours. It's why the most overused word in football is 'hopefully'. I never heard José Mourinho say 'Hopefully'. He has an unshakable belief that he will enjoy good fortune again, because he knows he will keep on applying the attitudes, beliefs and behaviours which made him successful before.

Alternatively, just like Mourinho when he left Chelsea, people sometimes go through a temporary setback. Sometimes in life, you have to go backwards in order to go forwards. There is no shame in that.

Backwards Can Sometimes Take You Forwards

Looking back, there are a small number of times when you have to signal your intent quite clearly if you are to move towards your aspirations. There was one time in particular when I had to do this quite forcefully. I had to take a massive risk. It saw me go backwards before I was able to go forwards again. I had to back my belief in good fortune and remain positive.

Part of me says that maybe I acted unprofessionally. Part of me says that it is your professional right to express professional concern if you are not happy with something. So when I felt that I thoroughly deserved to consistently be the US national team no. 1 keeper, I decided I had to take a stand.

I've always taken the view that you shouldn't become embroiled in disagreements with colleagues or the boss. My attitude has tended to be that if I know in my own mind that I am right, then I will take the high road. I will try to rise above the situation, my philosophy being that if you do the right thing then you will get where you want to be.

I still believe that to be true for the most part. It's just that every so often you come up against a barrier; a blockage which is stopping you from being where you rightfully feel that you belong.

When this happens there are actually five things that you can do. You can use logic and state the reasoning behind your belief that you should be where you want to be. You can compromise by accepting a halfway house kind of solution. Then you could bargain by saying, 'Look, if you do something to help me, I'll do something to help you.' Fourthly, you could use emotion to show how strongly you feel. When you have tried all of these and the barrier to your progress is still there, then there is something that should be used only as a last resort. You have to issue an ultimatum. The basis of an ultimatum is that if things don't change, then something bad is going to happen.

I'm not a big fan of ultimatums, but when I had exhausted all other possibilities, it helped me to highlight how determined I was to get to where I wanted to be.

When Bruce Arena was coaching the US national team, I think he saw me as someone who would train hard, always be there when needed, and he knew that if he chose not to select me, I wouldn't go banging on his door.

Kasey Keller was my fellow US keeper and of course both of us wanted to be no. 1. There was a period when Kasey was in and out of different clubs. He left Leicester City, then went to Rayo Vallecano in Spain for a while and then joined Tottenham Hotspur. He wasn't playing regularly at the time. Meanwhile I had established myself as the no. 1 at Blackburn and was in a rich vein of form. Prior to internationals Bruce would contact both of us. When Kasey and I talked on the training ground, we realised that both of us felt that we had been given the impression that we would be in as no. 1. In actual fact we were playing alternate games. I didn't like this situation at all, and the frustration was beginning to build up inside me. The excuse in the past with Steve Sampson was that I was not playing club football regularly and that Kasey was. That was difficult to argue against because while I was trying to get a work permit that was true. But now that I was playing regularly the roles were reversed. The reason not to play me had been removed, and, even though we were now under a different manager, there was no logic behind the situation.

Something else was sowing a seed of discontent in my mind too. I felt that political games were being played. The US team was sponsored by Nike. Kasey was sponsored by Nike. At this time, I was sponsored by Adidas. There was always this idea in the back of my mind that Nike guys were being pushed forward. I'm not saying that this idea had any basis in fact; it was just in my mind, but nevertheless it was another niggling factor to add to the sense of injustice and absence of any logic to support the status quo.

During the World Cup qualifiers, Kasey and I were alternating again, and we had to play Jamaica and then Trinidad before we were scheduled to meet Mexico. Prior to this I'd been in, then Kasey, then me again. Now Bruce said he was giving Kasey the Jamaica and the Trinidad games, and that I could have the Mexico game, making it three games each.

I could not contain myself any longer. The logic said that I should be the no. 1 choice; I'd gone along with the compromise so as not to cause any upset; if there was a bargain being made, I wasn't the beneficiary and I'd tried to hold back my emotion.

I wanted more than anything to go to the 2002 World Cup and to play well for my country. The way things were my chances were 50:50 and I was feeling unhappy about the whole situation. When I boarded the team bus after the Trinidad game, I announced to the guys that I was retiring from international soccer. Of course it was the last thing I wanted to do, but I wasn't prepared to be walked on any more.

I'd delayed my honeymoon because of the World Cup qualifiers, so I took the chance to go on honeymoon. Bruce called me as well as all the Federation guys including the president. They asked me to reconsider.

I did not like doing this. I did not want to quit the US national team. Full stop. I wanted to be acknowledged for the work that I had put in for the team so I felt I had no option. I dislike ultimatums. I think they are unprofessional and disrespectful. I did not like doing it at all. It is the only time in my career that I have issued an ultimatum. I have never behaved that way since, nor do I believe that I will ever behave that way again.

It is a last resort, and the thing about ultimatums is that once you have issued one, you have to follow through otherwise you totally lose your credibility. If I am honest with myself, I feel a little bit ashamed that I behaved in this way.

The idea of retirement didn't sit well with me, but I held firm to my position. A few months went by and then Bruce called again. Kasey was not playing regularly and Bruce wanted to tell me that they really needed me. He flew over to England and came to see me. Just the idea of him getting on the plane filled me with hope that something good might come of this. If I heard anything that was remotely like what I wanted to hear I was going to come back to the team. I told Bruce that I wasn't feeling valued and that I didn't want special treatment but I wanted him to be honest with me and to play me or not play me on merit. It wasn't about me wanting to be Bruce's buddy; I just wanted to be the man if I played well. It was as black and white as that.

Things worked out, which is ironic really. You ought to get rewarded for doing the right thing. Issuing an ultimatum and following through with it didn't feel like the right thing for me, and yet it brought me what I wanted. It seems to be an unfortunate truism that in life you don't get what you deserve, you get what you negotiate.

Make no mistake, doing what I did and the way I did it really hurt me. It was a high-risk strategy and completely against my character. If you go against your character, your values and beliefs, you should not be surprised if it makes you feel bad about yourself. I was ashamed of myself and even today still feel a sense of unease about it. I would like to take this opportunity to apologise to all concerned: my coaches, my team-mates and the US soccer fans. It was an action that came out of many years of pent-up frustration. Afterwards I did play in the 2002 World Cup and I feel that I did very well for my country, so perhaps someone 'up there' forgave me for doing it.

Everything was really professional from that point on. We knew now that whoever was playing well was going to be in the team. It meant that I had to stay on top of my game. That was fine because it was all that I wanted. I just wanted to be selected or deselected on merit. In doing that, Bruce Arena was able to stay true to his word and I'm sure that Kasey much preferred this situation as well.

The message here is that you should set aspirational goals. If you believe that you are going to make them happen then adopt the right behaviours and show as much dignity as you can for as long as you can. If you hit a blockage try to negotiate your way around it. Just occasionally, you have to crack a few eggs to make an omelette. Take a stand on things that you believe in and, if you need to, then take some calculated risks. Stay positive for as long as you can, and you have a right to believe in good fortune.

Accentuate the Positive

Phil Thompson had an amazing career as a footballer. He was the captain of Liverpool during one its most successful periods ever. He won an incredible seven championships, two European Cups, two UEFA Cups, two League Cups and an FA Cup.

He was a leader who battled for his hometown club. He had belief. He was a winner.

I'm not sure what happened to him after he gave up playing. He changed from a guy who believed he was destined for great things into a coach who maintained a negative disposition.

Our paths crossed during my two and a half seasons at Anfield. He had returned to the club as assistant manager under Gerard Houllier. Usually when a player has been very successful, as Thompson undoubtedly had, they are positive people. Generally they are the ones that if they are in coaching roles will try to divulge their experiences and portray them in a positive way, so that others can try to emulate them and their achievements. Sometimes it doesn't work, sometimes times change and their ways wouldn't work today, but that's irrelevant, because they are trying to do the right thing.

With Phil Thompson, the approach was Negative. Negative. Negative. The team was ill-disciplined at the time and perhaps he was brought in with a brief to try to do something about it. That's fine, but once the new players are bedded in and the ones they wanted out are gone then behaving like a workplace bully isn't the way to do that. It is a sure way to get players to mistrust you.

Thompson would rant when things went wrong, often using the most foul and abusive language imaginable. The foreign players had never experienced anything like it. It was always after-the-fact stuff that he would pick up on. 'Why did you do this? You should have done that.' It was all shoulda, woulda, coulda, put over in a way that could sometimes either belittle or humiliate people. Perhaps he genuinely thought that this was a way to get the best out of the players. I don't know if he thought this way, but I do know that it had an adverse effect on most of them. A good coach has an instinct for the players who will give a response when they are challenged strongly and those who need to be picked up in order to get a response. With Phil Thompson this was too fine a distinction.

There were times when he was angry after games when you could see that Gerard Houllier was uncomfortable with it. Houllier and his coach Patrice Berg had a more calculated approach. They didn't like to say too much after games. They were trying hard to create a cohesive unit and they wanted us to win together, lose together and speak about it on Monday together.

I don't want this to sound like I have a complete distaste for Phil Thompson, because I don't. I admire anyone who has had the success that he has had as a player. He was a driving force behind a period of great success for Liverpool. All that I am trying to point out is that the trouble with negativity is that it breeds only one thing: more negativity. For me, that is not a recipe for success in any walk of life. There is a time and a place to come down hard on certain players. I absolutely believe that. It just cannot be incessant and unrelenting. Arsene Wenger says that if you make more than three changes in a team you disturb its chemistry. Maybe the chemistry wasn't quite right between him,

One in 5000: Scoring the very late equaliser in open play against Charlton Athletic in February 2004. Unfortunately, we couldn't hold out for the remaining two minutes so my celebrations were cut short (*Getty*).

In a game of three penalties, Sheffield United and Blackburn played out a 0-0 draw and I saved two of them (*Action Images*).

Semi-final display: Michael Ballack scores the winner against the run of play in the 2007 FA Cup semi-final (*PA photos*).

…bbie Savage is one of the great characters I have played with…you certainly know when
…is in the dressing room (*PA photos*).

oman Pavlyuchenko and Martin Laursen compete for the ball in one of my first matches
r Villa against Spurs in September 2008 (*Colorsport*).

My debut for Villa against none other than Manchester City. I could easily have been turning out at Villa Park in City's colours (*PA photos*).

After an eventful summer, this was my first outing in a Villa shirt at a pre-season friendly against Reading in August 2008 (*Action Images*).

Soccer in the US is still a mid- to upper-class sport. The Academy is open to people of every social class and background and is a supportive environment which encourages its students to thrive in whatever it is they want to do, not just soccer (*Premier Soccer Academies*).

My record-breaking game against Fulham on 29 November 2008. A great run of 167 consecutive Premiership appearances which began at Blackburn Rovers (*Action Images*).

Houllier and Berg. Watching Phil actually taught me an enormous lesson in life, which has helped me a lot in my time at Blackburn. I learned that you can always draw a positive from a negative, which is something that I now always try to do. Working with Phil Thompson meant that I was in the presence of a high achiever. That's always a good place to be because good things can rub off on you. It also served as a reminder for me to always try to accentuate the positive.

No More 'Hopefully's

In life you can't choose your parents. In football you can't choose your team-mates. You can, though, choose your friends and, if you want to maintain your belief in good fortune, if you want to continue heading towards your aspirations, surround yourself with people who are positive.

You can choose what you want to believe about yourself. If you believe that great things are going to happen and are prepared to be positive and go for it, you will find that you start to act out the behaviours that will take you to where you want to go. If you have setbacks, look to your positive friends for support, inspiration and encouragement. Positive breeds positive just as negative breeds negative.

So forget the 'shoulda, woulda, coulda's and 'hopefullys'. Believe that you can do great things and go for it.

Bouncebackability

For a goalkeeper, the net usually means bad news. If you come into contact with it you are invariably pulling the ball out of it. You have had a setback. The opposition has scored a goal.

You may have suffered an injustice, been dazzled by a flash of genius or been party to a mistake, maybe even an instant public humiliation. There is no time to sit and wallow. No time to feel sorry for yourself. Goalkeepers, perhaps more than anyone, have to become masters of 'bouncebackability'.

Just how is it that some people are able to bounce back from setbacks, while others seem to struggle? How come some people often go on to greater things after some form of failure while others resign themselves to doom? What are the attitudes and behaviours which contribute to the success of those who are able to get back up off the floor?

If there were ever questions that were made for a goalkeeper, it is surely these. Bouncebackability is something a keeper may have to draw on several times during a game. His mistakes and misjudgements are amplified. If a striker misses a chance, the crowd feel the excitement of an opportunity. They get an adrenaline rush which compensates for their disappointment. They also know that the score remains unchanged.

When a goalkeeper makes a mistake or misjudgement, things are different. The consequences are likely to be serious and immediate. Rather than producing an adrenaline high for the crowd, it produces anxiety and fear. Goalkeepers are under intense scrutiny all of the time and when they get it wrong they may have to wait some time for forgiveness.

All goalkeepers will tell you that from time to time this has bothered them. The greats are the ones who can rise above it. But how?

Whoever you are, and no matter how much of a charmed life you may lead, there is no doubt that at some time you will be faced with disappointment, a setback and an occasional disaster.

It has happened to me. It has happened to people who have been close to me on and off the field. It has emphasised to me that one of the most important aspects of being able to bounce back is maintaining a sense of perspective.

Bouncebackability I – Acceptance

In 2000, I was involved in World Cup qualifiers for the USA. The US Under 23 squad was in Australia preparing for the Sydney Olympics and the goalkeepers were first choice Aiden Brown, who now plays in Norway, and a young Tim Howard who was later to join Manchester United and then Everton. Tim was untried and untested and when Aiden got injured, the coach

Clive Charles called me up as one of the three overage players.

Clive was a very likeable man, whose approach to his own adversity showed that he was also a great man. He had broken through as a youngster at West Ham in the 1970s before being loaned to Montreal Olympique in the old North American Soccer League. He then had a spell with Cardiff City before finishing his playing career in the US Indoor Soccer League. When his playing career ended, he really took to coaching, beginning as nothing more than a high school coach. His coaching ability and his way with people saw him rise to become no. 2 to Steve Sampson in the US national team set-up.

Shortly before flying out to the Sydney Olympics, Clive was diagnosed with fatal prostate cancer. When you see it in print like this, it does not do justice to the way people feel when they receive this kind of news. Who could fail to be floored by this? Imagine having to break the news to the family and having to deal with their pain as well as yours.

Clive did all of this and then decided he was going to bounce back. He made sure that no one knew of his prognosis other than those closest to him, then he flew out to the Olympics and behaved as if nothing had changed. The players were totally oblivious to the situation. Looking back, he gave absolutely no clue as to what he might have been going through. He was elated when we won and he was upset when we lost. We lost to Chile in the bronze medal game, which is a shame, because it would have been a nice gift to Clive and his amazing spirit.

I'll never forget Clive Charles and the way he managed to bounce back from catastrophe when his whole world must have felt like it had crumbled around him. It also offered a lesson in how easy it is for us all to become self-absorbed. At the time, there was a young player breaking into the American scene. He later became an established international and served his country well over many years. The player's father, though, was not happy about Clive's judgement in the Olympics and wrote a disparaging letter which became public, running Clive down. Shortly after-wards Clive passed away. It was sad to see Clive treated that way at the best of times, when he could easily have used his illness as a get-out or an excuse. He didn't and maintained his dignity until the end. Here was a man motivating his team, while he knew inside that he was dying, being lambasted by a father who was upset because he thought his son should have played more games. This was disrespectful to Clive, his staff and the other players.

I understand the parent's reaction. It's a normal emotion which as a father myself I can relate to. If you see what you think is an injustice your natural instinct is to stand up in support of your child. I know that. Yet in football it is always best, especially when you are on the outside of the team, to keep your feelings and emotions to yourself. Even as a parent of a player you are part of the team. There is a duty to be supportive to the team.

I don't wish to demean this player or his father in any way, which is why I have chosen not to name them. I use it purely as an illustration of how we can get carried away. Football is a game that excites the passions, but it is a game. It is not a matter of life and death. The issues that Clive was dealing with at the time, in his courageous humility, were about life and death.

Sometimes, like this particular parent, we lose perspective and small things grow out of proportion. That is when we make misjudgements. In the face of adversity, somehow, Clive maintained his perspective. Maybe that helped him to bounce back and continue making a contribution right up until the end.

Having lost three close family members to cancer myself, I have noticed something with all of them. Somehow, they reach a point of acceptance. This is the point where they seem to set aside the anger, the feelings of injustice and the fear. The point where they feel able to bounce back, even if it is just a little.

Surely, if people can bounce back in this horrendous situation, we have the power to bounce back in our everyday lives; in our workplaces; in the course of a game of football.

I think that maintaining perspective and acceptance of your situation are the keys to bouncing back quickly. If I concede a goal, I may indeed feel angry and sometimes I will feel a sense of injustice. Yet the sooner I can get to a state of acceptance, the sooner I can put the incident into perspective by thinking about it in the context of the game, and the game in the context of the season, the sooner I can bounce back. Once I have done this I can address all of my mental energies forwards, towards the future, towards influencing events that I *can* influence. You cannot influence the past. You cannot wipe out a goal by dwelling upon the injustice of it all.

Bouncebackability II – Control

As a young man, money did not come easily to me. I am from a normal working-class background, and for a time I was an international goalkeeper on $35 a day. It was a far cry from the salaries that Premier League players can command today. When I did eventually make some cash, the last thing I wanted to do was to lose it. I took advice and invested in the stock market, only to see the shares I had invested in nosedive. I lost a chunk of money.

Most likely, though, it's difficult to prove. It was what they call a 'pump and dump' scheme. I'm sure that some people made money as the shares rose in price quickly. Within a short time the 'in-the-know' investors cashed out. I was just not close enough to it, I wasn't privy to the information about the company, and even if I had been I probably wouldn't have known how to act on it at that time . . . I watched as one stock I held rose to a high price per share, then collapsed so that within a week or so they were worth just a few cents. They 'pumped' and I got dumped. What struck me about this was that the broker still made his money even though the shares had plummeted. I lost yet he still won. As a young kid still figuring out how these things worked I was intrigued about this and thought I should think more carefully about investments in the future.

On top of this, when I was trying to get my work permit, I was approached by someone who I can now see was a very unscrupulous individual, who promised to use his influence and connections to help to get my application through the system. I naively paid him $25,000. Basically he took the money and ran, while my work permit applications kept on being rejected.

Of course, I felt duped, maybe naive; some may even say I was stupid. The way I bounced back from these incidents was to focus on control, rather than dwelling on the people who had knowingly or unwittingly let me down. I thought about what I could take control of. I made myself responsible for the decisions I had made and determined that I would take responsibility for future investments. I may make bad decisions in the future, and if I do they will be my bad decisions and I will have to face up to the situation. Taking personal responsibility and exercising control is another key to bouncing back.

Bouncebackability III – Was Shankly Only Joking?

He was a legend and a wit, and one of Bill Shankly's greatest lines was: 'Some people think that football is a matter of life and death. I can assure them that it is much more important than that.' Did he really mean that or was he being tongue-in-cheek? Who knows, but sometimes I think that people often believe that this is true.

I love football as much as anyone, but of course football is not more important than life and death. On Saturday, 25 August 2007 at Everton's Goodison Park this was a message which was brought home to me vividly. Just a few days earlier, in the Croxteth district of Liverpool, 11-year-old Rhys Jones was murdered. He was an innocent young boy, going about his business, a boy who loved football and was an Everton season ticket-holder.

I was playing for Blackburn Rovers in the first game at Everton since the appalling tragedy. Our captain Ryan Nelson was suspended, so I was acting captain for the day. It was my job to present a bouquet of flowers to Rhys's parents, in a little room off a corridor near the tunnel. I can, without hesitation, say that it was the hardest thing I have ever had to do as a footballer. No words, no gesture could fill the void that had been left in the lives of the Jones family. Nothing I could do could ease their pain. As a father myself I can only imagine what they were going through.

It puts things into perspective. The game at Everton was meaningful because football is my profession. It was important and we wanted to go and win it. Yet it was one of those times when you gain perspective. In the context of the whole scheme of things, the setbacks that we face in football and in our day–to-day lives are for the most part surmountable. We can, if we want to, do something about them. By maintaining perspective, accepting situations for what they are and taking control of what we can control, we can all develop our own 'bouncebackability'.

Inside the Mind of a Goalkeeper

A goalkeeper, even though he may not realise it, has to perform thousands of mathematical equations, taking account of geometry, the laws of physics and physiology. This happens in real time and the questions he is trying to answer are: 'Where should I move my body in order to make a save?' and 'Can I move it quickly enough?'

Of course, few goalkeepers ever think about what they do in these terms, nor do they stand in the goalmouth with clipboards and calculators trying to resolve the most complex of simultaneous equations. Instead, they become adept at using something that we all have, yet many of us have forgotten how to use. Instinct.

It is the ability to make complex decisions with very little information. As humans we all have this ability in some shape or form, yet as our society has been subsumed by ever more data and information, we have begun to rely less on our instincts in favour of more deliberative analysis.

Instincts have a role to play in football and in life, and if we can hone our abilities to use instinct effectively, we can all improve our performance in whatever it is that we do.

As footballers, because we train or play virtually every day, we develop an ability to pick up what is happening on a football field very quickly. Sometimes when things happen, it is almost as if you know what is going to happen before the ball has left a player's foot. The brain picks up on all sorts of visual cues, memories and analysis that you may have performed to give you advance warning of what may unfold. Sometimes it can be the shape of the body, the position of the planting foot or some scouting that you may have done which reveals to you how a situation is likely to turn out.

Other times, the position of defenders suggests to you where the ball is most likely to go. There are all sorts of things that you pick up on to help you to perform your calculations. Yet you only have a split second to decide what to do.

I can tell you that if the average man in the street were to stand in my goal and try to deal with some of the shots that come in, they would find it hard to believe the pace, bend and swerve of the ball. They would feel that the ball was nothing more than a marble in terms of its size, but it would feel as though it had been fired from a rifle.

For a top-class goalkeeper at the top of his game, the opposite is true. The ball seems to be the size of a beach ball, and somehow the mind seems to slow down the action so that unstoppable shots become great saves.

I know that when I watch games on TV after I've been playing, the action seems ten times faster than I remember it being. Sometimes during a game I will think, Well that was a pretty decent save, then often I'll watch a replay of it and think, Wow. That was good. It is as if you are acting out of intuition, without thinking. When you are on your game in this way and fully concentrated, it feels like nothing can get past you and the ball seems big and slow.

A business friend of mine in California has been trying to develop his ability to instinctively suss people out. He's been involved in deals that have wasted a lot of his time by choosing to associate with the wrong people. Instinct in business is as important as it is for a goalkeeper. Being able to make rapid assessments of people and situations, almost without thinking, is the key to making good decisions quickly.

Something that helps me to do this started because I tore a quad muscle in 2003–04 season. I went into a rehabilitation regime as normal, and then I tore it again in the pre-season. It was then that, with the help of my friend Barry Venison, I got into the practice of yoga and I can say that I've been doing it ever since. It makes your mind and body feel brilliant. It involves meditation which I find calms the mind and helps me to focus, which in turn helps me to fine-tune that natural talent that we all have: our natural instincts. Those, combined with a goalkeeper at the top of his form, can make a volley from a world-class striker appear like a beach ball tossed at you by your daughter on a calm summer's day.

Measure for Measure

I spend a lot of time staring out from my goalmouth at the action when it is down at the other end of the field. During a lull in play, I might look around a bit and survey the scene. A constant feature at football grounds these days is the multicoloured electronic scoreboard. It tells you how things really are; you cannot hide from the truth of the score. It is there. It is factual. You cannot kid yourself that if you are losing, you are actually winning. You can, though, decide what to do to try to change what the scoreboard is saying.

I think it is very important for a professional person and a footballer in particular to find his own ways of measuring his performance. You have to get comfortable looking at yourself in the mirror, even when, with warts and all, it can be an uncomfortable thing to do.

When I was at Liverpool, the coach Ronnie Moran said something to me which really made me think, and has influenced my attitude to looking at my own performance ever since.

We were in Liverpool playing a pre-season friendly against Inter Milan. During the game, I had an awful lot of saves to make. After the game he came over to me and asked, 'What do you think was the best save you made in that game?' I shrugged and said that I didn't really think about things like that. He persevered with me and went on to describe in detail which save he thought was the best and why. He then said, 'What do you think was your biggest mistake?' This time I joined in and told him where I thought I had made a mistake. He then gave me a word of advice. He said, 'Let me tell you something. Every game, even the best game you will ever have, always reflect on something that you could do better. It will help to keep you grounded and more focused for the future.'

His philosophy was that you should remember your mistakes even when you win. In football somebody has to win and somebody has to lose. Just because you won doesn't mean that you did everything right, and just because you lost doesn't mean you did everything wrong. It's right to be delighted when you win and to enjoy the euphoria for a while, but as a professional it is important to find a quiet time to reflect on what could have been better.

In this way you produce a more objective measure of yourself and your team which can help you improve if you are prepared to face up to what you see and do something about it. In football, the minute you think you have made it you are setting yourself up to fall flat on your face. Reflection and measurement can help you to avoid this.

You see it with teams often: they achieve something and struggle the year after. This happened at Blackburn when we came back into the Premier League. We progressed very well and in time achieved a top six place. Then bang. The following year we struggled and had to flirt with relegation before securing our place in the Premier League. The truth is that some players were strolling. They felt that being in the top six guaranteed them something. Last season's league position is not a good measure to be using for yourself. Your last performance and your next performance are the measures that you should be concerned with. Some of our players had it in mind that we were a top six team and that somehow would make everything all right. Last season's league tables are for historians and statisticians. Footballers should reflect upon their last game and think about the next game.

Most players these days have some form of reflective routine. When I was a kid at UCLA, I used to do the Pavlov's dog routine, going over and over a mistake on the training field until I had hard-wired the correct manoeuvre into my brain. I would beat the crap out of myself.

These days I don't need to do that. I find that through concentrated reflection I am able to achieve the same thing in my head. Now I effectively do Pavlov's dog in my head. I reflect and think about things that I could have done better – not in a 'shoulda, woulda, coulda' sense – but by thinking positively, and saying, 'Next time I will do it like this.'

I often find myself doing this in the evening after a game. It takes longer for me to settle down to sleep these days after a game and often I am still awake at three or four in the morning. This is a quiet time when the kids are asleep and I can reflect properly. My adrenalin continues pumping long after the game, and even though people may think it is easy for a keeper to get through a game, I can tell you that it isn't as easy as it looks. Of course, aerobically it is not as demanding as being an outfield player, but mentally it is very tiring. The concentration takes a lot out of you so that after the game my mind will be racing, and I become overtired so that I cannot sleep.

There was a time when I used to think, If only he had done that we could have done this, for example. I don't do that any more. I still make mistakes, of course, but now we try to support each other as a team. If I can help someone who had a bad game I will try to. Likewise, my team-mates will come to me and tell me if I have done wrong. Some will do it more forcibly than others, but I can take that. These days we tend to take more collective responsibility for mistakes. It's a team game and if you are not willing to accept that you will always be mediocre. I don't kick myself if I have made a mistake. I may not be happy about it, but I don't kick myself about it. I try to instil confidence in myself that I won't do it again.

Fight the Fear

I would imagine that at some stage, every elite athlete and professional has a fear of failing. It may not be there all the time, but it can come on during matches sometimes, and you have to fight that fear. You have to take that fear and make it work for you because if you don't it will work against you. If you are so nervous that you cannot concentrate then you will be looking over your shoulder and thinking too much about what other people think; your fear will inevitably get the best of you. To a certain degree this is what happened to me at Liverpool.

You really have to acknowledge your fears and take them on board. The reason you are nervous is because you don't want to lose. In order to win I have to get myself in the right state. If I make an individual mistake then we must look to overcoming it as a team. Take control of your fear.

It happens every season. Somebody will exhibit the symptoms of fear. As a goalkeeper you are well positioned to see the symptoms. Sometimes, I may be wanting to distribute the ball, and a certain player will consistently fail to 'show' himself for the ball through fear of failure.

There are ways to get through it. My former team-mate Tugay shows the way. If he knows that he is having a bad day, he doesn't hide from it, he begins to adapt his game. He will cut out the long passes, which give him a greater probability of failure and could reinforce his belief that he is having a bad game. Instead he will make a series of short passes, each one rebuilding his confidence. Soon he will be spraying the ball all over the pitch again. He doesn't hide from fear, he acknowledges and adapts.

Younger inexperienced players who are frightened will make a run just a little bit behind a defender, so you may want to play the ball to him, but he knows there is no way that you can get it to him.

Some players hide away from their fear, others take responsibility, while others have occasional confidence issues. This is something which tends to affect goalkeepers more than most. You have to be careful how you handle these situations. You have to be especially careful not to commit what I regard as a cowardly act: the act of yelling after the fact. A player makes a mistake and he gets slaughtered after it has happened. What is the value in this? I think that when players do this they are often trying to distance themselves from any responsibility for what has happened. There is an old adage in football: 'If you tell a player once that's OK; if you tell a player twice that's OK; if you have to tell him three times take him out.' In other words, give people a chance, and if they are not good enough remove them from the situation. Don't lampoon and pillory them.

When I see players who are suffering from a temporary confidence crisis, I will try not to yell at them. I'm not saying that I have never done this, but nowadays I'm a bit more careful about it. I will do it only with players that I know will be able to take it, or when a player's mind is not switched on to a particular game and it is imperative to switch them back on to the game quickly. Mostly I will try to speak to them in a way that will build them up. That's the theory anyway, which I always try to apply. Yet football is a passionate, intense and fast-moving game. Sometimes you do get caught up in the moment, sometimes you find yourself focusing on the wrong things and, with the best will in the world, we can all lose our rag from time to time.

Acknowledging the difference between players is important. I can pull one player and say something to him that I could not possibly consider saying to another player. Often a quiet word has an effect with a sensitive player. He will respect that more than having me shouting at him. If he is a good player, there is no need for me to try to make him look a bad player simply because he has made a mistake. I'll say, 'Come on, you're better than that.' It's better that way than to have all the arm raising and shouting, because when the crowd see that, if he makes another mistake, the crowd will jump on his back. We all have to overcome crowd criticism sometimes, but as a team-mate you don't need to be instigating it. If the crowd get on your players' backs you should be helping, not making things worse. You learn this when you have been around for a while. Partly, this is one of the factors behind really successful teams. They tend to have been together for a while, and they develop a good understanding of strengths, weaknesses, dispositions and attitudes of players and how to get the best out of them.

You see a lot of things as a goalkeeper from a viewpoint that nobody else has. As an experienced goalkeeper, you will have seen certain situations time and time again. Good coaches understand this. At Blackburn they acknowledged this. They would come to me quite often and ask me what I was seeing. They would ask other senior players too. A goalkeeper has a tremendous vantage point and I would throw in my ten cents and they would add it to their thoughts as they went into thinking about the next game.

One thing I will always see from time to time is fear. You cannot eradicate it, you can only deal with it. As a goalkeeper I see that as a big part of my job.

Thinking Outside the Box

A goalkeeper's job is pretty well defined. There are strict rules and regulations about what you can and cannot do, which means that you spend 99% of your working life inside a rectangular box. If you are not careful, your thinking can become boxed in too.

I've found that to create opportunity it's really important to be able to think 'outside the box' as well. I think that we all come in for a bit of brainwashing. When you grow up, everything seems to be quite structured. You go to nursery; primary school; secondary school; college; be an intern; get a job; pay off your student loans; get married; have kids and … Well, there you go, that was your life.

So what if you are ten years old and you say, 'I don't want to do what the other kids do, because I like this.' Is that wrong? Is it rude? I've always been allowed to think that if it's not illegal then I should be allowed to go and do something if I want to. I've been brought up as an individual with a streak of independence. Mom and Dad remind me often how they would just see me sitting on the floor, lost in a world with my toys, hour upon hour. I was never really that bothered what other people thought.

If somebody were to come to me and say, 'You have to do this' or 'You have to do that,' then I'm quite clear on where I stand. Wherever there is a team aspect to it then I take the view that I do have to do it. In a team sport there are others that you have to respect and you need their respect in turn. You don't necessarily have to be good friends with them, but there has to be mutual respect and team unity.

By contrast, in my own life I have tended not to do things just because somebody has asked me to. I don't conform to other people's expectations unless I think that it is right and it is what I want to do. I don't want to be troublesome or a rebel. I don't want to be disrespectful, but I will do things that I feel are the right thing to do, and I want my kids to do that as well.

The time I was offered a sponsorship deal by Adidas, and rejected it for little known Sondico is a good example of this. It was regarded as not a cool thing to do, and there was even the implication that it could damage my chances of being selected for the national team, which was sponsored by Adidas.

Adidas offered a modest sponsorship. Sondico offered me something that excited me and had potential. As well as a sponsorship, they gave me a share in the equity, so that as the company grew from its small beginnings I would benefit too. I also had a say in the design of the glove, which added another level of interest. It may have been uncool, but Sondico grew into a decent name, I enjoyed being part of it and as a by-product I made a heck of a lot more money than I would have had I gone with Adidas. I thought outside of the box and tried something different.

Again, back in 2002, I made a decision that every agent on the planet would have disagreed with. An awful lot of players would have said I was crazy, too. I had one year left on my contract at Blackburn. I could have gone to the World Cup and made an impact, knowing that other clubs would be interested and that I could either go elsewhere or use the increased demand for my services to escalate my wages at Blackburn.

The received wisdom was that that was exactly what I should have done. I actually chose not to do that and, before I went to the World Cup, I signed a three-year contract extension. That is not because I am stupid. I knew the situation and I still chose to sign in advance.

It is something called loyalty. Genuine loyalty is a state of mind which money cannot buy. I happen to believe that it is very important.

Blackburn gave me an opportunity by bringing me in from

Liverpool, where I wasn't playing regular first team football. They put their necks on the line, because the supporters at first could not understand why they did it and it was not a popular move in the eyes of the other three goalkeepers. I will always be grateful for that opportunity, so I thought that if clubs were going to come in for me after the World Cup, then Blackburn should benefit, by having me on a four-year contract. They would get a suitable transfer fee so as to be able to go out and get a quality replacement, and have money left to reinvest in the team. Regardless, if a transfer fee wasn't forthcoming, then I was more than happy to continue playing for Blackburn Rovers.

My agent at the time, Paul Stretford, would have handled things differently had he had his way, but that was not how I wanted to live my life.

The World Cup in 2002 went very well for me and, as expected, there was serious interest from other clubs. I know that Manchester United came in and had discussions with my agent, and I am not sure whether they formally discussed the transfer fee with Blackburn. Graeme Souness had told the press that anyone wishing to continue a conversation about me going elsewhere would need to come up with £10 million. I'm not sure if he was being serious or not, but I think that when United got wind of this, they may have considered the transfer fee to be a little high because with a 32-year-old keeper on a three to four-year contract, it would have to be written off – they would not have got that money back. I would be lying if I said I wouldn't have been interested; of course I would. Any professional with any ambition would want to play for one of the top teams. Blackburn had sold Damien Duff and David Dunn and so I don't think they were going to sell me in the same summer and lose three influential players. Still, I could have pushed for it, but I wanted to do right by Blackburn, and I decided I wasn't going to force the issue. At the end of the day, United plumped first for Tim Howard and then for Edwin Van der Sar.

Arsenal were also interested, but they were dogged by spiralling stadium costs as the Emirates Stadium was being built, and again I'm sure the transfer fee would have proved to be a stumbling block. I've always admired Arsenal Football Club and Arsene Wenger as a manager, but in the end they did a very good piece of business by acquiring Jens Lehmann for a reported €1.5 million.

Had I gone I would have been happy because Blackburn would have been properly compensated and I would have behaved honourably. In the end I stayed and I'm equally happy because I had an immense feeling of loyalty towards Blackburn Rovers and its supporters. By signing before the World Cup I was able to demonstrate that loyalty.

I went against everyone's advice and thought outside of the box. Had I not done this, doubtless I would have been wealthier and more famous. Yet I would have lost my integrity.

I am so glad that I keep thinking outside of the box.

How Fascinating! I Made a Mistake

Success or failure for a player or a team is not about what brand of boots they are wearing, how much they are getting paid or whether they are playing against a 'bogey' team.

For the most part the big difference between them is in terms of what goes on inside the head. There are some exceptions of course. Certain extraordinary players set themselves apart from their peers on talent alone. Ronaldo, Rooney, Adebayor, Van Persie, Fabregas and Henry – players like these have a special talent.

Other players may be very, very good but they don't stand out. I believe certain players put themselves above others because of the way that they deal with mistakes and the way they handle pressure.

The outstanding players tend to be outstanding because they have an exceptional talent and they also tend to be mentally very strong. I imagine that if Wayne Rooney had a run of ten games without scoring, he would still walk out onto the pitch believing that he was going to score or set someone up to score. I know that the better goalkeepers walk out onto the pitch thinking that they are not going to give a goal away today.

That can be hard because goalkeepers' mistakes get noticed

more than most so you need a particular mental toughness. Peter Schmeichel was one of the great goalkeepers of all time. I've seen him make mistakes, though perhaps fewer than most. You very rarely saw him make two mistakes in a game, or consecutive mistakes in consecutive games. That's because he did not allow his mistakes to put pressure upon him. He would think, I made a mistake, but I'm big, I'm strong, I'm confident, I'll carry on.

Pressure is something that people place upon themselves. Nobody else is responsible for the pressure that you feel other than you. You can have performance anxiety by worrying about what everybody else thinks, rather like I did at Liverpool. It can be detrimental to your game and the likelihood is that under such circumstances you will make mistakes.

The ones that go up or down in performance and are not consistent either; they lose concentration or suffer from the effects of putting pressure upon themselves by the way they think about things. Driving a car, once you understand the basic elements, is not a difficult thing to do. Yet you see people have accidents because of lack of concentration, fear that something bad might happen, or being unaware of the consequences of taking excessive risks.

It's the same in football. People can put pressure on themselves in exactly the same way. You have to let things flow, and a match-day routine is an important part of this. There is a range of feelings that I go through on a match day from the moment I wake up until the moment the whistle blows. If you heap pressure upon yourself during the build-up you will be hampered when you get out on the pitch.

I try to relax as much as possible and then begin to focus my energies towards what I have to do. Then there is an adrenaline rush, and an excited feeling, a bit like butterflies in the stomach, but not a nervous feeling; a feeling of anticipation that I am going to do something good in this game. I think all of the consistent performers have this on a game-by-game basis.

I worked with the young keepers and I would watch them sometimes when they made a mistake. You can see them shaking their heads and yelling at themselves. I tried to tell them that they must take the view that if they have made a mistake it doesn't matter. What matters is that you don't make that mistake again. I say that if you are going to have a long career you are going to make many mistakes. But if you react by berating yourself after each one you are setting yourself up to keep making mistakes in the same game. If you can develop this ability to acknowledge but not dwell on mistakes you also earn respect from players, coaches, supporters and the media. Everybody wants to see how people react when they have made a mistake. It's better to respond positively.

Mistakes should be fascinating because every time you make one, you have an opportunity to become more positive, wiser, stronger and, by acting upon them, even to become outstanding. How fascinating.

Rock & Role Model

You are your environment. We as a society are responsible for the environment we create for future generations. I feel that we are allowing the media and big business to create an environment for our kids where excessive drinking and drug taking is becoming normalised. Footballers are an easy target for anyone wanting to point a finger and identify a cause of this malaise.

Most footballers are excellent role models. A very small number are not. I neither condone nor support the behaviour of the few, but I must stand up in support of my many fellow professionals who set a good example for young people to follow.

I believe that when you sign a contract to play football professionally, you are signing a contract which puts you in the public eye and part of that agreement should be an undertaking to behave in a way which creates a positive role model.

It both amazes and concerns me that as a society we seem to be standing by and allowing the corporate world to hypocritically frown upon the drink and drug culture while using it as a springboard to make money.

I know quite a number of musicians, actors and actresses, and I know that their industries have been enmeshed in a drug culture for many years. It seems that it is acceptable to behave appallingly and be constantly strung out on drugs if you are an 'artist'. The media are culpable. They decry the behaviour of these people while dedicating their lives to filling page after page about their antics. Corporates throw money at the likes of Kate Moss despite the drug allegations about her. What kind of a message is that sending out to our kids? Don't artists like Amy Winehouse and Britney Spears have a duty to be role models? They are in the public eye as much as footballers.

I would agree that some footballers could behave better, but very few footballers end up strung out on heroin or crack. Of course there are drugs in the game, but nothing like on the scale of other role model professions. We get drug tested often, so the performance-enhancing drugs have a minimal presence if they exist at all. If any player is taking any form of banned substance, obviously some things stay in the system longer than others, but he is taking a huge risk. We are educated very well about the effects of all kinds of substances, so there is no excuse. Players know that they will be tested, and if they are tested positive the chances are they will be out of a job or suspended. All I would say is that if you took a sample of actors, actresses and rock musicians and a sample of footballers, I would be willing to bet my house that the artists' group would be taking more drugs on a regular basis than the group of footballers would have even seen in their entire lives.

That's not acceptable given their role model status. When I open the papers I think, Give me a break. You get a Lindsay Lohan or a Paris Hilton, both of whom have had their problems, and the corporate machine continues to pour millions of dollars into their pockets – they have a perfume deal or a fashion endorsement or a movie. The corporates are condoning their behaviour. That's dead wrong. When you go into one of these positions and get the big pay cheques I believe that you do have to exercise some form of responsibility.

It seems to have become the norm to criticise football players. The received wisdom is that they are poor role models. I'm sorry but there are a lot of other people in the public eye that have got a lot more to do to clean up their act than footballers have. Maybe we get a bad rap because people see a footballer as a mindless idiot when he does something stupid, whereas they think that artists are suffering for their art and that's considered more acceptable.

It's not. They then use rehab as a badge of honour, almost as a must-have designer label. It's often not a device for tackling their problems but rather a quick fix to cleanse their tarnished image so that companies can feel it is legitimate to keep on giving them cash.

Against all of this nonsense, footballers, for the most part, are excellent role models that we can and should be proud of. I don't like to disparage fellow professionals, but there are certain things which happen that make you think that the privilege of being a professional footballer and role model should be taken away from some people for good.

Joey Barton of Newcastle United has been found guilty of two separate charges of serious assault. In my view, he should no longer have a football contract. You cannot keep behaving the way he does and he should have his pay packet taken away for good and be taken out of role model status, otherwise football is seen to condone his behaviour just because he happens to be a very good footballer. I'm all for giving people chances, but it's just as I said earlier about player selection: tell someone once; tell someone twice; but if they have to be told three times then they are out.

I've known lots of players who have had the inability to control their emotions on and off the pitch over the years. In order to be a top footballer you must be able to demonstrate controlled emotions as consistently as possible. Of course there are times when we can all lose our cool. Take Zinedine Zidane's outburst in his last ever professional game, for example, but by and large the best players are able to control their emotions, including Zidane most of the time. It is not coincidence, or bad luck, that Joey Barton has found himself in these situations; it is behavioural. If he can change, and I hope he can for the sake of the game, there should definitely be a place for him. If he cannot change then there should not be a place for him in a profession where you are a role model. Had someone in Newcastle's finance department, or their IT manager, for instance, behaved in this manner, they would be dismissed on the spot. Yet, because there has been a major investment on behalf of the player, the club has put itself in a bind.

Newcastle United may have made a bad business decision when they chose to buy him. What I think Newcastle needs to do now is to try to stand by Joey Barton and to help him to deal with his issues. He has had more than three strikes against him, so I'm not sure if he can ever change. I hope he can because he is a very good player, but if he can't then Newcastle should bite the bullet on this one. I don't like to see fellow professionals having problems in their lives, yet at the same time I don't like to see a bad role model have an effect on even one youngster. Sometimes in life and in business you have to lift your head towards things which are more important than money.

Football has a duty to try to help fellow professionals when they are having issues in their lives. It also has a duty to try to maintain a good image for our youth. We have a duty as a society and as parents to take on the media and corporate world which are complicit in creating an environment where drug abusers are heroes. It is not a drug abuser's fault if they are offered a fortune to endorse a product. Are they going to say no? Of course not.

The company is wrong for making the offer. These days all of the big corporations talk about their ethical strategy, and how good they are. They think it is just about stocking a few organic products or reducing their carbon footprint. Really it is about everything you believe in and everything you do. How can it be morally or ethically right to pour millions of pounds into the pockets of drug abusers? What kind of a world are we creating for our kids?

I think as footballers we have a duty to be positive role models and overall I think footballers deserve more credit for this than they get. Maybe we should introduce random drug testing for musicians. I wonder, how many would be left on stage?

14

There's No Business Like Good Business

What's brave, what's noble,
Let's do it

Anthony and Cleopatra, *William Shakespeare*

Way back in the late Victorian era, about the time when those 17 men gave life to Blackburn Rovers Football Club in a room above the Leger Hotel, a kind of enlightenment was occurring. The industrial revolution had brought immense wealth to a small number of entrepreneurs. They lived well, but living well was for them not sufficiently fulfilling in itself. It was almost as if the acquisition of wealth gave them a different perspective; enabled them to see a bigger picture; one which saw entrepreneurs become philanthropists. They used their experience, vision and a portion of their accumulated wealth to improve the lives of others.

Philanthropists such as George Cadbury, Joseph Rowntree and William Lever, to name but a few, did more to improve the conditions, outlook and opportunities for their workers than the governments of the day. Many set examples which created blueprints for new approaches to housing, education, health and social care. Why?

Why did they do these things, when they could have settled for an easy life? The romantics would say that there is a human need for fulfilment which cannot be attained simply by accumulating greater wealth. In other words, it feels good to do good. Cynics may say that by improving the conditions of their workers they were effectively improving their own prospects by having healthier, happier, more educated and therefore more productive workers.

Maybe there is some truth in both these explanations. I like the romantic view because I think that there is some truth in it. Doing good does feel good. I also can accommodate the more cynical view. In fact, I have absolutely no problem with it. If you make money and then use it to do some good, and as a result you make more money, I say why not? That's good business. It's also *good* business if you see what I mean.

It is funny how I am one of the few people in the world who can say that their job has changed hardly at all since the late Victorian era. There has been an industrial revolution, a technical revolution and two World Wars, yet a goalkeeper still does pretty much what goalkeepers did in the 1870s. It's also funny how, almost by accident, I fell into something outside of football which saw me behaving as an entrepreneur. Then without thinking about the parallels with the late Victorians I instinctively developed a philanthropic nature.

They say that man cannot live on bread alone. We all need something more than the material to feel fulfilled. I don't yet know where my entrepreneurial and philanthropic journey is taking me. All I do know is that it is an exciting time …

Respect for the Dollar

I think that, since my dad had some serious financial problems when I was growing up, I have a respect for the dollar that I might otherwise not have. As a family we had to stick together to get through some very difficult times and I think, subconsciously, I never wanted to experience that kind of situation again.

So even when the money started to flow, apart from a short-lived indulgence with cars which have been a passion since as a boy I played with my model cars on the floor of our Bay Village home, I've never really needed much. I've never been a big follower of fashion. I don't have a watch any more and my phone is the free one that comes with the contract.

That's not to say that I am mean. My wife Tracy more than makes up for my lack of interest in these things. I find that I can be happy with the little things and maybe my real desire is to ensure that the security we almost lost when I was young is always going to be in place. Perhaps that's what drives me a little bit.

The other thing that drives me is an experience that I had when I was a young man. After the Barcelona Olympics, I'd had a living expenses grant and various fees for this and that, and for the first time in my life I had a little money. I went to a financial adviser thinking that I should make this money work for me. I was an impressionable young college kid, with no experience of money matters. The adviser would say to me, 'Do this, invest in that.' Naively I would just say, 'OK.' Then I lost some money, which came as a bit of a shock, and I thought to myself, I should have looked into that a bit more. What really hit me was that even though I lost money, the financial adviser didn't. He still made his commission. I realised that I knew nothing about mutual funds and I knew nothing about the stock market, and I vowed never to make more investments like that until I did. It's impossible to go through life only winning, and on this one I lost, but I treated it as a learning curve. What intrigued me about this was that while I lost, the adviser still won. He was the clever one in that deal. So from there, I decided that I was going to take my own advice.

You can see how I was quite naive with my little bit of money in those days. In today's Premier League you sometimes see young players being just as naive as I was, but there are much bigger sums involved. I watched one player who was earning about £1 million a year go and buy £750,000 worth of cars. I tried to explain to him that after deductions his £1 million was about £600,000 take home pay and that his cars were worth a heck of a lot less than £750,000 the moment they drove out of the showroom. Hey, but who am I to talk? The figures may have multiplied a lot, but young men and money will always be easily parted.

More Turkish Delight

As the years went by and I had money to invest again, I talked to a friend who was in business. I asked him what advice he would give me. He said, 'Go and buy yourself a good solid property.' This sounded like a sensible idea. Properties can go up in value and are less likely to fall in value than shares.

So I made my first property investment. I remember it well because it was in my hometown of Bay Village, Ohio. It cost me $269,000; I got together with some builders and renovated it a little. Then I moved my parents in, which in itself gave me a great feeling. Three years later we sold it for $330,000. I'd done something good for my parents and as a by-product made $61,000.

As I began to reflect on this and contrast it with my previous loss-making investments, it occurred to me that there was something in this. It kind of lit a spark in me and I began to realise that property could be a great investment if you thought about it in the right way. I know that there are thousands of people around the world who understand this, some making millions of dollars, but I was young and I was learning, and this was a kind of enlightenment for me.

What I noticed was that there were many different ways that developers went about shaping and structuring their business deals. So, I asked a lot of questions to the business people that I knew and to friends of friends. What this did was encourage me to learn more about moving up the property ladder.

I took the view that there are very easy ways to renovate a house by reversing the normal way of doing things, so I began to find good builders as partners and work on an incentivised profit-sharing basis. That way I didn't get builders trying to inflate their prices and then hiding problems in the house. We all had a real incentive to make it work.

When I was playing for Galatasaray in Turkey, they had an unusual approach to paying the wages. Firstly they were rarely on time. They had a really relaxed attitude about paying you, which for me was not such a problem. I was a single guy with everything taken care of, but for some of the married players this kind of thing was a real irritation. The second thing was that you only got paid twice a year, so you got your money in quite substantial lumps.

At that time, Turkey was trying to open itself up to trade in all sorts of ways. Tourism development was a big theme for them as they were trying to develop places like Malvasia and Marmaris.

When I went out to the coast one day, I noticed that they were offering plots of one quarter of an acre at very low values compared to what I was used to in California, Florida and places like that. These were magnificent ocean plots. Istanbul was always very expensive, especially around the Bosporus, but there were other parts of the country where the weather is beautiful all year round and they were really trying to attract people there just as they still are today. So with my two-year contract at Galatasaray, I was due four lumps of money. I felt that I had to make this money work for me. I could take the safe route and put it in the bank, or I could invest in something that could yield good returns. So that's what I did: I began investing in Turkish property.

This provided a useful little insight. Don't just go into any property investment. Look for places where land values are low and the potential is high. This can be difficult when you are scouring the neighbourhoods of your own town, but with my roving lifestyle as a globetrotting goalkeeper, I could keep my eyes open for opportunity wherever I went. As a result, I've been able to develop all sorts of properties in Turkey, Mexico, the USA and, of course, the UK. I understand that this isn't a magical new way of earning money, but it was new for me at the time. I was young and I had to learn about it as I went along.

Good Business Is Good Business

Way back in 1993 a germ of an idea was sown. I'd played in the US national team with a player named Desmond (Desi) Armstrong, who played 81 times for his country.

In the off season he would come up to Bay Village and we would run some soccer camps for kids. It was no big undertaking, it was fun and we were able to make a little money out of it. We were thinking that maybe we could develop the idea a bit more and make it into a business. It was then that I went overseas in pursuit of the illusive work permit, and there was no way I could follow through on this idea.

I guess we both got busy with our own lives and Desi and I lost touch. Then in 2001 Desi called me up out of the blue. He said he wanted to pick up on the idea that we had had all of those years ago. Of course, I'm older now, I've travelled a million miles, taken risks and learned to manage investments and property. I couldn't see myself going back to doing some summer coaching camps. I wanted to do something more than that.

Each day I would drive from home to training at Blackburn Rovers' training ground in a small Lancashire village. Each day, my journey took me through Brockhall village, past the Rovers' football academy, which is in fact one of the most advanced in the country. It is the kind of thing that all Premier League clubs now have as a means of developing their own players. The Blackburn academy has done well in that respect, bringing through players like David Dunn, Damien Duff and Matt Derbyshire.

It began to occur to me that though the European clubs were highly evolved in terms of academy development, there was nothing of the sort in the USA. I also had this feeling that the Premier League academies were very football focused and didn't look at the whole person. Sure, they do some educational work as well, but the whole ethos is about spitting out players capable of playing in the Premier League. I felt that, by looking at things slightly differently, so much more could be achieved.

By this time my old friend Barry Venison and I had started to do some business deals together. We had met at Newcastle and played together at Galatasaray, where we struck up a good friendship, and stayed in touch ever since. Barry and his wife Julie are the godparents of our first daughter, Izabella. We have learned some of the ups and downs of business together, which has been very valuable, and as families we have a very tight bond. Barry and his family have now based themselves in California.

After the conversation with Desi and my thoughts about how

an academy could be, Barry became involved in the thinking process, which is really one of his strong suits. He and Desi both have very creative minds. These two people are an interesting combination because they are both creative, Desi being more the 'artist' type, while Barry, when not in creative mode, brings structure to the way things are done. I was more the person who could get things done because once the decision to go into the Cleveland area was made I had a lot of people who were able to help me out. So between us we began to develop a very exciting concept.

The idea was to create a fantastic football academy, at least to the standard of a Premier League academy, and to build around it a proper educational and vocational programme. I wanted to be able to bring into the United States an academy system that considered the youth development of the players as the sole goal. In the US we can have the best of the best of facilities, yet in soccer our kids train on some very poor facilities. It has a lot to do with the perception of soccer as a sport in America. We wanted our academy to make a strong statement about the importance of soccer by getting top-class facilities at grass-roots level. The primary aim is to build well-rounded people who may have a future as professional footballers, or may not. We will support them in whatever it is that they want to do in life. So with a concept in our heads, we now had to work out how to bring it to life.

What I knew from my own experience is that soccer in the US is primarily a middle- to upper-class sport and is much more popular than you would imagine. In fact it is the second largest participation sport in the USA, with 18 million people playing on a regular basis. The vast majority of club teams in the US at the elite level charge a fee to play, sometimes up to $5,000 a year. What I wanted to do with this academy idea was to include every social class and people from every walk of life and to give them the opportunity to develop a love of soccer. But first we needed a site.

We began the search in 2001. I knew that my name meant something on my home patch back in Ohio and, of course, I have a soft spot for that area. Parts of the region are very 'blue-collar' so it was a natural thing to want to search for a site in that area.

We set up as a non-profit organisation known as a 501(c)(3). It means that I don't take a penny from the academy and it allows us to get sponsorships and donations in and donors can get a tax break for their donation. When word of what we were trying to do spread, six other locations around the US came forward inviting us to go and set up there instead. All had warmer climates than Ohio. I could have saved $2 million on construction costs because I would not have needed to build the indoor soccer pitch to cope with adverse weather. But as far as I was concerned there was only one place where this thing was going and that was in my hometown. If that meant finding another $2 million then so be it.

A disused golf course became available and we were able to buy this at a reasonable price because we had had discussions about what we were trying to do and began to develop a win-win situation.

We worked very hard to purchase the golf course and get the planning permission changed in a way that enabled us to build the academy and also have room for commercial development on the property.

The land was in a part of Ohio called Lorain, quite close to Bay Village where I grew up and still have a home today. This is a huge feather in the cap for the local area because Premier Soccer Academies is the best thing the US has seen in soccer youth development in the history of the sport. We would build and fund our academy and make the facilities available to as many local people as possible. This is a win for local people, in that they have access to great sporting facilities, and a big win for people who come as academy members. We decided to use 29 acres for the academy and 3.53 acres of the site for retail and commercial development. The retail and commercial development will contain businesses that can be complementary to the academy. That's a win for us as developers and as people who wanted to make a philanthropic dream come true.

After a year-long search for a site and another six months to change the planning permissions on the old golf course, we then had to develop a business plan which would in time lead to a situation where the academy could become completely self-sustaining. This is not an easy thing to do and, as I write, we are still in the process of working on this.

For the first year we set up a soccer camp at Oberlin College. Desi Armstrong opened registration and 115 players signed up to come to the camp; most paid on this occasion, but we had set up a scholarship programme for those that couldn't pay. I went over and coached along with Desi Armstrong, Scott Sellars and my old goalkeeping coach from Blackburn Rovers, Roy Tunks. We were able to spend some time together and put our thoughts on how to scout players who might be resident players when the academy opened.

The camp was really successful and helped us bring our ideas to the attention of local businessmen and women. The most difficult thing was to get the soccer side of things sorted out, to find coaches and people who have soccer minds in the US, so I spent a lot of time doing that while also talking to architects on a day-to-day basis.

My first hire was a lady called Kay Catlett. She had expertise in running camps and organising smaller-scale events and trips, and she was really helpful in getting us going in these areas. Kay is no longer with us but played her part in getting us off the ground.

As things really started to roll, it became more and more difficult for me hold down a job as a goalkeeper in England and attend to the 1,001 issues that needed to be dealt with regularly. It was then that Craig Umland was introduced to me. He was a vice-president in IMG which represented the interests of 150 US and international soccer players and organised big events. Craig's responsibilities included North American golf events with some of the biggest names in the PGA, LPGA, nationwide and Champions tours in the US, Mexico, Bahamas and Korea. He had great connections with top athletes and, importantly, with the sponsors of major sporting events. When he heard that I was looking for someone to lead the academy operations he immediately asked if we could meet. His track record was really impressive on running events and after meeting with him I knew that he really cared about what we were trying to do. I obviously felt the interview went very well and, in September 2006, Craig became the impetus behind the project.

Funnily enough, soccer had never even featured on his radar screen. All he knew at the time was that his five-year-old daughter had an interest in playing.

Around about the time Craig arrived, a massive snow dump hit Lorain and the building programme began to slip. Everything was geared towards opening in August 2007, and for a while it looked in jeopardy. By the late spring of 2007, Craig and the construction team had begun to catch up and we were back on track to bring in our first intake of athletes. In the first year of Craig's tenure at Premier Soccer Academies I had to ask him to do a lot of things that were not in his specialist area. Some of these were because of funding issues and some were due to the fact that there was not an American who would be sufficiently in tune with all the soccer issues. It's been a real learning curve for all of us. Now that we are over a year into the running of the academy, Craig has turned into more of a soccer enthusiast than I think he could ever have imagined and the academy operation is running very smoothly.

The concept is incredible in that we offer full all-year-round scholarships, worth about $35,000 per player per year, to young players from around the world. We select them purely on ability and the scholarship system means that they don't have to pay anything. We have an arrangement with Amherst school system for our American players. Our overseas players attend a private school called Lake Ridge Academy, so all of them attend a proper programme of education. The only reason why they are split between the two schools is due to visa issues relating to study arrangements for foreign players. Other than that, they spend their time together at the academy.

Premier Soccer Academies runs combines or selection camps as well as other events around the world to decide who should be offered a scholarship. We also tap into our scouting network, based on contacts that we have built up between us; some of these relationships go back 20 or 30 years.

Once we have identified players with potential we can bring them in for more extensive trials. When this long scouting process has taken place and boys are selected, they live two to a room in one of the most amazing rooming facilities that a school could offer anywhere in America. We have tried to develop an atmosphere inside the academy where players intermingle with each other no matter where in the world they may come from. They are encouraged to learn about each other's cultures as well as their own.

We have a chef that is responsible for their diet and nutrition, strength and conditioning coaches, world-class football coaches, tutors, academic advisers, house parents, kit men and everything that they need to help them develop.

There are facilities to accommodate 30 scholars, and at present all of these are boys. As we continue to develop the business plans around the academy, we are looking at ideas to extend it, both in terms of the number of players we are able to accommodate and in terms of possibly opening up to talented young girls as well. Right now these are possibilities for the future.

The boys are on a year-to-year scholarship, which could run for four years. To maintain their right to a scholarship, players have to keep up their performance both on and off the football field. They must show progress in football and in their studies in order to have their scholarship rolled on.

Anyone who is familiar with sporting facilities in Europe may well have in their mind's eye a picture of a breezeblock building and a couple of football pitches. Nothing could be further from the truth.

The Premier Soccer Academies, as we call it, has a main building which is 32,000 square feet. It is designed and fitted out very much like a five-star hotel, and as you enter the entrance lobby with its wood-panelled walls, marble floors and chandeliers you could be forgiven for thinking that you had arrived at the wrong place. Our ethos is about quality, and that runs through everything that we do, from the design of the building, to the materials and finishes, through the programme and the educational curriculum. When you give people quality, you usually get a quality response, which is what we want.

We have four full-sized football pitches and one half-sized pitch. When the weather is bad we can play all year round because we also have a full-size indoor soccer pitch. The state-of-the-art fitness centre is 5,000 square feet and fitted out with top-of-the-range equipment thanks to the generous support of Gatorade, Adidas and StarTrac. In addition, we have our own classroom and conference area.

Our facility is set up for top-class professional training. With the exception of the school system, our coaches, who have been educated in soccer throughout their lives, run their sessions and organise the diet so that we can develop top-class athletes. We also have combines with youth club teams as PSA affiliates, as this is another way that we can extend our scouting network.

In terms of the academy activities for people other than the year round players, we offer numerous levels of programmes during the year including camps for boys and girls, five-a-side tournaments across the United States, the PSA World Youth Tournament, and three-day combines in various cities in the world.

You can imagine my delight and the sense of achievement that I got when, on 20 August 2007, 15 boys arrived from all over the United States to become our first intake of scholarship players. Four days later our nine international scholars arrived from South Africa, Brazil, Trinidad, Chile, Bolivia, Venezuela, Canada and Mexico.

We are not only here to develop players, but good well-rounded human beings as well. We want everyone to respect each other. We have players from all over the world thrown in together. Some speak English, some don't, but eventually they will all have to. It is incredibly satisfying to see them develop as they are starting to become not only team-mates but good friends as well.

Having set this up at a cost of just over $10,000,000, we obviously have to work very hard to make sure that our business plan comes to fruition each year in order to keep it going.

All of us are committed to what we have built from a germ of an idea, and if we don't find that money from sponsorships, donations and trading then we have to find it out of our own pockets. I do this already, in that now when people come to me with sponsorships or endorsement propositions, I ask them to make a tax-free donation to the academy. Giving money to the academy is just as good as giving money to me. What's great is that the academy has become a focal point in terms of the regeneration of the area and we are now developing 3.53 acres to the front of the site. Right opposite, Home Depot has developed on a 63-acre site as part of the Lighthouse Village comprising 400,000 square feet of retail space. The junction, which once had a traffic count of 12,000 cars a day, now sees 30,000 cars a day.

This has increased interest in what's going on at the academy and it has also made our site very attractive for the business sector. We took some calculated personal risks; we tried to do something good and due to a combination of factors our commercial site has increased in value. That's good business. It happened because we wanted to also be in the business of doing good.

For me the icing on the cake has to be this. If you were to ask my parents what they are most proud of, they would pause for just a moment. Mom would recall the moment when the hairs on the back of her neck stood on end as they played the US national anthem before our first game at the Barcelona Olympics; Dad might recall me playing at Wembley Stadium, just as I had told him I would when he took me there as a small boy. But then they would pause again and exchange glances. They are able to agree that the opening of the academy was their proudest moment of all.

To feel the sense of achievement that I felt when we opened the academy is enough for me. I don't need any extra bonuses or accolades. Yet the thought that it has been my parents' proudest moment is something that makes me extra proud of what we have done.

I like business. I especially like good business.

15

Expect the Unexpected

The most beautiful adventures are not those we go to seek
Robert Louis Stevenson

Everybody who saw Mark Hughes working at close quarters knew that it was only a matter of time before he was snapped up by a big club. When he left Blackburn Rovers for Manchester City in the summer of 2008 it was no surprise but it was still a little unexpected.

Then there came the inevitable speculation about a successor for Mark Hughes. If you were to believe the papers and the rumour mill everybody from Sam Allardyce to Avram Grant was packing their bags and heading for Lancashire. There was even talk that my old friend Paul Ince was an outside candidate.

His progress as a young manager had been short yet meteoric. In less than two seasons he had saved Macclesfield Town from what seemed like certain relegation and then taken MK Dons to promotion at the first attempt.

Impressive form indeed, but few pundits really believed that he could see off managers with Premiership management pedigree. Gradually, he nosed his way to the front of the shortlist and the unexpected happened again.

As for me, watching this from a distance during my summer break it was intriguing. I was delighted for Mark Hughes of course. Sad to see him leave Blackburn Rovers but there had been no doubt in my mind that it would happen sooner or later.

I still had two years to run on my contract at Blackburn and I was happy and excited to be going into pre-season with one old friend replaced at the helm by another of my good buddies. It was going to be interesting to watch Paul Ince the manager, having known him as a player and a pal.

Despite being the Premiership's draw specialists Blackburn had had a decent season in 2007–08, finishing seventh, which meant we had missed out on a European place. That and the fact that we exited the FA Cup early was a disappointment for all of us, and by the time the end of May came we were all ready for a vacation.

Tracy and I packed up the kids and headed for Barbados. Hot, idyllic and well away from it all. We had planned some relaxing family time, followed by a short burst of neon in Las Vegas, before heading over to Ohio to spend some time at Premier Soccer Academies and to be with family.

Tracy feels that I have something of an obsession with my phone, so in the family holiday spirit I had it turned off for a time in Barbados and of course during the flight to Las Vegas.

There's always that feeling of anticipation when you switch your mobile on as you head to pick up your suitcases at the airport. Still in relaxed mode as we arrived in Vegas, my heart sank a little when I looked at the screen of my phone. "You have 22 new messages". My head began to whirl thinking of all the possibilities. What could all of these messages be about?

I wondered if there were problems at the academy and perhaps I was going to have to get involved to sort them out. As I ploughed through the messages, there were a lot of calls from all sorts of journalists asking if there was any truth in the rumours that I was leaving Blackburn to go to Manchester City or Aston Villa.

I thought 'rumours? What rumours?' This was the first I had heard of it. Alan Nixon of the *Daily Mirror* was the first person to get through to speak to me. He asked me if I knew of any impending transfer. I think that he thought I was being coy or something, but I genuinely knew nothing. In any case I didn't give much credence to it. I knew that Mark had gone to Manchester City, but they had a perfectly good keeper in Joe Hart.

Of course, I'm in an unusual situation because unlike pretty much every other player these days, I no longer have an agent. So, any interested club would not be allowed to contact me directly, and Blackburn was under no obligation to keep me informed of offers. I was under contract and they had the right to refuse any offer if they felt like it.

As for the speculation about Villa, well as far as I knew they were trying to do a deal with Liverpool to sign Scott Carson on a permanent deal. Maybe there was a game of cat and mouse being played because Liverpool wanted to sign Gareth Barry from Villa. Whatever. As far as I was concerned this was a matter for the sports journalists and had nothing to do with me.

Then, it began to dawn on me that there may be some truth in these rumours. I started to get calls from people outside of the journalistic world. There were too many calls coming in from too many people for there not to be something in it.

So as we left Vegas for Ohio, I was intrigued, yes of course, but I had things to do at my academy and I wanted to spend time with my dad, who had been ill, as well as with the rest of my family, so we just got on with our plans. Ohio of course is the home of my favourite NFL team the Cleveland Browns, owned by Randy Lerner. That's the same Randy Lerner who owns Aston Villa. I'd only met Mr Lerner once before so I can't say that I knew him as such, but I did know people in Cleveland that knew him and others that had worked for him and I had heard good things.

I know that he bought Villa with the best of intentions, wanting to make it bigger and better on and off the field. Relatively speaking he had come into football quietly and seemed to be making an impact. So, all of this Villa speculation became more intriguing.

John Williams, Blackburn Rovers' Chief Executive called me up whilst I was still in Ohio. He wanted to let me know that the club was about to appoint Paul Ince as manager. Naturally I was delighted for Paul. Then John mentioned that there had been some informal enquiries about my availability, confirming that there was some truth behind the rumours.

John was adamant that he wanted me to stay at Blackburn Rovers and having discussed it with Paul Ince, they were both of the same mind. He asked me what my thoughts were.

Now that was a tricky one to answer. A lot of things started to go through my mind. I spoke with Paul Ince as well and that made things even harder for me. I had been at Blackburn for eight years, I was really happy there and I felt we had been good for each other. I have massive respect for Paul Ince. I respected him as a player and team mate, and we are personal friends, yet it was hard not to consider the possibilities which were emerging.

Manchester City is a big club and now they had Mark Hughes and the backroom team that he had taken from Blackburn. There was absolutely no doubt that I could work with these guys; they are a fantastic coaching unit. We understood and respected each other and this management team with City's financial resources could in time be a force to be reckoned with.

Villa meanwhile, had finished one spot above Blackburn in the Premiership even though they had the smallest squad; they had the chance of progressing into the UEFA Cup via the Intertoto Cup; and in Martin O'Neill, they had an astute manager, who was beginning to add to the depth and quality of the squad. You had to believe that Villa's stated ambition of breaking into the Premiership's top four clubs was beginning to gain credibility.

At 37 years of age, I had to ask myself how likely it was that opportunities like this could emerge. They were unexpected. They were pretty exciting, yet by the time I got home and got ready for pre-season training, they were nothing more than interesting thoughts. There had been no formal offers as far as I was aware.

All I could do was to get my head fixed upon what I was paid to do – to go out and do my best for Blackburn Rovers. I went into pre-season training as fully committed as I always was. Now Blackburn is a tremendous family club and I will always have a deep affection for everyone associated with Rovers. Yet it is no secret that with their attendances and the absence of large corporate income, there is not the scope for major transfer spending.

As I have said before though, they can compete with most on wages. Whilst all of this talk about prospective offers coming in was going on in the background, I sat down with Paul Ince on several occasions to discuss developments. Paul's position was always absolutely clear, he wanted me to stay. Blackburn Rovers knew that they could do things about wages and so they presented me with a series of improved contract options, even though I had signed a new contract not so many months earlier.

Yet money was not what was going through my mind. Money alone would never have been a catalyst for me to leave Blackburn. As we got on with our pre-season tour and began getting into games we carried on talking about the possibilities and the probabilities but largely got on with the business of getting ready for a new season with a new manager.

Behind the scenes I believe that Villa put forward the first bid, which was then matched by Manchester City. Both were turned down. Then Villa had a second bid turned down and so too did City. Whilst we were out on tour in Portugal, Villa finally had a bid accepted which was contingent upon Blackburn being able to find a suitable replacement.

The Blackburn fans need to know that at no stage did Paul Ince, or anyone at Blackburn for that matter, want me to leave. It wasn't a case of bad judgement or of them showing me the door, they wanted very much for me to stay. I have to thank them for taking the considered view that they did. I was a free transfer when I came, I had served the club well for eight years and the transfer fee being offered meant that Blackburn would make money from the sale. They reluctantly agreed only after they had scoured Europe for a replacement keeper. Paul Robinson was lined up to come in from Tottenham Hotspur should I agree terms.

I flew back into Manchester having been granted permission to have discussions with Aston Villa. Whilst I was in the air City matched Villa's bid. So, I had a choice to make.

Thankfully, the way I like to operate is pretty simple and it makes dealing with situations like this a little bit easier. I like to stay as loyal as I can to people and do the right thing by them as long as it is also the right thing for me. With these two clubs making identical offers, whatever I did would not be to the detriment of Blackburn Rovers, so that element could be removed from the equation.

I didn't think I could make a wrong decision with either of these two clubs, yet Villa always seemed to put their foot forward first. Everything they said that they were going to do they did. They acted quickly, very professionally, and without causing problems for Blackburn. I liked that.

So, I made a decision to go and meet Villa. As I drove down to Birmingham I was very clear in my mind what I was going to do. I was going to listen to what they had to say, and if I liked it I was going to sign for them there and then, on the day, in that meeting. In that way I would not be muddying the waters for Manchester City by creating uncertainty. Neither was I interested in playing one off against the other. That's just not my style.

It could not have been simpler. The moment I walked into Aston Villa's training ground everything just seemed to fall into place. Randy Lerner and Martin O'Neill were there to meet me. We had a really enjoyable discussion and I knew that this was the place I wanted to be.

I agreed that I would sign subject to me making one phone call. The signal strength was poor so I excused myself and went outside. Mr Lerner, Martin O'Neill and a few others were all sitting about inside waiting. This was no last minute negotiation ploy I simply wanted to contact my wife Tracy to let her know that I had agreed terms. Eventually I got hold of her on the phone, she was still in the States with the kids, and though I know she really loved Blackburn Rovers she is happy when I'm happy. She said that she was delighted, so I went back inside and signed on the dotted line. Simple.

I don't have one single negative thing to say about Blackburn Rovers. I was coming up towards my testimonial year and that would have been nice, but there was this opportunity to go on what could be a big adventure right at the end of my career. That was an unexpected opportunity and one that I simply could not turn away from.

The Cleveland connection with Randy Lerner was a nice coincidence, but first and foremost I wanted to play football for Martin O'Neill. I like what he has to say, he has a great track record and has made great progress at Villa with a small squad. He has resources at his disposal and he tends to make astute purchases. Something very positive is beginning to grow out of this considered and intelligent approach. When I met the two of them, something just felt right. I was getting a gut instinct that the time was right to move and that this was the place to move to.

There's a substantial British contingent in the Villa squad. These days as well as being an American citizen I also have a British passport. Laughingly I wondered could that be why they wanted to sign me. They say that Britain and America are two great nations divided by a common language so maybe I was brought in to provide interpretation services for my fellow American and goalkeeping colleague Brad Guzan.

I joke. We are all there on merit and for what we can bring to the squad. It is unusual of course to have two American keepers at one club. The US seems to almost have a goalkeeping production line on the go. It's interesting to compare Brad's entry into English football with mine. Whereas I went through a five year work permit battle, Brad was turned down just the one time. Aston Villa put together a very convincing and professional case the second time around because Brad doesn't qualify based on the international games criteria. He has his work permit and can now concentrate on developing as a top flight keeper.

I don't have any official sort of brief to bring him on, but there is a kind of unofficial goalkeepers' union, which says that you try to help any of your goalkeeping colleagues wherever you can. The more backing a goalkeeper gets from the goalkeeping group the better. It makes everything more positive and more enjoyable whilst still being competitive. You are not looking for your colleagues to fail: you have to be positively competitive by trying to be better and sharper. This is the kind of healthy competition I've always thrived upon and it is what we are doing at Villa.

Brad Guzan is a young man with the world at his feet. I'll watch with great interest to see how he develops, and of course he knows that if he needs help with anything, then I will be there.

So there I was running out on the first day of the season at Villa Park. Five or six weeks earlier I had no inkling whatsoever that I would start the season in Villa's colours. Yet again football threw up one of those dramatic ironies, with Villa being paired against Manchester City on the first day. I could easily have been turning out at Villa Park in City's colours.

Nearly 40,000 people turned up to create an amazing atmosphere for my second debut at Villa Park. It was after all the place where I made my Premier League debut for Liverpool. It proved to be a captivating start to the season and a match that the fans will remember for Gabby Agbonlahor's hat-trick in just eight second half minutes. City attacked with vigour and I got to face my first penalty of the season which Elano converted. It ended 4-2 and we were off to a flier.

In any season there are ups and downs. We had progressed in the UEFA Cup and been knocked out of the Carling Cup. By the time my old club Blackburn Rovers came to visit in October we had broken into that magical top four spot. This was our sixth game in just over three weeks. We were pretty jaded but, to be fair to Blackburn, for periods of the game they just played us off the park. Despite this we found ourselves 3-1 up in the 90th minute and a very late free kick brought it back to 3-2. We had not performed the way that we know that we can, yet teams that do well over the course of a season have a knack of still eking out a win when they don't play that well. In one sense perhaps this was a sign of progress.

Had Blackburn won that night they would have pulled themselves within five points of us, but the league is so tight, with everybody seemingly capable of beating everybody else on the day. I think the changes will just take a little time to bed in and a couple of well-timed wins will see Blackburn up closer to where they belong. They are a really good group of players and I know that the team spirit is as good as it ever was. For Blackburn, I believe it is just a matter of time before things pick up.

You know, people often talk about the great supporters at Liverpool and at Newcastle and so on. To be honest I hadn't realised just how big a club Villa are and can be. We have fantastic passionate supporters who really get behind the team and Birmingham is a city of one million people with about two and a half million living in the Greater Birmingham conurbation. In fact as a city, Birmingham has twice the population of Manchester.

The potential for this club is enormous. I think that in Mr Lerner, we have an owner who recognises this. His work, and the work of the people he has brought in, is about realising that potential of the club, its brand and what it means to the people that really care about it. There is a real connection between the club and the supporters and it's good to see that the club recognises the reality of life for many fans in a period of recession.

The big picture at Villa is exciting and the day-to-day is fantastic too. I've gone from a great dressing room at Blackburn to another great dressing room of a different kind at Villa. The Villa squad is a lot younger than the Blackburn squad, yet I love going in to training in the mornings and I think it is helping to keep me young. At 37 I am by far the oldest player. I'm even making Martin Laursen look young and he's 31. After that most of the players are in their early to mid-twenties so there is a lot more to come from these lads.

Martin O'Neill has taken his time over his buys and has brought in a stream of new talent, so that Villa are beginning to develop the strength in depth that we will need to continue to make progress.

There is one thing that I have noticed, though, that has taken me slightly by surprise. Maybe it shouldn't have, but I have to be honest and say that it has. I have always known that Gareth Barry was a very good player. That goes without saying. It's just that I didn't realise exactly how good he actually is. Watching him every day and being part of big games with him you begin to see just how good he really is. Though he is a different type perhaps from Stephen Gerrard and Frank Lampard I think he is definitely up there at that level. Whether he is playing for Villa or for England he is one of the first names you would put on the team sheet. He is one of those players that I think you would find him very, very difficult to replace, regardless of how much money you had at your disposal. It was suggested by one of the papers that the best piece of business that Martin O'Neill did in the summer of 2008 was to keep hold of Gareth Barry. It was indeed a great boost for the club that we held onto Gareth. If he keeps doing what he is doing and the other signings keep delivering the goods we can reflect on the merits of Villa's wheeling and dealing at the end of the season.

What I am seeing is that these new additions to a squad that finished sixth last year are resulting in a group of players who have many talents. Essentially, and importantly, this talented group have a collective work ethic which is quite remarkable. When you add talent to application you have got a chance of doing something.

It's exciting also because a lot of the talent in the team is still young and will develop further. Gabby Agbonlahor has terrific pace. We have pace elsewhere though. Ashley Young is quick and John Carew deceptively so. With the passing ability of Gareth Barry and Stiliyan Petrov we can unleash this pace and cause other teams some serious problems. I'm pleased with the way we have begun to gel at the back. It inevitably takes a bit of time for players to get used to each other and, all in all, I think we are developing a good understanding. Add all of these ingredients together, the pace, the passing, the overall work ethic, the depth of the squad, the solidity at the back and you begin to feel that we have got something really good to build on. Let's see where it takes us.

I'm as enthusiastic as ever about the future and what it may hold. I don't feel my age at all, and I've always seen it as my absolute duty to stay as fit as I can possibly be and to keep my form at a high level as consistently as possible. Since I retired from international football I've had the opportunity to rest up a little between domestic games, and over the past few years when I have received the odd knock it always seems to have coincided with the break, giving me a chance to recover.

I just love playing football and I concentrate on the game in hand and doing the best I can for the team. Until it was brought to my attention by the statisticians I hadn't noticed that the game against Fulham on 29 November 2008 would be my 167th consecutive Premiership appearance and a new record.

The record is an interesting statistic which I can look back on in future years, but that's all. I'm happy that I have had such a run of games. I'm under contract to play football and it's what I love doing. That is what is important. I would be more pleased to help Villa qualify for the Champions League or to win a cup competition than to accept an individual accolade.

That is what I am focused on at present as are all the squad and it's great to be a part of it.

What does the season hold for us? In a word, we want to make progress. I think we can. One thing we can be sure of is that this is football and we should always be certain of one thing.

We can expect the unexpected.

16

The Wonder Years Part II

To everything (turn, turn, turn)
There is a season (turn, turn, turn)
And a time for every purpose, under heaven

Soundtrack to Forrest Gump, *The Byrds*

It's been an eventful life so far. Just as I thought that I had signed my last contract, an unexpected turn of events saw me moving to Villa. By the time my current contract expires I will be 40 years old. At my age I am 'mature' for a footballer, but in everyday terms I am still a young man with an exciting life continuing to open up before me.

My life began with 'The Wonder Years' created for me by my parents. It taught me the power of love, security and family. I created the next amazing phase of my life against the odds. I aimed high, set goals, tried to stay true to my values and do the right thing. Now having looked back on everything that has happened to me, I'm beginning to think about the next phase of my life. The picture is unclear and the possibilities are endless. Whatever we do as a family, wherever we go, the one thing I am sure of is that I will refuse to live on past glories. I want to create 'The Wonder Years Part II' …

Life Is a Sigmoid Curve

Think about the greatest football managers that you have ever known, that is, those who consistently achieve success over long periods. Football managers tend to have an increasingly short shelf life these days, with the average Premier League manager staying in a job for less than 60 games. That's only about one and a half seasons.

When you actually think about it, there are very few managers who enjoy prolonged success over a sustained period. These managers are not just very good at what they do; they are extraordinary.

The names that spring to mind are Bill Shankly, Sir Alex Ferguson, Brian Clough and Arsene Wenger. Sure, there are and have been many other very good managers that you could add to this list, but how many of them have enjoyed success at one club, by building one successful team after another?

That's what these four greats have in common. They all have managed with a different style and had their own individual ways of doing things, yet they all achieved over long periods by reinventing their teams.

That's because great managers like these have an instinctive understanding of the sigmoid curve. That's what they all have in common regardless of their style and approach.

The sigmoid curve, also known in business as the life cycle curve, can be a very useful tool for thinking about things. All sorts of things, from football teams, to mobile phones, to what to do about your life and your future.

If you imagine a letter 'S' placed on its side, and quite lazily drawn so that it lies at a slight angle rising a little from left to right, then that is the sigmoid curve. Imagine it as a graph so that as you move along from left to right it represents a movement in time.

In terms of football teams, when you look back over history, you can see the sigmoid curve in action time and time again. At first, a team comes together and they take time to gel. So the beginning of the curve dips. Players begin to get used to each other and the curve begins to level off. Then a team may just click, and so the curve takes off on an upward trajectory as the team begin to win and achieve success. But remember, the sigmoid curve is a side-on 'S' shape, and that curve sooner or later is going to start going down again.

It is inevitable. Nothing lasts for ever, and great teams will eventually grow old, break up or burn themselves out. The difference between the truly great managers and the rest is that they recognise the importance of constant change and have a special knack for judging just the right time to change things.

In football, as in life, what many of us do is wait too long before we instigate a change. We wait until we are on the downward slope of the curve. We are too busy enjoying the heady days of success to imagine that one day they will be taken away from us. The key is to change when you are approaching the top of the curve because a new curve will have to begin and that will take a bit of time to bed in. How many footballers wait until their career ends before they wonder, what am I going to do now? How many people in everyday life wait until they are made redundant or there is a death in the family before thinking about creating a new curve? If you don't create a new curve for yourself, sooner or later circumstances will force it upon you. You will be on a downward slope and acting from a position of fear and uncertainty.

It is much better to envision a new future from a position when all the signals you are getting are telling you that everything is OK, you are doing brilliantly. Here you can create a vision from a position of strength.

And that's about where I am now. My career conforms to the sigmoid curve almost perfectly. I started well, then I felt as if I was on a downward slide as my work permit applications were rejected. Then came a period where things levelled off a bit, before things really clicked at Blackburn and my curve began to take off. I'm really excited about my move to Villa and I'm going to savour every moment of the next few years. Though I know that I am approaching the top of my current curve, my life as a professional footballer, and it is almost time for me to reinvent myself and create a new curve which I can climb to the top of.

Old Footballers Never Die . . .

I really want to create a new kind of future for myself. Something that I can strive towards, that will excite me and which will give me fulfilment.

There has been a wealth of stories over the years of great players who refused to acknowledge the inevitable logic of the sigmoid curve. The fact that one day it was all going to come to an end. Many players are totally unprepared for a new kind of life after football and sometimes it saddens me to see them, forever dwelling on the past, like old soldiers who find it difficult to adjust when the adrenalin rush that had become a feature of their lives is taken away.

This is partly why we have endless comparisons about players 'in my day'. These tend to come from players who seem to dwell in some kind of 1970s or 1980s time warp that was their era. In the mists of time and romantic nostalgia things always seem better in the past. The way I see it is that you cannot compare players from different eras. I really do hope that you don't see me in ten years' time on the TV saying it was better in my day. What I will want to say is that it was different.

Can you say that Pelé was better than Ronaldinho? Could Pelé play today? Who cares, he was just great. Why don't we just leave it at that?

Things in football will keep on improving, and in ten years' time there will be players who will be better than the greats of today. People will say, 'Well, back in the day the pitches were not as good and the play was slower,' but a player from a past era, if he were playing today, would be trained using today's methods in today's conditions. So would a great player like Sir Bobby Charlton be as good as a great player like Wayne Rooney? If everything was evened up all we can say is that they would both be fantastic players. Let's just leave it at that and appreciate players for what they are in their own time.

So you can hold me to this. If you see me on TV in ten years' time, I will just be saying that different eras in football are better enjoyed rather than compared.

When I think about a block of time like ten years, it seems a long, long way away. Yet we all know that as we get older time seems to speed up with every year. I know that ten years will pass very quickly. I'm thinking about what to do, but I haven't decided for sure yet. When I imagine the future, I really do hope that if I were out for a meal and somebody came over and said, 'Hey, I remember you playing, you were great,' I would be the one who says, 'Thank you very much,' and that that's where that conversation would end. It's because I want to be successful in inventing a new curve for myself, and therefore I would want the person to say, 'So, what are you doing now?'

I would want my response to mention something that I was really excited about. The person that asked may very well regret it because, in my excitement for whatever my new thing is, I may very well bore the ass off them. Yet that's how I want things to be. To politely acknowledge the past and all that has gone before, while living in the moment and looking to an exciting future.

Some players find this a hard concept to get to grips with but, with the lifestyles we have led and advances in medicine, many of us may live to be well over 100 years old. That's a lot of time to spend telling your old football stories over and over again.

It's natural that players find it hard to let go. Football is an exciting profession, where you get a lot of attention from people and, of course, enjoy the camaraderie of your team-mates every day. It is a big thing to have all of that taken away from you. For some players, it is possible to stay involved through management and coaching. Many now make a good living and retain their involvement through working in the football media. These are good ways for players to create new curves for themselves, but not everyone can do these things. For some players their feelings of self-worth are completely intertwined with playing football. This is something that they must address for themselves in due course and, as I said earlier, it is far better to do it when your curve is still on an upward trajectory, rather than wait until you are on the way down.

One of the greatest transformations occurred in a great friend of mine. Barry Venison, who is also my business partner, was absolutely football crazy. He lived and breathed it. He clung to it for a while after he finished playing. He became a media pundit and he was very good at it.

He has moved to California and created a different kind of lifestyle. We are involved in the Premier Soccer Academies together and we are jointly developing the 3.53-acre frontage. Barry is finding this all immensely exciting and stimulating, so much so that this total football nut very rarely finds time to even watch the games any more. He has found a new curve to replace his old one and is on an upward trajectory. That's exciting and it gets the utmost respect from me.

I've met Gary Lineker only once or twice in my life, but looking from the outside in, he appears to me to be another great example. He has forged a new life as a professional presenter. He went at it from the bottom up. I think he has gone at it from the point of view of making a new and fulfilling career for himself rather than saying to himself, 'How can I cling on to football for just a little while longer?' Consequently, you see him doing all sorts of things and not just football. As a presenter, he is as good as they come, and I am sure that there will be young kids watching *Match of the Day* that have no idea that the grey-haired fellow used to play for England. He has truly reinvented himself.

Whatever it is that you do, it is important to get out of this 'living in the past' routine and create an enjoyable life. The thing that I have noticed when people don't do this and stay locked in their time warp is that they tend to become disgruntled, invariably negative and in time very boring people to be around.

Footballing Philanthropists

And what of football's future? Pundits have been predicting that the 'bubble will burst' for decades now. It hasn't happened, and English football has evolved from a working-class game to the point where the Premier League is one of the world's most valuable brands. Where it was once a game of 11 men against 11 men, it is now 11 millionaires against 11 millionaires.

Football has become big business, and I don't see anything

changing that in the near future. Transfer fees may become less significant, with the switch of Andy Webster from Hearts to Wigan Athletic. Webster moved clubs by taking advantage of Article 17 of FIFA's Player Status & Transfer Regulations. This allows a player to buy out the remainder of his contract after three years if it is due to end before he is 28 years old. Players over 28 can buy out after two years. Premier League clubs are looking hard at the ongoing implications. It may mean that transfer fees will fall and players end up with bigger pay deals so that it becomes harder for them to leave by buying out their contract.

One thing is for sure: the business of football has transformed in recent years. The Premier League has created a megabrand, and this has attracted foreign owners of Premier League clubs, a move not always welcomed by the fans. Where once local clubs were owned by local businesspeople in the town – the butcher, the baker, the candlestick maker if you like – now they are attracting a different form of ownership.

Whereas in the past the club was a source of local pride and owning a piece of it was an honour which gave you status in your town, now it is strictly business. Though we may hanker after the romantic image of those days where running a football club was part hobby, part honour and only some part business, those days will never return.

If we consider the upside, the emergence of American owners will bring a healthy business discipline to football. You know that American businessmen are more detached from the romance. They are not coming in to lose money and they will look at things differently; they are wealthy because they are good at seeing ways to make money. In Premier League clubs there is a chance to get into a great business that is only going to grow. Granted, Manchester United wasn't cheap; the Liverpool takeover has had its share of problems but looks like it may turn out to be a good business for its owners; while Aston Villa could turn out to be an incredible bargain for Randy Lerner.

The Lerner family had paid a mega sum for the Cleveland Browns American football team, so when Randy Lerner paid about $110 million for Aston Villa he got, in my opinion, something of a bargain. Just look what he and Martin O'Neill have done in a short space of time at Villa; the two of them seem to have come together well as a team.

I see the future of football as being very bright. It is inevitably going to have to continue to evolve like any product. If you stay still, you will be overtaken by something else. The attempt to play some Premier League games overseas is a natural progression to this. A global brand needs global reach in order to stay in the game and football, as a premium product as it now is, needs to embed itself into the fabric of the world's emerging economies. This will sadden traditionalists, yet, just as players need to create new futures, the game of football must too.

Now every aspect of the product gets looked at in great detail; football as a business is not just about what goes on within the confines of a green rectangle for 90 minutes once or twice a week.

As businesses grow to the scale that we are seeing in the Premier League, they begin to follow the pattern established by the Victorian philanthropists. They achieve a critical mass and regular profitability, and then they begin to consider their wider impact on society and the environment. Listed companies do this and rather than calling it philanthropy, they tend to call it Corporate Social Responsibility (CSR). They realise that doing good is good for business.

That can only be a good thing. The power of football to engage people, to lift and motivate is immense. Football can be a powerful force for change, and having circumnavigated the globe several times and seen real poverty and real pain, I know that there is still much that we need to change in our world.

For now the CSR activities of clubs are modest when compared to, say, the pharmaceutical industry or the finance sector. Yet, as football extends its global reach, so must it extend its concern for its stakeholders. No longer are these simply the residents of the town in which the club is based; they are people who form an extended global fan base.

For example, Manchester United have a CSR programme which has three tiers: work with local communities around its sites, work with national charitable organisations around the UK and a partnership with UNICEF supporting projects like AIDS/HIV relief in Africa.

This is a well thought through strategy and, where Manchester United lead, others tend to follow. In 2008/9 Aston Villa announced that it would be giving its shirt logo space to Acorns Children's Hospice. This charity looks after 600 children with life-limiting illnesses and provides support for their families. The value of having the Acorns logo on the Villa shirt has been esti-mated by pundits to be worth £2 million and Acorn reckoned it had £1 million worth of PR in the first month alone. With this there is the prospect of a new breed of successful hard-nosed businessmen beginning to raise their sights in terms of what football can do for the world. It makes sense because, as I have already found out, good business is good business.

So, on the broad front there is a bright future for football, one which I believe will lead to a brighter future for society as football begins to properly establish itself as a vibrant and genuine change agent, helping to tackle some of our toughest social problems.

Yet there is a mixed message being given out. The public's per-ception of the modern-day professional footballer is not all that it could be. Looking at some of the tabloid revelations I am not surprised. There are many great people who are playing in the game today, yet, as always, it is the not-so-great people that the papers love to write about.

Surely more has to be done to avoid the kind of situations that do nothing but give football and footballers a bad name. Though the Professional Footballers' Association do a lot of great educa-tional work, it tends to focus on preparing players for a life out-side the game. This is commendable and I am all for it, yet, for me, there is something missing in the academy system which we have in this country.

If at the age of 16 you show promise as a footballer, you are essentially out of school. Yes, there is a token gesture to an aca-demic programme, but in my view it is little more than a token gesture. These kids, great footballers that they may be, often have little education, and from an early age rarely engage with anyone who is not a footballer.

I contrast this with some of the players I have played with from overseas. The Scandinavians, in particular, the Dutch and the Germans often speak anything from two to five languages; perhaps have a college education and have interests other than football. They tend to be well-rounded people who are able to cope with the attention and the wealth that is thrust upon them. I've also noticed that they think quite early on about what they are going to pursue after they have finished playing.

If we don't make a proper attempt to produce well-rounded young footballers, then perhaps we should not be too surprised when they are constantly bringing the game and us as professional footballers into disrepute.

This is why I have approached the development of our Premier Soccer Academies from the point of view of seeing the whole person, not just creating fodder to be eaten up by a footballing machine. I know that the young people we produce will be successful in life, whether or not they are successful in football.

As for me, I have some thinking to do. What kind of new future do I want to create for myself and my family? I'm sure that I will continue to engage in philanthropy in some form. Offers and ideas arrive on my doorstep on a regular basis. The thing I have to be aware of is that no matter who you are, there are only seven days in a week and 24 hours in a day. These things can take up a lot of time and whatever it is that I do in that field I want to be able to do it justice.

My business ventures excite me a lot as well. I don't know for sure what I will pursue on this front in the future. I do know that whatever it is that I do I will do it to my fullest and I will pour my heart and soul into it.

Don't forget that I dropped out of UCLA and, as far as I know, with my credits still intact. My scholarship is still open and I still have the right to go back and finish my final year. How about that? A retired footballer-entrepreneur-philanthropist as an undergraduate student.

Now that's thinking outside the box.

Watch this space.

Index

Index

Index